LEARNING TO READ TALMUD

What It Looks Like and How It Happens

The research for this book and its publication were made possible by the generous support of the Jack, Joseph and Morton Mandel Center for Studies in Jewish Education, a partnership between Brandeis University and the Jack, Joseph, and Morton Mandel Foundation of Cleveland, Ohio.

LEARNING TO READ TALMUD

What It Looks Like and How It Happens

Edited By JANE L. KANAREK
and
MARJORIE LEHMAN

Boston
2016

Library of Congress Cataloging-in-Publication Data:
the bibliographic record for this title is available from the
Library of Congress.

ISBN 978-1-61811-513-3 (hardback)
ISBN 978-1-61811-514-0 (electronic)
ISBN 978-1-61811-577-5 (paperback)
©Academic Studies Press, 2016

Book design by Kryon Publishing, www.kryonpublishing.com
Cover design by Ivan Grave

Published by Academic Studies Press
28 Montfern Avenue
Brighton, MA 02135, USA
press@academicstudiespress.com
www.academicstudiespress.com

For our parents, who first taught us how to read

Anna C.V. and David J. Kanarek
Sheila K. and Wallace B. Lehman

Contents

Acknowledgments		vii
Introduction	Learning to Read Talmud: What It Looks Like and How It Happens *Jane L. Kanarek and Marjorie Lehman*	viii
CHAPTER 1	Stop Making Sense: Using Text Study Guides to Help Students Learn to Read Talmud *Beth A. Berkowitz*	1
CHAPTER 2	Looking for Problems: A Pedagogic Quest for Difficulties *Ethan M. Tucker*	35
CHAPTER 3	What Others Have to Say: Secondary Readings in Learning to Read Talmud *Jane L. Kanarek*	57
CHAPTER 4	And No One Gave the Torah to the Priests: Reading the Mishnah's References to the Priests and the Temple *Marjorie Lehman*	85
CHAPTER 5	Talmud for Non-Rabbis: Teaching Graduate Students in the Academy *Gregg E. Gardner*	117
CHAPTER 6	When Cultural Assumptions about Texts and Reading Fail: Teaching Talmud as Liberal Arts *Elizabeth Shanks Alexander*	137
CHAPTER 7	Talmud in the Mouth: Oral Recitation and Repetition through the Ages and in Today's Classroom *Jonathan S. Milgram*	159
CHAPTER 8	Talmud that Works Your Heart: New Approaches to Reading *Sarra Lev*	175
POSTSCRIPT	What We Have Learned about Learning to Read Talmud *Jon A. Levisohn*	203
Contributors		219
Index		223

Acknowledgments

Learning to Read Talmud: What It Looks Like and How It Happens is a work that emerged from a research initiative supported by the Jack, Joseph and Morton Mandel Center for Studies in Jewish Education at Brandeis University. We are deeply grateful to the Mandel Center and its director, Jon A. Levisohn, for sponsoring and supporting this project. Dr. Levisohn's wise guidance, his challenging and insightful questions, and his enthusiasm for our work helped make this project a richer and more meaningful process. We also thank Susanne Shavelson, Associate Director of the Mandel Center, and Sharon Feiman-Nemser, Jack, Joseph and Morton Mandel Professor of Jewish Education, for their ongoing support of our work.

We are deeply grateful to our co-contributors to this book, who opened their classrooms to research and who gave generously of their time in workshops and in writing: Elizabeth Shanks Alexander, Beth A. Berkowitz, Gregg E. Gardner, Sarra Lev, Jonathan S. Milgram, and Ethan Tucker. We learned an immense amount about teaching and reading Talmud from each of you. We thank Shira Horowitz for guiding us through the intricacies of how children learn to read and for helping us to conceptualize our first workshop. We thank Jennifer Lewis for providing us with a rubric for doing evidence-based pedagogical research and for helping us to conceptualize our second workshop. We thank Elizabeth DiNolfo of the Mandel Center for her expert and efficient charge of the administrative aspects of our workshops. We also thank Baynon McDowell for her attention to detail in her invaluable copy editing of this manuscript. At Academic Studies Press, we appreciate the work of Deborah Furchtgott, William Hammel, Kira Nemirovsky, and Meghan Vicks in helping us bring this work to publication. We also thank the anonymous reader, whose comments made this work stronger.

We dedicate this book to our parents, without whom we would not have become readers, learners, and teachers of Talmud.

INTRODUCTION

Learning to Read Talmud: What It Looks Like and How It Happens

Jane L. Kanarek and Marjorie Lehman

Sparked by an intensification of interest in the study of talmudic literature, we are experiencing a revolution in the teaching of Talmud and rabbinic texts in North America.[1] While the teaching of talmudic literature has long been a focus in Jewish religious institutions, the types of institutions offering courses in rabbinic literature and the range of adults studying it have grown exponentially in recent years. Talmud is now taught in secular universities and in adult education courses to undergraduate students as well as to rabbis-in-training. Recognizing this expansion in interest, audience, and pedagogical potential, this book, *Learning to Read Talmud: What It Looks Like and How It Happens*, represents both a response to and a search for enriched pedagogical methods, using a series of classroom studies by professors of talmudic literature that reveal both *how* teachers teach their students to read and *how* students learn to read the Talmud. These studies analyze the teaching of Talmud to adults in a range of North American settings of higher education,[2] from seminaries to secular universities and from novices to advanced students.

---

[1] This book focuses on the teaching of the Babylonian Talmud, or Bavli, a corpus of literature composed between the third and seventh centuries in Sassanian Persia (modern-day Iraq). We have included one chapter that discusses the teaching of Mishnah, the foundational work of rabbinic literature and around which the Bavli is organized. The Mishnah was edited circa 200 CE in the Land of Israel. The term sugya refers to a smaller unit of literary discourse within the Bavli, which is often composed of a web of various voices from different time periods.

[2] One author, Sarra Lev, taught her course in a Jerusalem yeshiva (a religious institution for the study of rabbinic texts). As her students were all North American, we include her within this group. For an examination of her teaching at the Reconstructionist Rabbinical College, see "Teaching Rabbinics as an Ethical Endeavor and Teaching Ethics as a

Through analyzing an array of teaching and learning practices, we elucidate a broad expanse of conceptual ideas and practical tools that will aid other teachers who similarly seek to teach their students how to read the Talmud using tools that encourage student investment in learning. As such, we address a known shortage in published descriptive material that articulates and analyzes what teachers do in order to effectively teach their students to read this significant literary corpus.[3] To clarify the teaching goals with which we are concerned, we have structured this book around three main questions: (1) What does it mean for students to learn to read Talmud? (2) How do we, as teachers, help them learn how to read? (3) What does learning to read look like when it happens?

This contribution to expand the burgeoning field of Talmud and pedagogy breaks new ground. Specifically, *Learning to Read Talmud: What it Looks Like and How it Happens* is the first book to present a series of extended inquiries into the teaching of Talmud. As the following chapters demonstrate, each contributor participates and investigates a tradition of practitioner inquiry or performs practitioner research into their own teaching method.[4]

Rabbinic Endeavor," in *Turn It and Turn It Again: Studies in the Teaching and Learning of Classical Jewish Texts*, ed. Jon A. Levisohn and Susan P. Fendrick (Brighton: Academic Studies Press, 2013), 388-414.

3 See, for example, our own work, Jane Kanarek and Marjorie Lehman, "Making a Case for Rabbinic Pedagogy," in *The International Handbook of Jewish Education*, ed. Lisa Grant and Alex Pomson (New York: Springer, 2011), 581-96; Jane Kanarek, "The Pedagogy of Slowing Down: Teaching Talmud in a Summer Kollel," *Teaching Theology and Religion* 13, no. 1 (2010): 15-34; reprinted as "The Pedagogy of Slowing Down: Teaching Talmud in a Summer Kollel," in Levisohn and Fendrick, *Turn It and Turn It Again*. See also Marjorie Lehman, "Examining the Role of Gender Studies in the Teaching of Talmudic Literature," *Journal of Jewish Education* 72, no. 2 (2006): 109-21; Jeffrey Kress and Marjorie Lehman, "The Babylonian Talmud in Cognitive Perspective: Reflections on the Nature of the *Bavli* and Its Pedagogical Implications," *Journal of Jewish Education*, 69, no. 2 (2003): 58-78; and Jeffrey Kress and Marjorie Lehman, "Dialogue and 'Distance': Cognitive-Developmental Theories and the Teaching of Talmud," with Jeffrey Kress. *Jewish Education News* (Spring 2004): 21–23. See also Jon A. Levisohn, "A Menu of Orientations to the Teaching of Rabbinic Literature," *Journal of Jewish Education*, 76, no. 1 (2010): 4-51; reprinted as "What are the Orientations to the Teaching of Rabbinic Literature," in Levisohn and Fendrick, *Turn It and Turn It Again*.

4 On the terminology of practitioner, inquiry, or practitioner research, see Marilyn Cochran-Smith and Susan L. Lytle, *Inside/Outside: Teacher Research and Knowledge* (New York: Teachers College Press, 1993) and Marilyn Cochran-Smith and Susan L. Lytle, preface to *Inquiry as Stance: Practitioner Research for the Next Generation* (New York: Teachers College Press, 2009), viii-ix. K. Patricia Cross and Mimi Harris Steadman

INTRODUCTION | Learning to Read Talmud

All of the chapters here reflect the work of trained scholars in the field of Talmud, accustomed to researching Talmud, rabbinic culture, and Judaism in late antiquity. Together we have undertaken a different form of research, in which the objects of research are our own teaching and our own students' learning of Talmud. We are passionate scholars of Talmud, engaged in trying to understand the past as we seek to translate it for and with our present-day students. Yet, as academics, we are often charged and motivated with furthering the scholarly agendas of the field of Talmud rather than focusing on our pedagogical aims.[5] This project aims to reset if not align that balance. Not only do we see the teaching of Talmud by scholars of Talmud as a central academic endeavor, but we also believe that thinking about the Talmud as scholars is fundamentally the same as thinking about teaching Talmud.[6]

As scholars who have invested a considerable amount of time in learning how to read the Talmud and who are intimately familiar with what makes the

---

term this method "Classroom Research" and define it "as ongoing and cumulative intellectual inquiry by classroom teachers into the nature of teaching and learning in their own classrooms." K. Patricia Cross and Mimi Harris Steadman, preface to *Classroom Research: Implementing the Scholarship of Teaching* (San Francisco: Jossey-Bass Publishers, 1996), xviii. See also *Going Public with Our Teaching: An Anthology of Practice*, whose editors contend that teacher-research into their own practices can serve as the basis for local theories that then become, "a powerful knowledge base different from—but no less important than—the knowledge bases that [have] emerged from conventional research on teaching and learning." *Going Public with Our Teaching: An Anthology of Practice*, Thomas Hatch, et al. ed. (New York: Teachers College Press, 2005), 2.

5 See Jonah Chanan Steinberg, "Academic Study of the Talmud as a Spiritual Endeavor in Rabbinic Training: Delights and Dangers," in Levisohn and Fendrick, *Turn It and Turn It Again*, 377-87. In this chapter, Steinberg discusses the challenges faced by the teachers of rabbis who are trained as academics, but who also are responsible for shepherding people on their spiritual journeys. He argues that the students learn that they can engage with their most challenging questions "over and around and through" classical Jewish texts (ibid., 377).

6 See Mary Taylor Huber's discussion of Brian P. Coppola's teaching chemistry at the University of Michigan in her book *Balancing Acts: The Scholarship of Teaching and Learning in Academic Careers* (Washington, DC: American Association for Higher Education and The Carnegie Foundation for the Advancement of Teaching, 2004), 74 and Lee S. Shulman, "Teaching as Community Property: Putting an End to Pedagogical Solitude," *Change* 25, no. 6 (1993): 7, each of whom stresses the importance of reconnecting teaching to the disciplines. See also Michael Chernick, "Neusner, Brisk and the *Stam*: Significant Methodologies for Meaningful Talmud Study," in Levisohn and Fendrick, *Turn It and Turn It Again*, 105-26.

Talmud the multivalent document that it is, we are particularly well-suited to explore the pedagogical process of and objectives in teaching Talmud. Those with expertise and more formal training in educational research certainly can and should contribute to understanding better how students learn to read Talmud. As talmudic "insiders" with rigorous training in this discipline, we are also well-prepared for this enterprise. Our understanding of both what the Talmud is and the vast range of approaches useful for reading it open up the possibility of our being both uniquely reflective teachers of this document as well as thoughtful researchers of our teaching and the learning processes of our students. We *know* when our students are reading with the aims we have in mind. As articulated by K. Patricia Cross and Mimi Harris Steadman, "Teachers who know their discipline and the problems of teaching it to others are in the best position to make systematic observations and to conduct ongoing investigations into the nature of learning and the impact of teaching upon it."[7]

As Talmudists, we speak the language of other Talmudists. We are rooted in the research traditions that define us as scholars of our discipline—scholarship that we apply in the classroom to teach our students to read Talmud.[8] We hope that this commonality of discipline will encourage other scholars in the field of rabbinics to become both active researchers of the Talmud *and* of their teaching methods. As such, this book, while focused on excellent classroom teaching that is carefully prepared and well-designed, is also about teaching that involves inquiry into a type of learning that emerges from the very nature of the text in question.[9]

---

7   Cross and Steadman, *Classroom Research*, xviii. See also Pat Hutchings, who comments on "the power of the disciplinary context in shaping the way faculty think about and design their approaches to the scholarship of teaching and learning," in her article "Introduction: Approaching the Scholarship of Teaching and Learning," in *Opening Lines: Approaches to the Scholarship of Teaching and Learning*, ed. Pat Hutchings (Carnegie Foundation for the Advancement of Teaching, 2000), 6.

8   Huber, *Balancing Acts*, 23.

9   For a deeper analysis of the relationship between knowing one's discipline and the practice of teaching, see Barry Holtz, "Across the Divide: What Might Jewish Educators Learn from Jewish Scholars?" *Journal of Jewish Education* 72 (2006): 5-28. Citing Joseph Schwab, Holtz argues for the importance of understanding the large organizing, interpretive frames that define a field prior to making decisions about practice. The very essence of the discipline needs

With this book and its publication, we join the growing field of the scholarship of teaching and learning (SoTL), a field that seeks to expand the research agendas of scholars in a particular discipline to include research into the teaching or learning of that discipline or both.[10] Familiar with posing questions and using specific interpretive methodologies in researching the answers to these questions, we tasked the contributing authors represented here to think more self-consciously about how their students learn to read Talmud. Paralleling their own research paths in the field of Talmud, the contributors to this book began their inquiries by posing a set of questions at the beginning of the teaching semester, with the result that their classrooms became the subject of their research.[11] Each author's answers were therefore grounded in his or her specific institutional context—from which grew the course-specific experiential evidence you will read here. By assuming a dual role as reflective teachers and teacher-researchers, we provide windows into our actual classrooms, into our profession, to see what our teaching practices and student learning looks, feels, and sounds like. When did our students learn to read and when not?[12] Each of us believes that *teaching is an inquiry into learning,* and each of us has opened up our classroom for review and critique by writing about it here.[13] We have designed and implemented select learning experiences, examining

---

to inform the practice of teaching (ibid., 10-11). See also Joseph J. Schwab, "Education and the Structure of Disciplines," in Ian Westbury and Neil J. Wilkof, *Joseph J. Schwab, Science, Curriculum and Liberal Education: Selected Essays* (Chicago: University of Chicago Press, 1978), 229-272.

10 In the field of Jewish studies, see Levisohn and Fendrick, *Turn It and Turn It Again*. See also the editors' articulation of the scholarship of teaching and learning in their introduction (SoTL), "Cultivating Curiosity about the Teaching of Classical Jewish Texts, ibid., 14-18.

11 On the importance of beginning with questions in the scholarship of teaching and learning, see Hutchings, *Opening Lines*, 3-6.

12 For further on this topic, see Elie Holzer and Orit Kent, *A Philosophy of Havruta: Understanding and Teaching the Art of Text Study in Pairs* (Boston: Academic Studies Press, 2014), 26-27. The authors also designed a program dedicated to teaching Talmud through *havruta* learning and then studied their own practice and their students' learning.

13 Huber, *Balancing Acts*, 23; Hutchings and Shulman, "The Scholarship of Teaching: New Elaborations, New Developments," 13.

how well our students responded.[14] We have charted the discussions that ensued in class each week by keeping extensive teaching journals; we have experimented with different types of assignments and then evaluated our students' work; we have audio recorded and taken videos of our classes, analyzing each record as evidence. This close attention to detail represents an integration of content and pedagogy, of scholarship and practice.

In presenting a range of perspectives on what it means to read a talmudic text, the chapters in this book highlight the distinct challenges of teaching instructional courses centered on this classical Jewish canon. Our exploration of a select array of our own teaching practices, coupled with the variety of assessments used to determine whether our students achieved the goals we each had set for them, created a framework for understanding the different types of choices we make as contingent on the contexts in which we teach our courses and the nature of the students we encounter. For example, Elizabeth Shanks Alexander, who teaches an undergraduate course at the University of Virginia to students who had never been exposed to the Talmud, worked only with translated texts and emphasized the importance of attention to detail in comprehending talmudic material, even when reading translations. Jonathan Milgram, who similarly taught an undergraduate course but at the Jewish Theological Seminary to students who could read Hebrew, emphasized the importance of the oral repetition of the Hebrew/Aramaic talmudic text in learning to read.

As a result, these eight chapters highlight a collection of focused, pragmatic teaching strategies, each informed by a set of different epistemological, religious, and political stances as well as different educational goals. We have long dismissed the idea that there is one *best* successful method of teaching Talmud or one *best* approach to reading, as the variables that have an impact on teachers' reading goals and student comprehension are numerous. These chapters reinforce the concept that students of Talmud do not learn to read in a linear fashion. The chapters also importantly add to the literature on the scholarship of teaching in describing these distinct practices, cultivated by

---

14 Huber, *Balancing Acts*, 27-28.

the authors' different reading goals. Taken collectively, they show that studying one's teaching practices has a profound influence by creating a context "in which students engage in productive learning activities with greater intensity or focus than previously."[15] Actively turning our classrooms into sites for our research made us better teachers and our students better learners.[16]

The chapters in this book explore aspects of learning *how* to read that are highly particular to understanding Talmud: its complex manner of expression in Hebrew/Aramaic, its dialogical nature where challenges are posed and refuted, its integration of source material from different historical time periods, and its centuries-old history of commentary. The vastly different preconceptions that students—from the seminary to the secular university—bring to Talmud study also add a layer of complexity to learning to read this document. Yet, while we write here about the peculiarities and particularities of teaching the primary text of Talmud, we also contribute to a larger conversation within general education of how students learn to read primary texts, whether historical, philosophical, religious, or scientific. We join a broader discussion that supports students in becoming critical and proactive readers of primary material.[17] Thus, while our book will be useful for teachers of Talmud in a range of settings, it can also speak to those who teach students how to read primary texts in many areas of higher education.[18]

---

15 Huber, *Balancing Acts*, 21 and Daniel J. Bernstein, Jessica Jonson and Karen Smith, "An Examination of the Implementation of Peer Review in Teaching," *New Directions for Teaching and Learning*, no. 83 (2000): 77-78.

16 By challenging ourselves to define precisely what we want to convey to our students about the Talmud and through seeing how our students learn to read, inquiry into teaching also enables us to become better practitioners of our central academic discipline, Talmud.

17 See, for example, the contribution of Samuel S. Wineberg, "On the Reading of Historical Texts: Notes on the Breach between School and Academy," *American Educational Research Journal* 28, no. 3 (1991): 499 and Sam Wineburg, "Reading Abraham Lincoln: An Expert/Expert Study in the Interpretation of Historical Texts," *Cognitive Science* 22, no. 3 (1998): 319-46.

18 While this book contains studies of teaching Talmud in higher education, its chapters can also inform teachers of younger students in Jewish Day schools, congregational schools,

Inside Our Process: Constructing the Book

These classroom studies evolved from a research initiative supported by the Jack, Joseph and Morton Mandel Center for Studies in Jewish Education at Brandeis University that brought together eight scholars of Talmud in a year-long process to investigate their own and each other's pedagogy. This work built on a previous research project of the Mandel Center, the Initiative on Bridging Scholarship and Pedagogy in Jewish Studies (2003-2010). The Bridging project focused on the teaching of Bible and rabbinic literature in a variety of educational settings, including Jewish Day Schools, synagogue adult education contexts, seminaries, and universities.[19] Our current initiative seeks to deepen the understanding of one aspect of this earlier work: the teaching of talmudic literature in higher education settings.

As part of our work lay in introducing scholars of Talmud to the scholarship of pedagogy, we brought this group of eight scholars together for two workshops at the Mandel Center, the first in December 2013, before we had taught the courses that would form the basis of our inquiries, and the second in June 2014, after we had taught them.[20] The first workshop focused on an investigation of our own reading practices: how each of us defined for ourselves what it meant to learn to read Talmud, how we think people learn to read in general, and what we thought our reading goals would be for our students in our specific Talmud courses. The second workshop, convened after we had taught our classes, was an opportunity for us to reexamine our courses within the context of the scholarship of pedagogy. These two workshops, thus, were part of a reflective process that bookended a semester of teaching.[21]

---

and non-religious schools. Of course, the practices described will have to be molded for those settings.
19 For further information on the Bridging Initiative, see "Bridging Scholarship and Pedagogy in Jewish Studies," accessed April 22, 2015, http://www.brandeis.edu/mandel/projects/bridging/.
20 Shulman, "Teaching as Community Property," 7.
21 A longer process would likely have enabled us to deepen our reflective process and apply the insights we had gained from investigating this one course to another and then, in

INTRODUCTION | Learning to Read Talmud

Guided by the research of Ellin Oliver Keene and Susan Zimmermann on teaching students to read, portrayed in their book *Mosaic of Thought: Teaching Comprehension in a Reader's Workshop*,[22] we felt it essential to begin our first workshop by thinking about our own reading comprehension strategies before we could examine how we would teach reading to our students. As described by Stephanie Harvey and Anne Goudvis, Keene and Zimmermann argue that, "as the custodians of reading instruction, teachers must be readers first. Of all professionals who read, teachers must top the list."[23] Whether we are teachers of undergraduates in secular universities, of rabbinical students in seminaries, of graduate students of ancient literature, or of young adults in egalitarian yeshivot, and whether our students are Jewish or non-Jewish, studied rabbinic literature previously or not—we needed to understand our own processes of proficient reading before we could attempt to think about the ways in which we wanted to teach our students to read. With this in mind, we meticulously studied a brief Talmud passage in *havruta* (study pairs) and then as a full group, asking everyone to read attentively in order to be able to articulate well how he or she made sense of the passage.[24] We asked everyone to think about the point at which they felt they had "understood" the text—what it means to them to read a text of the Talmud proficiently.

When we reflected back on the group conversations that followed our *havruta* study, we were able to conclude that as proficient readers of Talmud we approach unfamiliarity, including difficult words, concepts, and ideas, with a sense of familiarity. We know when we do not comprehend something, we know why it is unclear, and we develop strategies to solve our

---

turn, research and evaluate that course.

22 Ellin Oliver Keene and Susan Zimmermann, *Mosaic of Thought: Teaching Comprehension in a Reader's Workshop* (Portsmouth, NH: 1997). This book is also available in a revised edition: Ellin Oliver Keene and Susan Zimmermann, *Mosaic of Thought: The Power of Comprehension Strategy Instruction*, 2nd ed. (Portsmouth, NH: Heinemann, 2007). For our workshop, we found the way in which the material was presented in the first edition to be more useful.

23 Stephanie Harvey and Anne Goudvis, *Strategies that Work: Teaching Comprehension to Enhance Understanding* (Portland, ME: Stenhouse, 2000), 7.

24 For a discussion on the contributions of *havruta* learning to learning to read Talmud, see Holzer and Kent, *Philosophy of Havruta*. We chose to study a passage from B. Avodah Zarah 8a.

difficulties. For example, some of us relied on the medieval commentator Rashi (Rabbi Shlomo Yitzhaki, 1040-1105) for sense-making at the local level; others of us turned to Rashi only later in the process and instead began with dictionaries or parallel talmudic passages.[25] While our individual strategies may have differed somewhat, we all modeled proficient reading. In other words, each of us could automatically activate a prior schema and use prior knowledge to solve the reading challenges and make sense of the passage in front of us.

We next turned from the specifics of our own reading processes in Talmud to thinking about learning to read in general. As we prepared for our workshop, we were surprised to find a gap in the scholarship on teaching college and graduate school students how to read.[26] Unsurprisingly, however, we were able to uncover a greater amount of scholarship on teaching reading comprehension to elementary school children.[27] We turned to an expert kindergarten and first-grade teacher Shira Horowitz, who has extensive experience instructing teachers on reading and teaching children how to read, including reading Jewish texts.[28] Proficient readers, she pointed out, no

---

25 Rashi is renowned for his almost comprehensive commentary on the Babylonian Talmud. His commentary, part of the standard talmudic page, is distinguished by its attachment to the word or words being explicated as well as to the local sugya.

26 For material on teaching students to read and understand primary texts, see Robert Scholes, *Textual Power: Literary Theory and the Teaching of English* (New Haven: Yale University Press, 1986) and his *Protocols of Reading* (New Haven: Yale University Press, 1991). In both books, he discusses teaching students to read texts critically. See also Dennis Donoghue, *The Practice of Reading* (New Haven: Yale University Press, 1991), who argues for reading texts closely and imaginatively, without necessarily theorizing about them. And see Sophie Haroutunian-Gordon, *Turning the Soul: Teaching through Conversations in the High School* (Chicago: University of Chicago Press, 1991) regarding her experience teaching high school English students, stressing the importance of classroom discussion. These researchers had a great impact on the work of Holzer and Kent, as they note in their book, *Philosophy of Havruta*, 29-30.

27 See Keene and Zimmermann, *Mosaic of Thought* (1997, 2007) for a fuller articulation of this process and its application in teaching children to read; Harvey and Goudvis, *Strategies that Work*; Cris Tovani, *I Read It, but I Don't Get It: Comprehension Strategies for Adolescent Readers*, (Portland, ME: Stenhouse, 2000). See also Sophie Haroutunian-Gordon, *Learning to Teach through Discussion: The Art of Turning the Soul* (New Haven: Yale University Press, 2009), in which she stresses the importance of asking questions for cultivating understanding in elementary school children.

28 Shira Horowitz, "'Torah Talk': Teaching *Parashat Ha-shavua* to Young Children," in Levisohn and Fendrick, *Turn It and Turn It Again*, 324-51, where she narrates her approach to

matter what age, are always thinking as they read, monitoring their own comprehension, and working to create new images from material that is already present in the text. She referred to this as text-to-text reading. In addition, proficient readers are adept at utilizing personal connections to their own life experiences to trigger meaning. She referred to this as text-to-self. And ultimately, readers with these skills apply their ideas about how the world works to further understand what they read and to comprehend better the world around them (text-to-world). She wanted to show us that proficient readers stop and think and stop and rethink.[29] Although none of us teach Talmud in precisely the step-by-step fashion that Horowitz modeled,[30] this approach to reading helped us to see and articulate the necessity of breaking down our own more intuitive reading processes into their respective components, defining the process of sense-making so that we could better help our students to make sense of the Talmud.[31]

Once we had examined our own reading-steps and thoughts with Horowitz at the workshop about the field of elementary school teaching and how children learn to read, we then turned to the individual instances of our courses and the reading skills and strategies that we wanted our students to learn. Each of us wrote our reading goals for our own courses on large posters. As we walked around the room and read the individual list of goals each of us had authored, it quickly became apparent that while there were some overlapping reading goals, each of us had a different sense of what it meant for our students to learn how to read. There was no single overarching rubric. Every one of our approaches was intimately connected to the different contexts in which we found ourselves (for example, an undergraduate class at a seminary vs. an undergraduate class at a secular university), as well as to

---

teaching young children to read and understand the weekly Torah portion.

29 In fact, one of the techniques Horowitz utilizes with her students (and demonstrated for us) is a stop sign. At various points while reading a story to her students, Horowitz holds up a stop sign and asks them to pause and think about a particular question. Then she continues to read and repeats the process at select intervals. The process is meant to teach students how to "bookmark" particular details as important and to slow down the reading process in order to better help students make sense of the story.

30 See Keene and Zimmermann's *Mosaic of Thought* for a fuller articulation of this process and its application to elementary teaching of reading.

31 See Horowitz, "Torah Talk," 332-33 and her reference to Lucy M. Calkins, *Lessons from a Child: On the Teaching and Learning of Writing* (Portsmouth, NH: Heinemann, 1983).

the different assumptions we made about what the Talmud is and why one should study it. In fact, it became clear when we returned for the second workshop that teaching students to read the Talmud was an incredibly complex process involving student, text, and teacher and included all prior experiences and expectations of both teachers and students.[32] Additionally, our own scholarship and the different contributions that each of us have made to the field impacted our approaches to teaching students to read and the choices we made in the way we taught.

While the first workshop focused on thinking about the process of reading, the second workshop, which convened after we had taught our classes, focused on bringing everyone to a point where they could write the chapters that culminated in this book. To that end, we invited Jennifer Lewis, a professor of education at Wayne State University, to join our workshop. Lewis' work centers on how teachers learn about teaching and learning mathematics by researching their own teaching. Lewis had us do math problems and analyze a video of a grade-school teacher teaching those same problems—all with the goal of introducing our workshop participants to the importance of heuristically evaluating their own evidence-based research. With Lewis present, we revisited the reading goals that we had established for our courses and began to explore, based on evidence that we had gathered, what our teaching and student reading experiences looked like. For each of us, what did it mean for our students to learn how to read? How could we describe the learning processes of our students such that these processes could be duplicated by others?

Inside Our Classrooms

The chapters in this book will take you inside our classrooms and give you a remarkably close experience of a diverse range of approaches to reading. Strikingly, while some of the skills that the authors ask their respective students to master are similar, the goals of skill acquisition often differ. To be

---

32 This articulation is similar to the complexity of the *havruta* process which, as aptly described by Holzer and Kent, involves an active dialogue between the learner and text, learner and learning-partner, and each learner's preconceptions, values, and beliefs. Holzer and Kent, *Philosophy of Havruta*, 34-59.

INTRODUCTION | Learning to Read Talmud

sure, all of us want more from our students and from ourselves as teachers than to have our students learn only *about* the Talmud. Our group was in agreement that to achieve a competence, a rich understanding of the Talmud—to understand its structure, its message, and its cultural power among Jews over the centuries—the students needed to intensively engage in reading the texts that comprise it. They needed to experience the intellectual journey on which it takes them. We shared the belief that our students would not be able to do this until they developed the skills to truly read Talmud, delving into its depth and multiple-voiced narratives, whether in translation or in Hebrew/Aramaic.

And yet, during our conferences and workshops, we learned that we approached our courses with very different reading goals, partly out of the necessity of students' desires and partly out of our own. Some of us were concerned about training rabbis to read the Talmud as a way of approaching central existential questions through a specifically Jewish lens that was simultaneously connected to a wider world of theological, philosophical, political, and emotional questions. Some of us wanted and some of our students wanted to become life-long readers of Talmud, while others of us recognized that many of our students would probably never read the Talmud again. Some of us wanted our students to value the Talmud as an essential part of a liberal arts curriculum, while others were concerned with how to read the Talmud to gain a better understanding of antiquity. Some of us hoped that reading the Talmud could make us better people and the world a better place through a commitment to reconstructive ethics. For this reason, the classroom descriptions and analyses represented in the following eight chapters provide not only examples of different teaching techniques but insight into how one teaches reading *for* different results. Yet, a common thread to which each contributor remained sensitive and will be observed in all of these chapters, whether the teaching context was secular or religious, is that students needed to find meaning, however differently defined, in order for them to succeed in learning to read Talmud. We therefore felt it important in presenting studies of classrooms from a range of contexts with a range of students, to highlight both what *all* students need to learn in order to read Talmud and what is context specific. These chapters thus question a strong dichotomy between religious and secular educational frameworks and suggest a softer one of overlapping but not identical processes and goals.

Beth Berkowitz, in her chapter, "Stop Making Sense: Using Text Study Guides to Help Students Learn to Read Talmud," discusses the use of a series of text study guides in a Talmud text study course taught at Barnard College. The class was composed primarily of students who had significant experience studying Talmud in high school or in a post-high school setting. However, as Berkowitz discovered, her students did more poorly on these study guides than students without previous experience in Talmud study, which seemed counter-intuitive. Berkowitz used the text study guides to invite the students to temporarily suspend their sense-making, slowing them down and preventing them from relying on what they already knew from their past experience studying Talmud. This, so they could ultimately make better sense of the text.[33] Her study guides enabled students to read on three necessary levels, moving from reading *for* an understanding of the basic building blocks of a talmudic sugya (its vocabulary and grammar) to a recognition of the subtle shifts and textual variations that require reading on a deeper level, and finally, to reflect on their "newly made sense" of the sugya by exploring the gaps and curiosities it provoked in each of them. Berkowitz was intent on teaching her students that learning to read Talmud was about understanding the Talmud as constrained by place and time: seeing the text as grounded in a context that rendered certain interpretations implausible and others plausible. She wanted the students to understand themselves, like the rabbis, as similarly rooted; that is, simultaneously constrained in terms of their interpretive visions by the worlds they inhabit, but also as creative and imaginative thinkers. For Berkowitz, the teaching practice of requiring her students to complete extensive study guides effectively brought her students to read Talmud with this realization.

Ethan Tucker, in his chapter, "Looking for Problems: A Pedagogic Quest for Difficulties," also proposes a step-by-step process that sets students up for making sense of the talmudic sugya. While targeting the more advanced Talmud student in a North American egalitarian yeshiva,

---

33 For a larger discussion on the value of and strategies for slowing down, see Jane Kanarek, "The Pedagogy of Slowing Down," *Teaching Theology and Religion*, 15-34; reprinted as "The Pedagogy of Slowing Down," in Levisohn and Fendrick, *Turn It and Turn It Again*.

INTRODUCTION | Learning to Read Talmud

Tucker contends that learning to read for difficulties involves a number of distinct steps that range from formulating a coherent reading of the talmudic passage to identifying the ways in which medieval and modern commentaries disguise problems as explanations. He begins by instructing his students to formulate a coherent reading of the chosen relevant sugya. But, as he aptly recognizes, producing a coherent reading often yields additional questions. Tucker encourages students to name these difficulties, because, as he argues, locating these difficulties is the basis for all subsequent analyses. Ultimately, Tucker's goal is to lead students to look to medieval and modern talmudic commentaries, not only to uncover the difficulties that these master readers of the Talmud encountered and to compare such questions to their own, but also to generate new challenges. Indeed, as the students learn to read through the lens of earlier expert readers and interpreters of the Talmud, they learn from them more about how to read for the *dilemmas* that impede sense-making in a talmudic sugya rather than solutions. Like Berkowitz, Tucker exposes, through his process of teaching the students to read for the Talmud's difficulties, something about the Talmud itself. By seeing that the discovery of difficulties in a sugya is what has defined serious Talmud study for generations, the struggles of the students to understand the texts they encounter is contextualized within a wider conversation, and a deeper purpose of the Talmud is revealed. As students learn to read with these difficulties, they come to see themselves as part of the history of talmudic interpretation, building a long-term commitment to Talmud study and a reverence for the complex language of this text as well as the struggles encountered reading it.

Jane Kanarek shares Tucker's interest in reaching outside of the talmudic sugya in order to better understand the Talmud and the problems it poses for the student of the twenty-first century. However, instead of focusing on the use of classical talmudic commentary, her chapter, "What Others Have to Say: Secondary Readings in Learning to Read Talmud," discusses the use of academic secondary readings. Teaching an intermediate level Talmud course at the Rabbinical School of Hebrew College, she proposes that integrating secondary readings, some concerned with rabbinic literature and some not, improves students' ability to decode a sugya and contributes to a richer ability to read the Talmud itself. As students learn to read scholarly articles along with the Bavli, students come to see the Bavli's passages as linked to a wider range of ideas in the humanities, enabling them to uncover issues that are not readily apparent (or accessible) on the surface of a talmudic sugya. These exercises empower them to engage with their own questions about meaning. As such, in learning to read the Talmud in company with the work of modern scholars, students bring their personhood back to the world of the Talmud. Students learn how to read one text critically in order to better read another.

While all of the authors represented in this book were interested in developing the personhood of their students as a part of their Talmud study, Marjorie Lehman, Gregg Gardner, and Elizabeth Alexander chose additionally to take into account their students' previous educational backgrounds in designing their courses—allowing the contrast of teaching the experienced and the novice in Talmud to be explored directly. This moving between attempts to make the familiar strange to a group of Jewish students at the Jewish Theological Seminary and attempts to make the strange familiar[34] to a group of university students, who had far less exposure to talmudic texts, resulted in these scholars proposing contrasting methods of reading. For example, when teaching students how to read the Mishnah in the context of a required course for undergraduate Talmud majors at the Jewish Theological Seminary, Lehman discovered a resistance to reading the Mishnah's references to the Temple and the priesthood critically. As she notes in her chapter, "And No One Gave the Torah to the Priests: Reading the Mishnah's References to the Priests and the Temple," many students began the class thinking of the Mishnah as a testament to the rabbis, who created a type of Judaism that could function without the Temple in Jerusalem. Rabbinic Judaism, in their minds, was a natural outgrowth of Temple Judaism, a swift response to the crisis of the destruction of the Temple in 70 CE. For the undergraduate students who entered the class, references to the Temple in the Mishnah offered "true" evidence of a past Temple reality and a desire, on the part of the rabbis, to reinstate Temple life, leadership, and ritual exactly the way it had once been. Given

---

34 Jonathan Z. Smith, introduction to *Imagining Religion: From Babylon to Jonestown* (Chicago: University of Chicago Press, 1982), xiii; Jonathan Z. Smith, *Relating Religion: Essays in the Study of Religion* (Chicago: University of Chicago Press, 2004), 383, 389.

this conceptual framework for reading the Mishnah, the author focused on teaching these students to read more analytically, more critically, and with greater attention to a hermeneutics of suspicion, fueled by an ability to ask questions of the texts they read. Asking the right types of questions of the mishnaic material, the author argues, is what leads the students to articulate what the rabbis were asking themselves about the Temple and their role in a world without its physical existence. The author describes her reading goal as marked by the intention to make the students' sense of the relationship of the rabbis and the Temple more complex, to make the familiar strange, by enabling the students to read the Mishnah with a far more critical eye than when they entered the course.

In his chapter, "Talmud for Non-Rabbis: Teaching Graduate Students in the Academy," Gregg Gardner argues that learning to read Talmud must be expanded to include training students how to read talmudic sources, so as to assist them in their research in other fields. Thus, when Gardner thought about the experience of teaching rabbinic literature to graduate students in classics, archaeology, and early Christianity, many of whom entered his class with little or no background in studying rabbinic literature, he had to think carefully about how to break down the barriers that prevent many from approaching this discipline altogether. The study of Talmud can be quite insular, and the obstacles preventing one's entry can be high. And yet, even what was familiar to the students (their knowledge of historical detail) became strange to them when they encountered, for example, a talmudic narrative about Rome's siege of Jerusalem, a revolt well-known to them. References to Roman emperors acting in ways that were not supported by the ancient sources with which they were familiar confused them, especially given their prior graduate training in ancient history. Gardner's appreciation of the strategies for reading proposed by Ellin Keene and Susan Zimmermann in *Mosaic of Thought* enabled him to apply the ways in which proficient readers read by making connections between what they know and new information that they encounter in the Talmud itself. He was concerned with teaching them to resist their desire to dismiss talmudic sources on the basis of their misuse of historical facts. For Gardner, reading the talmudic texts became an exercise in teaching his students how to read the Talmud's questionable historical references as literary constructions. This reading technique, which also included the ability to utilize translations in this endeavor, was central to understanding the manner in which contemporary scholars develop their arguments—without which these graduate students would be constrained in their use of talmudic texts to meaningfully illuminate their own research in the future.

For Elizabeth Shanks Alexander, the undergraduate students she taught at the University of Virginia became true partners in their own instructional process. In her chapter, "When Cultural Assumptions about Texts and Reading Fail: Teaching Talmud as Liberal Arts," she describes a process where teaching students how to read Talmud involved making them responsible for monitoring their successes, failures, and pace of their development as readers. Drawing on what L. Dee Fink identifies as six components in which one kind of learning enhances the possibility of achieving other kinds of learning,[35] Alexander sought to teach her students (most of whom were reading the texts of the Talmud in translation) to "learn how to learn." This pedagogic emphasis provided an interesting hook for the students, motivating them to work with material that was difficult and unfamiliar, even when they were initially clearly discouraged. Through carefully constructed assignments that prompted students to answer questions about talmudic texts prior to going over them in class, Alexander emphasized, paralleling Tucker's observations, that reading happens, and therefore learning happens, when the students pay careful attention to difficulties, rather than skimming over them. Alexander's assignments revealed to her and to the students that they intuitively search for an overarching narrative when they read a text, often ignoring the role that textual details play in understanding a given passage with all of its nuances. Like Berkowitz, her students found that slowing down the pace of their reading was key to learning to understand a talmudic passage. Ultimately, it was about reading the Talmud to experience the intellectual thought process of the rabbis and, at the same time, to recognize that the text could become a platform for their own experiences of reading. In the

---

35 L. Dee Fink, *Creating Significant Learning Experiences: An Integrated Approach to Designing College Courses* (San Francisco: Jossey-Bass, A Wiley Imprint, 2003), 32.

end, the students would come to recognize that their questions, just like the rabbis' questions, had many answers. Indeed, the talmudic texts could foster multiple ways of sense-making, if only one's reading was developed to recognize this.

In marked contrast, Jonathan Milgram approached teaching his students to read the Talmud by employing an ancient pedagogical approach used in the transmission of rabbinic literature—group recitation and repetition. Milgram's chapter, "Talmud in the Mouth: Oral Recitation and Repetition through the Ages and in Today's Classroom," focuses on the use of oral recitation practices in an undergraduate class at the Jewish Theological Seminary. This method, where the instructor reads the sugya aloud line-by-line in Hebrew/Aramaic, followed by class repetition, results in a greater cognitive closeness to the Talmud, due to an internalization of its rhythms. "Simulation," as Milgram notes, prompts "stimulation." Engaging the students in a collective process peaked their interest and motivated them to engage with the text, which, in turn, resulted in better reading and understanding. Milgram detected that fears of embarrassment over pronunciation errors were very much reduced when students read aloud in unison, promoting a greater commitment to sense-making in the classroom structure. The comfort of mastering the more technical aspects of reading like punctuation and intonation through a group activity enabled students to approach learning talmudic content more confidently.

Differing from Milgram, whose pedagogical methodology echoed an ancient and medieval mode of reading, Sarra Lev aimed to create a new mode of reading the Talmud— reading *for* the formation of a more ethical society in her chapter, "Talmud that Works Your Heart: New Approaches to Reading." Drawing from the work of Hans Georg Gadamer and theorists of transformational learning, Lev articulates a methodology where reading the Talmud—even its more difficult texts—becomes a summons to interpret it and a summons to holiness. The Talmud does not tell us what it means to be holy but, rather, impels us toward holiness through our interactions with its texts—that is, its many voices. Lev's chapter thereby proposes a model where students learn to read the Talmud as a summons; they come to read with their minds *and* with their hearts, cultivating empathy.

Conclusion

As our work makes clear, learning to read Talmud is a complex and multi-faceted endeavor. It involves the mastery of base-line skills: learning the technical terminology and the particular dialogical style of argument for which the Talmud is well-known. But, as this book argues, learning to read Talmud is more than either of these two abilities. Making sense of the Talmud—whether in its original language or in translation—involves competencies in several cognitive processes: breaking a sugya into much smaller units in order to rebuild sense; simultaneously considering multiple answers as possible; viewing problems as integral to the text; integrating the ahistorical with the historical; becoming conscious of and rethinking prior religious, cultural and historical assumptions in the face of new evidence; learning to think with a different mode of reasoning; building bridges between the ancient and the contemporary; and confronting the unethical. Interestingly, in the end, we found that each author, while equally dedicated to teaching their students to read *for* meaning, whether in the seminary or secular university, emphasized different avenues of achieving this goal; each accentuated different interpretive methods. And despite their differences, each teacher agreed that a student learns more about the Talmud by including in the pedagogical process learning *how* to read the Talmud (even in translation).

And yet, behind this goal of searching for meaning lay an implicit question: Why study Talmud at all?[36] As we taught, each of us was aware that for many of our students studying this text is not a given; the value of investing in continued Talmud study was not always self-evident. Indeed, for some students, the course we taught may be the only one in which they would formally study Talmud. However, each teacher, through a chosen method of reading, aimed to help students answer the question, "Why study Talmud?" For one teacher, the "why of reading" lay in the value of creating a life-long Jewish practice of study; for another, the "why" lay in becoming a better

---

36 For a number of personal answers to this question, see Paul Socken, ed., *Why Study Talmud in the Twenty-First Century? The Relevance of the Ancient Jewish Text to Our World* (Lanham, MD: Lexington Books, 2009).

INTRODUCTION | Learning to Read Talmud

historian of antiquity; and for still another, it lay in helping to envision a more ethical society. Yet, whether the goal is a deeper understanding of a particular sugya, connecting the Talmud with the discipline of the humanities, rooting oneself in a chain of tradition, or understanding that one's personhood is simultaneously constrained by context and inherently imaginative—we knew that we wanted our students to learn how to read richly and rigorously. Our students may not answer the question, "Why study Talmud?" in the same ways that we do. But only through entering the world of the Talmud by *reading* it deeply and thoroughly will our students begin to answer the question for themselves, "Why study Talmud?"

CHAPTER 1

■ ■ ■

Stop Making Sense: Using Text Study Guides to Help Students Learn to Read Talmud

Beth A. Berkowitz

What do you do when the students who appear in your classroom are not the ones you expect? That is to say, how does an instructor adjust carefully laid plans when the actual students are different from the ones they had imagined teaching when they planned the course? I encountered this problem when I taught an Introduction to Talmud Text Study course in the spring semester of 2014 at Barnard College.

It was my second year teaching at Barnard after having spent a number of years teaching Talmud to undergraduate and rabbinical students at the Jewish Theological Seminary (JTS) across the street. At JTS, a major goal of my teaching had been helping students acquire technical skills for reading Talmud in the original languages, but at Barnard I was Chair of Jewish Studies and responsible for teaching broad survey courses such as Introduction to Judaism and Introduction to the Hebrew Bible. I developed such courses in my first year of teaching at Barnard, but by the time my second year arrived, I wanted to return to teaching Talmud text skills in the way that I had at JTS. I thought back to myself as a college student who knew Hebrew but had never studied Talmud and would have appreciated an introductory Talmud text course. My aim was to identify such students at Barnard and to open up the world of Talmud to them, just as I had strived to do for the students at JTS.

One can imagine my surprise then, on the first day of the semester at Barnard, when I read through the slips of paper on which the students had described their backgrounds and found that all the students with the

| 1

CHAPTER 1 | Beth A. Berkowitz

exception of one had gone to Jewish day schools since they were children. Some had recently returned from a year of yeshiva study in Israel. I had announced the course as an introductory course for those who knew Hebrew but had little to no experience in Talmud study, yet virtually all the students who registered had been studying Talmud for years. Did they enroll because they expected it to be easy? Were they dissatisfied with the Talmud instruction they had received so far? Were they looking for a distinctively academic approach to Talmud?[1] Could some students simply not get enough Talmud? I had thought that I would be playing the role of tour guide for a group of first-time visitors, but I realized that instead I would be holding a master class.

Why Weren't the Students Acing the Study Guides?
How the Same Assignment Works Differently for Different Students

I did what I think most instructors would do in this situation; I would use the materials I already had and change whatever I needed as I went along. The biggest problem was my text study guide. Each year teaching Talmud at JTS, I realized afresh how impenetrable a text the Talmud is. It is composed in two languages, Hebrew and Aramaic, that are mixed together on almost every line. Like legal contracts and medical handbooks, the Talmud uses technical terminology that takes years of training to acquire. Like the Bible, it is composed of literary layers that span centuries and empires and that must be carefully disentangled from each other. Its argumentation is famous for its logical twists and turns. Its primary commentator, Rashi, translates strange talmudic words into equally strange medieval French.[2] The solution

---

1   For an overview of the major questions in the academic study of Talmud, see Richard Kalmin, "The Formation and Character of the Babylonian Talmud," in *Cambridge History of Judaism Volume IV: The Late Roman-Rabbinic Period*, ed. Steven Katz (New York: Cambridge University Press, 2006), 840-876. For exercises in applying academic methods to particular sugyot, see Joshua Kulp and Jason Rogoff, *Reconstructing the Talmud: An Introduction to the Academic Study of Rabbinic Literature* (New York: Mechon Hadar, 2014).
2   Rashi is the acronym for Rabbi Shlomo Yitzhaki (1040-1105). On Rashi's commentary on the Talmud, see Jonah Fraenkel, *Rashi's Methodology in His Exegesis of the Babylonian Talmud* [In Hebrew] (Jerusalem: Magnes Press, 1975).

Stop Making Sense: Using Text Study Guides to Help Students Learn to Read Talmud | CHAPTER 1

I had developed to help students face these myriad challenges was a text study guide.

The guide is designed around a small "chunk" of Talmud text, no more than a paragraph, which is cited at the start of the guide (Figure 1):

Study Guide 7 for B. Sukkah 23a-b
Berkowitz, Barnard, Introduction to Talmud Text Study

בפיל קשור כולי עלמא לא פליגי דאי נמי מיית יש בנבלתו י' כי פליגי בפיל שאינו קשור למאן דאמר שמא תמות לא חיישינן למאן דאמר גזרה שמא תברח חיישינן למאן דאמר גזרה שמא תמות ניחוש שמא תברח אלא בפיל שאינו קשור כולי עלמא לא פליגי כי פליגי בבהמה קשורה למ"ד גזרה שמא תמות חיישינן למ"ד גזרה שמא תברח לא חיישינן ולמאן דאמר גזרה שמא תברח ניחוש שמא תמות מיתה לא שכיחא והאיכא רווחא דביני ביני דעביד ליה בהוצא ודפנא ודלמא רבעה דמתיחה באשלי מלעיל ולמאן דאמר גזרה שמא תמות נמי הא מתיחה באשלי מלעיל זמנין דמוקים בפחות משלשה סמוך לסכך וכיון דמייתא כווצא ולאו אדעתיה

Figure 1 Example of a study guide. This particular study guide is the last of seven that I distributed to the students in Introduction to Talmud Text Study at Barnard. This excerpt shows the study guide's initial quotation of Talmud text.

The study guide takes the student through a series of steps whose ultimate objective is a precise and multi-layered understanding of the selected passage. First comes translating and explaining technical terminology and expanding abbreviations into their full form. This is followed by translating and parsing the grammar of all Hebrew-language words, and then doing the same for all Aramaic-language words. The next step is to translate biblical verses that appear in the passage, to explain relevant halakhic concepts, and to identify the generation and provenance of named rabbis. These steps culminate in translating the text unit as a whole. The student then outlines the text unit's argument and answers questions about its logic. In the last step, the study guide poses questions that invite the student to engage in reflection on the passage. This procedure begins all over again with Rashi's commentary, for which the student goes through most of the same steps.[3] It is a laborious slog, as one can imagine, but the students at JTS, many of whom who had been made miserable by the complexities of the Talmud text, had thanked me over the years for throwing them this life raft. The study guide did not provide any answers, but it helped students to ask the right questions.

I worried, however, that my experienced Barnard students would not need the sense-making device I had spent years developing at JTS. They would know the right questions to ask without being told. They would be able to differentiate between Hebrew and Aramaic on their own, and they would be familiar with the technical terminology—or, at least, they would know that this is what they needed to know in order to read the text. The study guide would feel like tiresome busy work to them. But that was my main teaching tool, and I did not have the time to come up with a new one. I posted my first study guide on Courseworks (Columbia's on-line course platform) and hoped that the students would not stage a revolt.

What I found, inexplicably, is that the Barnard students did so poorly on the study guides that I felt compelled to let them correct and resubmit them. The students' work in the guides was careless, with mistakes littering every section and swaths simply left blank. If the Barnard students did have significant background studying Talmud, why did they perform more poorly than the JTS students, many of whom had little background and some none at all? On the one hand, I was happy to see that my study guides were still useful in my teaching at Barnard, but, on the other, I was puzzled that they were.

A Hypothesis about Sense-Making

For the remainder of this essay, I offer a hypothesis for why the study guides were still useful and for why the Barnard students did not ace them, at least initially. I then want to talk about the study guides in more detail and to

---

3   Because of space constraints, I will not discuss certain sections of the study guide (abbreviations, biblical verses, halakhic concepts, named rabbis, and Rashi) in this essay.

look at some of the student work in them, drawing on other evidence from the course, either explicitly or implicitly, including my teaching journal, reflection papers, the final exams, and a video recording of one session. I will use that collective evidence to explore how the study guides operate in practice. As I go along, I will reflect on the principles and objectives behind the study guides since I developed them intuitively over a long period of time and did not articulate for myself what theories might be driving them. I will close with some reflections on what does not work very well with the study guides and what I hope, nevertheless, the study guides accomplish, especially in the broader personal development of each student. I will suggest that, at its best, learning to read Talmud helps us to understand ourselves as simultaneously makers of meaning and creatures of context whose imaginations are constrained by who we are and by the worlds we live in.

First is my hypothesis about why the study guides were challenging to my experienced Barnard students. Many of the students with Jewish day school backgrounds were able to build up sense from the text on their own. They could sight-read and translate without having seen that particular text before. Some owned copies of Marcus Jastrow's *Dictionary* and Frank's *Practical Talmud Dictionary* and knew how and when to use them.[4] The students recognized halakhic terms and had heard of the named rabbis. They were familiar with the concerns of the text from their own lives of Jewish observance. All this familiarity, however, was precisely the problem. They had enough information to try to fill in the gaps in their understanding, so much so that they stopped being aware of those gaps. In the spirit of good guesswork, my students used what they knew to guess at what they did not.

But, in fact, most of the students seemed not to have been trained—either because their exposure was at a high school level or because it was a traditional setting where perhaps these concerns loom less large—to distinguish Hebrew from Aramaic, to parse the grammar of the words, to translate with precision, or to outline the logical arguments. They were able to fudge

---

4 Marcus Jastrow, *Dictionary of the Targumim, the Talmud Babli and Yerushalmi, and the Midrashic Literature* (Grand Rapids, MI: Baker Academic, 2005), http://www.tyndalearchive.com/tabs/jastrow/; Yitzhak Frank and Ezra Zion Melamed, *Practical Talmud Dictionary* (New York: Feldheim, 1991). Both dictionaries are also referred to in this essay as the "Jastrow" and "Frank," respectively.

these matters as they went about their sense-making. If a noun was singular or plural, a verb active or passive, a rabbi a second or fourth-generation amora, a biblical verse from Exodus or Leviticus—what real difference did it make? My conviction—a product of my academic training and intellectual orientation—is that it makes a big difference, for reasons I will elucidate further into the chapter. The study guide, rather than allowing the students to make sense of the text as it had done for the JTS students, required the Barnard students to *stop* making sense, but this was in order for them, ultimately, to make *better* sense. The study guide halted their process of sense-making, forcing them not to guess—but to know. I was not the tour guide for first-time visitors, it was true, but as a master for the already initiated, I found that the same steps proved just as important. While I had designed my study guide at JTS to make the strange familiar, at Barnard, my study guide had the opposite but just as salutary effect—the study guide made the familiar strange.[5]

The Course Plan

Before discussing the study guides and student work in greater detail, let me first give some of the background of the Barnard course. At JTS, a new rabbinical school curriculum had required me to teach materials from tractate Sukkah, so I had developed an introductory level course oriented around those materials. Using these materials again at Barnard seemed to make sense. In the JTS course, I had adopted a slow pace that I had at first feared the students would find torturous, but in fact, they, like me, seemed to enjoy luxuriating in the intricacies of the texts.[6] I therefore had taught only two

---

5 On making the familiar strange and the strange familiar, see Jonathan Z. Smith, *Imagining Religion: From Babylon to Jonestown* (Chicago: University of Chicago Press, 1982), xiii; Jonathan Z. Smith, *Relating Religion: Essays in the Study of Religion* (Chicago: University of Chicago Press, 2004), 383, 389.

6 On teaching Talmud at this pace, see Jane Kanarek, "The Pedagogy of Slowing Down: Teaching Talmud in a Summer Kollel," *Teaching Theology and Religion* 13, no. 1 (January 2010): 15-34; reprinted as "The Pedagogy of Slowing Down: Teaching Talmud in a Summer Kolel," in *Turn It and Turn It Again: Studies in the Teaching and Learning of Classical Jewish Texts*, ed. Jon A. Levisohn and Susan P. Fendrick (Boston: Academic Studies Press, 2013).

Stop Making Sense: Using Text Study Guides to Help Students Learn to Read Talmud | CHAPTER 1

sugyot over the course of the semester: the first sugya in the tractate that discusses the maximum height for a sukkah, and a later one in the second chapter about the permissibility of "mobile" sukkahs, that is, sukkahs built on top of various vehicles.[7]

As I had done with the JTS course, I decided with the Barnard course to supplement the study of the talmudic texts with contemporary scholarship about rabbinic literature, rabbinic history, and rabbinic perspectives on the sukkah. I interspersed the scholarly readings with Aramaic grammar paradigms. For each session, the Barnard students would prepare a "chunk" of talmudic text with the study guide and either a scholarly reading or a grammar paradigm. I discussed the scholarly readings and grammar paradigms usually at the start of class and did not discuss the study guide directly but would draw on information from it as we read and interpreted the day's Talmud text. Before we began using the Talmud study guides, I dedicated several sessions to studying passages from the Torah relevant to Sukkot as well as the first Mishnah and parallel Tosefta of the tractate.

Study Guide Section on Technical Terms

As mentioned above, the study guide starts with the text unit itself. At the beginning of the semester, the unit consists of only a few lines of text. As the semester progresses, the units reach the size in the sample above. I present the text unit to the students in as undifferentiated a way as possible, without any line breaks, punctuation, or vocalization (Figure 1).[8] I do this because the passage appears on the traditional printed Talmud page in a similar way, and my goal is for the students to study comfortably from such a page. It is also because I want to start with something that looks like "word soup," where no assumptions about meaning have been made and the job of

---

[7] This second sugya was of particular interest to me because it discusses a sukkah built on top of an animal, and my current research concerns animals in the Talmud. I discuss the material about sukkahs built on the top of animals in "Revisiting the Anomalous: Animals at the Intersection of Persons and Property in Bavli Sukkah 22b-23b," in *Festschrift for Steven Fraade*, ed. Christine E. Hayes, Tzvi Novick, and Michal Bar-Asher Siegal (Göttingen, Ger.: Vandenhoeck and Ruprecht, forthcoming).

[8] The complete study guide can be found in the appendix to this article.

producing meaning lies fully ahead. The text presentation is meant to stir up an air of mystery and perhaps even frustration.

I present the section on technical terms first because identifying and understanding each one is essential to understanding the sugya as a whole. These terms are the scaffolding on which the sugya is built. The student's task for each term that I have pulled from the text "chunk" is to copy its translation from the entry in Frank's *Practical Talmud Dictionary*, and if there is a description of function, to copy that too. In the first few study guides of the semester, I make explicit in the instructions that the student should look up the terms in Frank, but I omit that instruction in later guides. While copying a dictionary entry verbatim may seem like less than inventive pedagogy, in my view, the technical terms are so important that the value of getting them exactly right outweighs the rote educational experience. Moreover, the very notion of a technical term can feel quite alien—the idea that a word does not just mean what it means but embeds within it an entire network of argumentation. So, in many ways, the main objective of this study guide section is to introduce and naturalize the idea of a technical term. Finally, there is something to be said for starting with a task that is almost mindless, since it can act as a warm-up for the more challenging sections that follow. I found that students performed the task in this section more or less exactly as they were expected to, even the weakest students, and that the students were able to recapitulate almost all of this material on the final exam. Only a few students made mistakes or omitted content in this section, and I was always surprised (and exasperated) when they did.

I will give examples from two of the weakest performing students in the class, since their work best illustrates the pitfalls of the assignment. The two students, whom I will call Mara and Jamie, performed poorly for different reasons. Mara was slow in absorbing the language of the text and in grasping its logic, but she worked assiduously at it. She frequently asked questions after class either in person or by email, and she discussed with me other projects she was working on as well as larger life goals. Jamie, on the other hand, had spotty attendance and, when she did come, she sat in the back with one or two of her friends. None of them participated much, and Jamie participated least of all.

In the last of the seven study guides of the course (at which point the students were or should have been well-versed in the routine), in the entry for *ki pligi*, Jamie's translation was "when do they disagree" (Figure 2). Jamie's

Stop Making Sense: Using Text Study Guides to Help Students Learn to Read Talmud | CHAPTER 1

Technical Terminology

Term	Translation	Function
כולי עלמא לא פליגי	all would agree	n/a
כי פליגי	when do they disagree	n/a
אי נמי	even if	introduces new solution to problem yes, but not here
מאן דאמר	~~according to~~ the one who says	n/a
חיישינן	concerned	n/a
ניחוש	let him be concerned	n/a
שכיחא	common	n/a
איכא	there is	n/a
ביני ביני	between	n/a

Figure 2 The section on technical terminology in the study guide. Jamie's work is shown here.

translation is more or less accurate, but it implies that *ki pligi* is an interrogative statement, which it is not, and her translation would have been better without the helping verb "do." Many students who, unlike Jamie, did get the translation correct in their study guides ("when they disagree"), ultimately got it wrong on the exam in the same way that Jamie did, thinking it was interrogative rather than declarative. My guess is that what snags the students about *ki pligi* is, first, that speakers of modern Hebrew know *ki* to mean "because" instead of "when," which means they are facing a familiar word being used in an unfamiliar way and, second, perhaps more on point, people associate the English word "when" more with its interrogative sense than with its declarative: "When are you working on your study guide?" rather than "When I work on my study guide, I look up every word in the dictionary." Jamie neglected to write the function of the phrase—it restricts the scope of a rabbinic dispute—even though the Frank dictionary provides a description. My presumption is that Jamie did not consult the Frank dictionary entry, despite the explicit instructions to do so, and relied on her base of knowledge to guess at the translation instead. She must not have had enough knowledge to describe the term's function and perhaps thought that this was one of the terms in the section that did not have a distinctive technical function. The diligent Mara, by contrast, copied the Frank entry verbatim and had the correct answers for both translation and function, though there was a typo in her transcription (Figure 3).

Jamie seemed to have looked up other words in the dictionary, however, and my presumption is that these were words with which she was not familiar

Technical Terminology

Term	Translation	Function
כולי עלמא לא פליגי	all agree / all don't disagree	n/a
כי פליגי	in these circumtances [did] they differ	This formula defines the scope of a controversy that was previously quoted
אי נמי	or alternatively; even if	usually introduces alternative solution to a problem

Figure 3 The section on technical terminology in the study guide. Mara's work is shown here.

and did not have a base of knowledge from which to guess their meaning. But Jamie made mistakes even in those instances. For the rather uncommon term *beyney-veyney*, which according to Frank means "in the meantime" or "in-between" (the latter meaning fit our sugya), Jamie instead wrote "between," which is the meaning given for the previous entry in the dictionary, the related but simpler and much more common term *beyney* (Figure 2). Jamie seems to have stopped at the first entry (or, possibly, she relied on her knowledge of the Hebrew word *beyn*). The difference when comparing "between" and "in-between" is subtle, and it would have been possible to translate our text also with "between," so I (or, in this case, the teaching assistant, whose corrections are handwritten) did not take off points for her answer. But I did note that her selection of definition was part of a broader pattern of uneven dictionary work and, beyond that, uneven attendance. Jamie, in short, used what she knew to guess at what she did not and gave imprecise answers as a result. Mara, by contrast, took the stance of not knowing (perhaps she did know some of the terms, perhaps she did not) and attained a high level of accuracy. I will return to the question of whether Mara fully absorbed the information, but it is evident that at this initial stage she gave herself access to important information more so than did Jamie.

Study Guide Sections on Grammar

The grammar sections that follow are significantly more challenging for the students for a variety of reasons. I divide the grammar tables into two, Hebrew and Aramaic, because the grammar of the two languages is different and sometimes the meaning is as well, and because the student must look at

Stop Making Sense: Using Text Study Guides to Help Students Learn to Read Talmud | CHAPTER 1

different entries in the Jastrow dictionary depending on whether it is one language or the other. Jastrow's system for differentiating between Hebrew and Aramaic is unfortunate since he indicates Hebrew with the enigmatic abbreviation "b.h." (which stands for biblical Hebrew and is his term for what is generally called rabbinic Hebrew). Jastrow marks Aramaic with the even more enigmatic "ch." (short for Chaldean, which is generally called Aramaic).[9] In the early study guides, I issue explicit dictionary instructions for each grammar section but omit them in later guides (as I do with the technical terms section). I pull out each Hebrew word from the text unit and ask the student to identify part of speech, number if it is a noun or verb, and, if it is a verb, to identify the root, person, and tense. Finally, the student translates the Hebrew word. The student then turns to a similar table for the Aramaic words.

This sounds relatively simple, but I have run into a variety of problems with the grammar tables. For one, different categories apply to different parts of speech. "Number" applies only to nouns and verbs and not to adverbs, infinitives, or prepositions, while "person" and "tense" apply only to verbs. The result is a confusing checkerboard effect, with many boxes requiring the student to write "not applicable." Figure 4 shows one of the tables where I supplied "n/a" in the appropriate boxes to ease the students' burden.

If I had divided up the parts of speech initially when I was designing the study guides and created a separate table for each, the inconsistency in

Hebrew Language

	Root	Part of speech	Number	Verbs: person, tense	Translation of word as is
פיל	n/a			n/a	
קשור				n/a	
נבלתו	n/a			n/a	
גזרה	n/a			n/a	
סמוך				n/a	

Figure 4 The "checkerboard" effect in the grammar table.

---

9 I could ask the students to use the Sokoloff dictionary instead, but its scholarly orientation makes it a less appropriate choice for introductory students, despite Jastrow's outdated and non-user-friendly qualities.

| 11

categories would dissolve. But I had decided against doing this, not only because it would lead to a profusion of tables but also because I want the students to be able to determine for themselves what part of speech a word is. I am tempted to rationalize that there may well be a pedagogical payoff that offsets the confusion, since the "n/a"-filled boxes may prompt students to consider how parts of speech differ from each other. The student will see from the many "n/a's" next to the noun *pil* ("elephant"), for instance, that nouns are more static markers of meaning, while the row of empty boxes next to the verb *qashur* ("tied" or "tethered" in this passage) highlights the dynamic quality of verbs.[10]

I intentionally leave out a large amount of material from the grammar tables. I omit particular adverbs, prepositions, or conjunctions in the passage that I think the students either already know or can easily figure out. I focus almost exclusively on nouns and verbs, because they are the basic building blocks of a sentence. With verbs, I omit *binyan*, voice, and mood, because I thought an increase in the number of categories would overwhelm the student. With nouns, I ignore pronominal suffixes for the same reason. The study guide, therefore, may give a student the illusion of digging deep into the technicalities of the text while, in truth, there are many dimensions of the language that the study guide simply ignores.

Another problem is that many words can be classified in more than one way. For instance, in the chart (Figure 5), Jamie described *qashur* as an adjective. *Qashur* is used in the relevant text unit to describe an elephant who is tied down or tethered.[11] Jamie is correct that the word is used as a descriptor for a

Hebrew Language

	Root	Part of speech	Number	Verbs: person, tense	Translation of word as is
פיל	n/a	noun	singular	n/a	elephant
קשור	קשר	adj	singular	n/a	related to here, literally
נבלתו	n/a	noun	singular	n/a	carcass "tied up"

Figure 5 This is Jamie's work in the section on Hebrew language.

---

10 As explained below, I inserted "n/a" into the verb column for participles, thinking of them more in terms of their function as adjectives rather than as verbs.

11 I realize that one would not expect to read about a tethered elephant in a line of Talmud and that it merits some comment. The fact that I am not stopping to discuss it points to the suspension of certain kinds of sense-making that must transpire in order for other kinds of sense-making to happen.

Stop Making Sense: Using Text Study Guides to Help Students Learn to Read Talmud | CHAPTER 1

noun, so it does have an adjectival use and, moreover, in this case, without having thought about it too much myself beforehand, I placed an "n/a" under the verb column and, therefore, pushed the students in the direction of choosing "adjective" over "verb." But the word *qashur* comes from the root *q-sh-r* and is, in fact, the passive participle of the verb. As explained in Frank's dictionary, however, a passive participle is essentially a verb being used as an adjective. So is *qashur* more accurately described as an adjective or a verb? Should I accept both answers? Would it confuse the students if they show each other their papers and find that different answers were both marked as correct? I did not have much to worry about in this particular example, since many students probably knew this relatively common root from modern Hebrew. The problem of classificatory ambiguity was multiplied ten-fold when it came to the Aramaic tables, as the students did not know Aramaic grammar, and I was only gradually introducing the basics over the course of the semester.

A fundamental problem is that I am not particularly expert in grammar myself, nor do I expect the students to be. My assumption is that most students are not trained very well in *English* grammar, much less Hebrew, and certainly not Aramaic. Most of us know how to use words very well even if we cannot say what part of speech they are. So why bother, other than for pedantic reasons, to classify words in a talmudic text? My aim in all this is entirely pragmatic—understanding the particular text we have before us as best we can.

I maintain the conviction that classifying each word is an invaluable strategy for making sense of a text, especially one in a foreign language and from a foreign culture. Classification forces us to think about the role each word is playing and provides vital information about how all the words come together. If we encounter some ambiguities along the way, it does not mean the effort is not worthwhile, nor does it mean that we will not emerge understanding the text pretty well or even better than we would have otherwise. But how do I keep the students from getting tangled up in those efforts, especially when they are being graded for the study guides and are concerned with getting the right answer?

There is a variety of ways in which I try to preempt frustration and to model a workable, non-pedantic relationship to grammar, especially when grammatically ambiguous words come up. These strategies include (1) consulting grammar tools, providing the most accurate grammatical analysis that I can, and showing relevant sections from grammar guides on PowerPoint® slides during class session; (2) admitting my own ignorance when I cannot make a confident determination and conveying the message that incomplete grammar mastery is not an insurmountable handicap to sense-making, and that it, in fact, can add to their sense of the text's richness; (3) acknowledging that while most people are going to find grammar boring, it remains an indispensable step in getting to know the text; and (4) promising the students I will not test them on grammar per se but will expect them to know grammar only as it is folded into their translations and discussions of the text.[12] By framing the work on grammar in this way, my objective is for the student to use grammar to *deconstruct* the text, but not too much. The questions about grammar should challenge the student but should not hold her back from building new meanings.

Study Guide Section on Translation

While the capstone of the study guide is the translation section, it takes the students a number of study guides to realize that this is the case. The students stop making sense so enthusiastically (they become intent on breaking down each word and figuring out its form and function) that they forget the ultimate goal, which is to make sense of the passage as a whole. The problem begins in the initial study guide sections, where students tend to remain in the abstract world of dictionary entries and must be pushed to build a bridge back to the text unit that lies before them. I tell them that when Frank offers two or three definition options, they should not choose the first one or write them all down; they should choose the one that fits the context best. When Jastrow translates a root, the student should not write down that translation but rather choose the

---

12   I did break that promise when I decided to include on the final exam a table requiring the students to give the Aramaic past, present, and future tense forms of third-person, masculine singular and plural of the root *k-t-v*. I gave them advance warning that this table would appear, and I explained that knowledge of these basic Aramaic forms would give them much mileage in future Talmud study.

translation for the specific form of the verb that appears in our text. It sometimes takes a while for the students to absorb the nature of this task, and even once they have, it is often difficult for them to find the right definition for the context (unless one strikes a "Jastrow bonus," where Jastrow cites the same text one is studying). An example of such difficulty (Figure 5) is when Jamie translated *qashur* as "related to," which is a good translation but not for our text, where the word is used literally to mean "tied up," as my teaching assistant explained in his comments on her work. A similar occurrence happened with Jamie's and Mara's answers for *i nami* in the technical terms section (Figures 2 and 3). My selected text happened to be one of the few cases in the Talmud where the phrase is used literally and does not carry its usual technical function of introducing an alternative solution, as my teaching assistant indicates in his comments on Jamie's paper.

Ideally, the guide's sections operate synergistically. The right choice for each word depends on the right choice made for all the other words. The translation section is where the student pulls all the words and phrases together, where she goes back to the earlier sections and reconsiders her translation choices and how they fit into the larger composition, changing her answers in the earlier sections when necessary to accommodate her translation of the passage as a whole. What often happens, though, is that the students start from scratch in the translation section, reinventing their own wheels, translating the passage anew rather than using the translations they had generated in the technical term and grammar sections, as can be seen in the example below.[13] When Mara translates *kule alma la pligi* in the translation section, she writes "do not disagree" and then in parentheses she writes "agree" (Figure 6). This more or less matches the translation she wrote for the same phrase in the technical terms section, where she had written both "all agree"

---

13 Easy access to published translations exacerbates the problem since the student ends up building her translation on someone else's rather than on her own prior work in the study guide. This problem was particularly evident in reflection papers that were due the last day of class, in which students were asked to write about ideas from the text that appealed to them. In her reflection paper, Jamie entirely abandoned the translation work she had done in her study guide and instead relied on a very dated English translation when she cited the Talmud as saying "our eyes do not descry it."

CHAPTER 1 | Beth A. Berkowitz

Translation of Text Unit

In [a case where] a bound elephant [is being used as a sukkah wall], all (Rabbi Zeira and Abaye, the two opinions regarding Rabbi Meir's position) do not disagree (agree), for even if it dies its carcass [still] has ten [tefahim of height to serve as a sukkah wall]. When they disagree [is] in [the case of] an unbound elephant. According to the one (Abaye) who said lest it die, we are not concerned. According to the one (Rabbi Zeira) who said [it is] a decree lest it flee, we are concerned. According to the one who said [it is a decree] lest it die, let him be concerned lest

Figure 6 Mara's translation.

and "all don't disagree" (Figure 3). But when Mara translates *ki pligi*, instead of writing "in these circumstances [did] they differ," as she does in the technical terms section (Figure 3), she writes "when they disagree." In fact, I prefer this alternate translation because it more accurately reflects the original Aramaic. But it is not the translation that is found in the Frank dictionary and not what Mara herself had written in the earlier section when she had first been asked to translate the term.

Mara introduces another discrepancy between the sections of her study guide when she translates *man da'amar*. Whereas in the section on technical terms she copies the Frank entry, which translates the phrase as "the one who says" (with the verb in the present tense), in her translation of the passage as a whole she uses the past tense, "the one who said." In fact, *amar* is the orthographic form for both past and present tenses, so both translations are correct. But I emphasize during the course the importance of consistency in translation when a word is being used the same way, as well as the significance of using early sections in the study guide to help with later ones. So, despite the correctness of both translations that Mara uses, her shift from present to past between the two sections of the study guide reflects a problem in her work, seemingly minor, but perhaps reflecting a broader misunderstanding of the process that the study guide actually is designed to facilitate, which is the continuous building of sense through microanalysis of the words and terms.

The reader may have noticed an unexpected profusion of parentheses and brackets in Mara's translation (Figure 6). I want to comment on them before I move on to discuss the final sections of the study guide. This mass of punctuation is not an idiosyncrasy on Mara's part but is a practice that I require of the students. I instruct the students to use parentheses to explain a word in the text whose meaning is unclear, and I instruct them to use brackets when they are filling in words that are necessary to make English sense of the text but do not appear in the original Hebrew or Aramaic. My aim here, and in the course as a whole, is to sensitize the students to their own process of sense-making, to make them aware of what exactly is in the text and what is not, and to encourage them to reflect on the project of translation and how making sense works differently in different languages. The first sentence in Mara's translation (Figure 6) is an excellent example of how the students implement this system. While the original text reads *be-pil kashur*, literally "in a bound elephant," Mara writes "a case where" in brackets, showing that she knows that she filled in these words in order to make sense of the text. On the final exam, however, when asked to translate the same text unit, Mara put the entire opening section in brackets, i.e., [in the case of] (Figure 7), suggesting that she may not have fully understood the bracketing procedure. In the study guide (Figure 6), Mara puts "Rabbi Zeira and Abaye" in parentheses, since the "all" in the talmudic text is vague, and she chooses parentheses here instead of brackets because she is explaining the referent of the text rather than filling in words to make it read smoothly, as she was doing earlier. Mara offered the same parenthetical explanation on her final exam (Figure 7). I might have put her phrase "is being used as a sukkah wall" (which she used in the study guide but omitted entirely on the final exam) in parentheses rather than in brackets, since, in my view, it functions more as an explanation than as a translation tactic. In truth, I am not preoccupied with the distinction as long as I feel that the overall goals of using the parentheses and brackets are being met. Judging from the

[In the case of] a bounded elephant, they all (Rabbi Zeira and Abaye's hypothesis of Rabbi Meir) do not disagree that

Figure 7 Mara's translation in the final exam.

comparison between her translation in the study guide and her translation of the same passage on the final exam, I would conclude that Mara has mastered the basic idea of the brackets and parentheses and can sometimes use them correctly but struggles with the subtleties of implementation. She is gaining awareness of her own role in sense-making as she distinguishes between straight translation and elaboration, but she has trouble distinguishing among the different kinds of elaboration that she finds herself producing.

Study Guide Section with Outline

The outline section takes the student full circle back to the beginning of the study guide, where the text unit first appeared in its "word-soup" form. The text unit now reappears in the outlining section, but this time broken down into sentences, with each sentence positioned under an empty box (Figure 8). In the box, the student is asked to describe the function of the sentence within the flow of the discourse of the text unit. When I initially present the text unit in undifferentiated lines, I am encouraging the student to strip down their assumptions about meaning. When I present it now, in outline form, I expect the student to have developed a robust understanding of the text based on the work they have done so far on the technical terms, grammar, and translation. I expect them to use that gathered understanding to grasp the fundamental discursive patterns of the text and to consider how its many micro-elements together produce the voice or voices of the text.

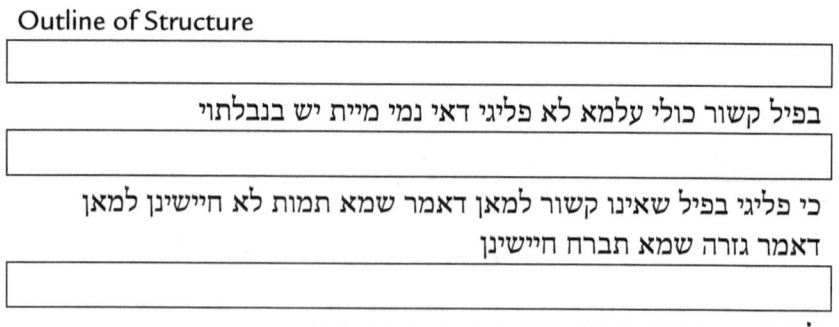

Figure 8 The outlining section of the study guide.

Stop Making Sense: Using Text Study Guides to Help Students Learn to Read Talmud | CHAPTER 1

If it takes the students a while to adjust to the expectations of the translation section, it takes them even longer for the outlining section. In the first study guide, I give lengthy instructions:

> In the boxes, describe in concise, abstract terms what is happening in the argument. Examples: "Question about a word in the mishnah"; "baraita contradicting the mishnah"; "an amora's explanation of the mishnah"; and "a resolution that restricts the scope of the mishnah."

As with the other sections, I abbreviate the instructions as we get further into the semester. An effective description of the function of a sentence in talmudic dialectic requires deft use of highly abstract terms and just the right amount of detail so that the outline comes to life and does not merely repeat the information in the text. Whereas the answers in the technical terms and grammar sections are relatively fixed, the translation section and, even more so the outlining section, allow for a good deal of individual interpretation.

I model outlining for them in class by speaking of the sugya in structural terms and using terminology of the type I describe in the outline instructions (e.g., the *stam's* question, the amora's answer, the *stam's* challenge to the amora's answer based on a baraita, etc.). The outlining labels that the students use often reflect the ones I used with them during our discussion. In Study Guide 7, Mara outlined the first two lines of the text unit using my approach to the sugya from class, in which I described three "cases" that are presented by the talmudic editor (Figure 9).

Mara describes here the first two lines of the text by referring to a case 1 and case 2, successfully reflecting our discussion in class. Another strategy I use in class to keep track of the talmudic back-and-forth is to use "smiley faces" to indicate when the Talmud has presented a positive proof or a

Outline of Structure ✓ Nice emoticons!

Case 1: ☹ the two opinions regarding Rabbi Meir's position agree on how he would hold
בפיל קשור כולי עלמא לא פליגי דאי נמי מיית יש בנבלתו י׳

Case 2: ☺ the two opinions regarding Rabbi Meir's position disagree (for now...) on how he would hold
כי פליגי בפיל שאינו קשור למאן דאמר שמא תמות לא חיישינן למאן דאמר גזרה שמא תברח חיישינן

Figure 9 Mara's work in the outlining section of the study guide.

satisfactory case and to use "sad faces" for a refutation or a problematic case. Mara here successfully adopts that practice and is complimented for it by the teaching assistant in the handwritten comments. This particular sugya entails a tricky application of smiley and sad faces, since the talmudic editor is looking for cases where two amoraim would disagree about what a tanna would think. The editor is counter-intuitively "happy" when there is disagreement. Mara was not tripped up by this. She also quite elegantly foreshadows in her parenthetical "(for now …)" that case 2 will be rejected. I would have liked slightly more elaboration, however, on the "two opinions" she mentions. She could have specified that Rabbi Zeira and Abaye are the holders of these opinions. I encourage the students to find the right balance between the specific and the general, and she may have concluded that mentioning the amoras' names would get her too enmeshed in the details. Mara also could have indicated that each sentence not only presents the opinions but also gives some explanation for one of those opinions (in the first sentence) or both (in the second sentence). I assume Mara knew that the explanation was there and either did not think to mention it or decided it was not important enough to include in her outline. Mara was able to recapitulate these labels in more or less the same form (she used slightly different language and left out the smiley and sad faces) on her final exam, where I divided up the text somewhat differently from on the study guide so that the student could not simply memorize the labels for each line but had to understand how they reflected the particular text with which they were associated. Mara thus showed herself to be capable of conceptualizing the structure of the text at a degree of removal from individual words and syntax. The study guide had taken her from the technicalities of terms and grammar, to the word-by-word work of translation, to a description of the thought patterns within the text.

Study Guide Sections with Questions

The final sections of the study guide consist of questions. The first set is called "Questions about Structure and Argument," and the second is called "Questions for Reflection." The questions on structure and argument adhere closely to the outline. If the student was successful in the outline they created,

Stop Making Sense: Using Text Study Guides to Help Students Learn to Read Talmud | CHAPTER 1

they should be able to answer every question in this set with perfect accuracy. These questions address what is usually called the *peshat*, or simple meaning, and require the student to know what each line of the Gemara does, how it follows from the previous line, and how it leads to the next one. The questions test whether the student understands the basics of the talmudic discourse. If the student cannot successfully answer these questions, then they have not really understood the sugya. These were some of the "Questions about Structure and Argument" from Study Guide 7:

1. What is the first case the sugya imagines, and what do Abaye and Rabbi Zeira each think Rabbi Meir rules on it?
2. What is the second case the sugya imagines, and how do Abaye and Rabbi Zeira each think Rabbi Meir rules on it?
3. On what basis does the Gemara reject the second case?
4. What is the third case the sugya imagines, and what do Abaye and Rabbi Zeira each think Rabbi Meir rules on it?

The second and more advanced set of questions (Questions for Reflection) includes two basic types. One type represents questions that the rishonim, the classic medieval Talmud commentators like the Tosafot, Rashba, or Ritba, would typically ask. These questions have to do with ambiguities or wrinkles in the text.[14] One question of this sort from Study Guide 7 is, "Think carefully about the flow of the argument and how the challenge about the animal's leg space fits into it. Whose position is this challenging?" The part of the sugya to which this question refers features a strange editorial patch-up job. It is hard to tell how the final back-and-forth in the sugya (about how exactly one would turn an animal into the wall of a sukkah) relates to the earlier back-and-forth (about when Abaye and Rabbi Zeira would disagree on Rabbi Meir's ruling on using an animal for the wall of a sukkah). The rishonim debate a number of options, as did my students in

---

14 The Tosafot (or tosafists, as they are sometimes known in English) were twelfth- and thirteenth-century Talmud glossators in France and Germany, the earliest of whom were Rashi's relatives or students. Rashba is the acronym for Solomon Ibn Adret, a Spanish Talmud commentator (1235-1310), and Ritba is the acronym for his student Yom Tov ben Avraham Ishbili (d. 1330). I do not usually show the students passages from the rishonim, but I present the questions in the name of the rishonim if that is where I encountered them.

class. This type of question requires an understanding of the text that goes well beyond the basics and that is sensitive to subtle shifts and textural variations.

The other type of question within the more advanced set requires the student to step back from the sugya altogether and to think about it independently and critically (not in the sense of being negative, but in the sense of being analytical). These questions invite the students to consider the Talmud at the macro-level as an intellectual, cultural, and religious project. An example of this sort from Study Guide 7 asks, "Is the Gemara serious about the tied-up elephant as the wall for a sukkah? Or the hanging, dead animal? What are we to make of these very strange scenarios?" These questions may or may not require the kind of text mastery that the other type does—ideally, the two types of advanced questions complement each other—but the "Questions for Reflection" ask the student to perform a certain kind of reality check. The degree to which the student is capable of this depends on their psychological maturity and intellectual creativity. The initial sections of the study guide (terms and grammar) ask the student to deconstruct the text and to penetrate deep into its details; the intermediate sections (translation and outlining) have the students recombining those details into a satisfying sense. This final section invites the students to reflect on that newly made sense and to explore the gaps and curiosities within it.

Problems with the Study Guides

The value of these questions may be canceled out by the fact that I do not require the students to answer them, and I have to admit the possibility that the questions simply vanish into the ether without the students giving them much thought at all. I have my reasons for not requiring answers: the earlier sections are taxing enough; answers to these questions could produce tomes and tomes; and grading these answers would, in turn, be too burdensome for me and my teaching assistant.[15] This leads me to talk about the problem of grading more generally as well as other problems with the study guides. To be blunt, the study guides are hellish to grade. The refrain in my teaching

---

15   I draw exam questions from these sections and tell the students to use them for exam preparation, so they do have some practical use for the students.

journal is dismay upon receiving a fresh batch. It is probably as much a hell for the students to fill them out. And that is another serious problem to consider—whether the study guides might just drain too much of the fun out of Talmud text study, even if the student does achieve at the end a richer, deeper, more satisfying reading. The students fill out each study guide once, whereas the teaching assistant and I have to review the same information as many times as there are students in the class. Few teachers enjoy mounds of grading, but grading the study guides feels particularly burdensome in the scheme of grading burdens. I say this not to complain or to get credit but because anything that seriously detracts from a teacher's teaching experience should be considered a pedagogical problem that has an impact on students, and that other teachers may want to think twice about before adopting.

An additional challenge that every instructor faces is plagiarism, and my study guides are particularly prone to that problem. It is very easy for one student to simply transfer another's work to their study guide, especially in the earlier sections. The plagiarism potential was further expanded by my decision to permit the students to work in *havruta*, though I tell them on the syllabus and in class that they must write down with whom they worked and on which sections. Even though cooperative work is relatively rare in the humanities, especially at the undergraduate level, I permit it in my text course because there is a tradition of *havruta* study for Talmud, and for some students, it can make study more effective and enjoyable (see my point above about displeasure as a pedagogical problem).[16] But, like all cooperative endeavors, they can easily turn sour, and it is quite possible that in the course of the semester weaker students had copied the work of stronger ones.

A final problem I want to treat leads me to my concluding reflections on the larger theories and goals of the study guides. The principle of the study guides follows the same logic as the well-known children's song "Bingo." As you keep singing the song, you take more and more letters away until you have only the music. The idea underlying the use of the study guide is that as you keep studying Talmud, you need the rubrics of the study

---

16   For references on the history of Talmud study in *havruta*, see Elie Holzer, "What Connects 'Good Teaching,' Text Study, and Hevruta Learning? A Conceptual Argument," *Journal of Jewish Education* 72, no. 3 (2006): 183-204. Ibid., no. 2: 183.

guide less and less in order to read Talmud accurately and meaningfully. Technical terms start to jump off the page, and you do not need to look most of them up as you progress through the text. Aramaic and Hebrew seem automatically and intuitively different from each other. You do not need to think about parts of speech because you know what they are. You do not need to outline because you know the function of each sentence. If you are unclear on any of these elements in the text, you know what questions to ask and how to get answers. You instinctively start to ask yourself questions about structure, and the same goes for second-order questions for reflection. The students, in short, are weaned off the study guides and become fully formed readers of Talmud without them. But how does this weaning happen, especially in a college setting where I teach students for only one semester? By nurturing them with all the steps, tables, rubrics, outlines, and questions, do I push them into a dependency and make their reading practices a mere replica of my own? Is my study guide a form of "helicopter teaching" (along the lines of helicopter parenting)? As I asked in my teaching journal at one point, "Do I over-teach?"

Conclusion: Learning to Read Ourselves

I might over-teach at times, but if I have to err, I would rather it be on that side than on the side of leaving students to "sink or swim," especially since many experience the study of Talmud as "sink or swim" and feel that they most decidedly sank. Perhaps some of my Barnard students had that experience in the past, and they came to my course in the hope that this time they would swim.

I call this concluding section "Learning to Read Ourselves" in order to exploit the double meaning of the syntax and, in so doing, to model an act of reading that recognizes and interprets ambiguity in the way that I am aiming for Talmud reading to do. I refer both to learning to read *by* ourselves, which ideally the study guide will foster even if it risks generating dependency, but also to learning to read *ourselves* as though we were a sort of text, as something that can be interpreted and reflected upon. These two meanings criss-cross, since my hope and goal is that we learn to read ourselves in the process of reading texts. As we come to know the text better and better, we begin to see what is there and what is not, and we are able to see what we are inserting or projecting in order to make compelling sense of it. Our own assumptions and perspectives and procedures of meaning-making emerge in a clearer light, so that as we get to know the text, we also get to know ourselves.

I will close with an example of what I mean. The second sugya I taught in my course provides commentary on M. Sukkah 2:3:

> One who makes his sukkah on top of a wagon or on top of a ship, it is fit,
> and one may ascend it on the festival.
> [One who makes his sukkah] on top of a tree or on the back of a camel,
> it is fit, but one may not ascend it on the festival.

We spent seventy-five minutes in class discussing these two lines. This mishnah presents four types of sukkahs—I call them "sukkahs in strange places," which include the top of a wagon, ship, tree, and camel—grouped into two, all of which are declared fit, but only the first two can be ascended on the festival. We spent most of our time discussing the following questions: (1) Why *these* four sukkahs? What common feature ties them together? (2) Why might you think that each of these would not be valid, and, then, why does the Mishnah consider them valid despite whatever problems they might have? (3) Why can you ascend the first two on the festival but not the second two, and what is the significance of this distinction? (4) Is there a deeper principle that runs through this mishnah? Is there some more abstract idea it is trying to point to, perhaps having to do with mobility on the holiday?

I posed these questions to the class (verbally and on a PowerPoint® slide), and we found—as I planned we would—that there are any number of possible answers. I noted in my journal that one student explicitly asked why the Mishnah is not clearer about its guiding principles. My answer to the student was that her guess was as good as mine and that while the Mishnah's terseness may be maddening, we would not have the two Talmuds without it.[17] The in-depth Mishnah discussion was part of my plan for the students

---

17 In fact, what I first said is that if we compare the Mishnah to its parallel in the Tosefta, which we had also studied, we find that the Mishnah is actually a little clearer about fundamental concepts, but I admitted that it's relative, and that neither is disposed toward abstract formulations, at least to the extent that the Talmud (and, specifically, the *stam*) is.

to recognize once we reached the Talmud that the Talmud represents one possible road of interpretation among many and that its perspective on the Mishnah is creatively selective. But then, as we study Talmud, I make similar distinctions within its literary layers, so I am asking the students to appreciate not just the creativity of the Talmud as a whole when juxtaposed with the Mishnah, but also the creativity of one strand within the Talmud when juxtaposed with another—the amoraic when juxtaposed with the tannaitic, the stammaitic when juxtaposed with both. Then the students will go on to see Rashi's interpretive choice as yet one more in a long line of choices before him. Since we studied the relevant biblical texts in a session early on in the semester, all of this rabbinic material is being juxtaposed with the Bible, where the interpretive project seems to have begun. But then I introduce the students to the idea of inner-biblical exegesis and the possibility that one biblical text may have been adapting earlier ones. I want the students to see that the interpretive path never ends. Each text we encounter is negotiating prior ambiguities and then generating new ones, which future texts will then, in turn, negotiate, and so on. We are learning, in the end, to appreciate the creativity of sense-making, and to see that creativity as happening at every moment, for every creature. That creativity is being exercised within the Bible, the Mishnah, the Talmud, and Talmud commentaries, and also within ourselves. When the students face the question in their study guides of whether to insert brackets or parentheses into their translations, when they consider whether a passive participle is an adjective or a verb, when they decide exactly how to label a line of Gemara—they are making interpretive choices akin to choices made within the Talmud when its authors encountered their inherited traditions, and like all the Talmud commentators who faced the same questions that the students and I face in our classrooms today.

My study guides halted the process of sense-making for the Barnard students so that, ultimately, they could appreciate their own sense-making as a creative act. When sense-making is working properly, it becomes invisible, and we do not realize the almost miraculous powers that each of us possesses to create coherence. But appreciation of our own sense-making, as well as that of others, entails experiencing not only our powers but also our limitations. When we recognize the particularity of the Talmud's perspective on the Mishnah, for instance, and all the roads it does not take, we can begin to see the Talmud as constrained by its place and time, as rooted in a context that makes certain interpretations possible, plausible, and worthwhile and others objectionable or unthinkable, and we begin to see ourselves as having that very same rootedness. We appreciate ourselves, and others, as creatures of both imagination and limitation.[18]

---

18 This kind of appreciation, however, is hard won. I wrote in my journal about the students' reflection papers that "a number of students could not successfully distinguish between Rubenstein (whose article we had read) and the rabbis and the Bible. It was still all a big soup to them, despite the fact that this is all I tried to do all semester!" I would like to think the fault was in my framing of the assignment, which had not sufficiently encouraged them to make such distinctions. The study guide cannot stand alone, however, and if it is to achieve its objective of fostering appreciation of our sense-making powers, then it must work in concert with class discussion, other assignments, and my own ability to articulate coherently and compellingly the vision I have here laid out.

Appendix—Study Guide

Study Guide 7 for Sukkah 23a-b

Berkowitz, Barnard, Introduction to Talmud Text Study

Text Unit

בפיל קשור כולי עלמא לא פליגי דאי נמי מיית יש בנבלתו י' כי פליגי בפיל שאינו קשור למאן דאמר שמא תמות לא חיישינן למאן דאמר גזרה שמא תברח חיישינן למאן דאמר גזרה שמא תמות ניחוש שמא תברח אלא בפיל שאינו קשור כולי עלמא לא פליגי כי פליגי בבהמה קשורה למ"ד גזרה שמא תמות חיישינן למ"ד גזרה שמא תברח לא חיישינן ולמאן דאמר גזרה שמא תברח ניחוש שמא תמות מיתה לא שכיחא והאיכא רווחא דביני ביני דעביד ליה בהוצא ודפנא ודלמא רבעה דמתיחה באשלי מלעיל ולמאן דאמר גזרה שמא תמות נמי הא מתיחה באשלי מלעיל זמנין דמוקים בפחות משלשה סמוך לסכך וכיון דמייתא כווצא ולאו אדעתיה

Technical Terminology (type in or add more space if necessary)

Term	Translation	Function
כולי עלמא לא פליגי		n/a
כי פליגי		
אי נמי		
מאן דאמר		n/a
חיישינן		n/a
ניחוש		n/a
שכיחא		n/a
איכא		n/a
ביני ביני		n/a
דלמא		n/a
לעיל		n/a
הא		n/a
זמנין		n/a
כיון ד		n/a

Appendix—Study Guide | CHAPTER 1

Abbreviations

Abbreviation	Translation
י׳	This *yud* stands for the Hebrew number 10. To what ten does it refer?

Hebrew Language

	Root	Part of speech	Number	Verbs: person, tense	Translation of word as is
פיל	n/a			n/a	
קשור				n/a	
נבלתו	n/a			n/a	
גזרה	n/a			n/a	
סמוך					

Aramaic Language

	Root	Part of speech	Number	Verbs: person, tense	Translation of word as is
מיית					
רווחא	n/a			n/a	
עביד					
הוצא					
דפנא					
רבעה	n/a			n/a	
מתיחה	n/a				
אשלי				n/a	
מוקים					
כווצא					

Translation of Text Unit

Please type here.

Outline of Structure

בפיל קשור כולי עלמא לא פליגי דאי נמי מיית יש בנבלתו י׳

CHAPTER 1 | Beth A. Berkowitz

כי פליגי בפיל שאינו קשור למאן דאמר שמא תמות לא חיישינן למאן דאמר גזרה שמא תברח חיישינן

למאן דאמר גזרה שמא תמות ניחוש שמא תברח

אלא בפיל שאינו קשור כולי עלמא לא פליגי

כי פליגי בבהמה קשורה למ"ד גזרה שמא תמות חיישינן למ"ד גזרה שמא תברח לא חיישינן

ולמאן דאמר גזרה שמא תברח ניחוש שמא תמות

מיתה לא שכיחא

והאיכא רווחא דביני ביני

דעביד ליה בהוצא ודפנא

ודלמא רבעה

דמתיחה באשלי מלעיל

ולמאן דאמר גזרה שמא תמות נמי הא מתיחה באשלי מלעיל

זמנין דמוקים בפחות משלשה סמוך לסכך וכיון דמייתא כווצא ולאו אדעתיה

Questions about Structure and Argument

1. What is the first case the sugya imagines, and what do Abaye and Rabbi Zeira each think Rabbi Meir rules on it?

Appendix—Study Guide | CHAPTER 1

2. What is the second case the sugya imagines, and how do Abaye and Rabbi Zeira each think Rabbi Meir rules on it? On what basis does the Gemara reject the second case?
3. What is the third case the sugya imagines, and what do Abaye and Rabbi Zeira each think Rabbi Meir rules on it?
4. On what basis does the Gemara reject the third case?
5. What rebuttal is provided for that rejection?
6. The Gemara next challenges exactly how one would use an animal as a sukkah wall: What is that challenge?
7. How is that challenge addressed?
8. What new challenge is posed to using an animal as a sukkah wall, and how is that addressed?
9. The response itself is now queried regarding Abaye's approach to Rabbi Meir: How does the understanding of the baraita that has just been presented actually satisfy the concern of Rabbi Meir as Abaye understands it?
10. How does the Gemara, in the last step here, revive the problem according to Abaye's version of Rabbi Meir?

Questions for Reflection

1. What is the overall aim of this section vis-à-vis Abaye and Rabbi Zeira's opinion and vis-à-vis the original baraita that they are addressing? What is this whole section trying to figure out?
2. Is the Gemara serious about the tied-up elephant as the wall for a sukkah? Or the hanging, dead animal? What are we to make of these very strange scenarios?
3. Think carefully about the flow of the argument and how the challenge about the animal's leg space fits into it: Whose position is this challenging?

Rashi's Commentary

קשור - דליכא למיחש שמא תברח.

What is the significance of the fact that the animal is tied up, acc. to Rashi?

| 31

דכולי עלמא - בין לאביי בין לר' זירא מכשיר ר' מאיר.
Rashi is responding to the fact that *kule alma* is being used in a slightly strange way here. How is Rashi explaining what exactly is the subject of agreement?

דאי נמי מיית - ויפול יש בנבלתו עשרה.
Why doesn't Abaye think that Rabbi Meir would have a problem with a tied-up elephant being used a sukkah wall?

מיתה לא שכיחא - ואפילו ר' מאיר לא פסיל.
Acc. to Rashi, what is the case that according to Rabbi Zeira even Rabbi Meir wouldn't prohibit the animal from being used as a sukkah wall, and why?

והאיכא רווחא - דביני כרעי שהיא פירצה ואפילו כשהיא חיה.
How does Rashi explain the challenge posed here to using an animal for a sukkah wall?

דעביד ליה - גדר בין רגליה.
According to Rashi, how is the Gemara addressing that challenge? What do you have to do to an animal in order to be able to use him or her as a sukkah wall?

בהוצא ודפנא - הוצא - לולבי דקל, דפנא - ענפי עץ שקורין לורי"ר +עץ הדפנה+ וגדל בו פרי שקורין באיי"ש +פירות עץ הדפנה+.
How does Rashi define the Gemara's words here?

רבעה - רובצת.
How does Rashi define the Gemara's word here?

אשלי - חבלים.
How does Rashi define the Gemara's word here? Notice: if Rashi thinks a word in the Gemara is unfamiliar or being used in an unfamiliar way, he will define it.

הא מתיחה באשלי מלעי - ואם תמות אינה נופלת.
Why would the hanging animal be acceptable as a sukkah wall not only according to Rabbi Zeira's understanding of Rabbi Meir but also according to Abaye's understanding of Rabbi Meir, according to Rashi here?

זימנא דמוקי לה פחות משלשה כו' - פעמים שאין בגובהה של בהמה אלא שבעה ומשהו, וסוכה עשרה דקאי לה בפחות משלשה סמוך לסכך, ואמרינן לבוד.

Appendix—Study Guide | CHAPTER 1

What does this wall look like that the sukkah builder is making, according to Rashi? How does Rashi use the *lavud* concept to describe this wall? See Halakhic Concepts below on what *lavud* means.

וכיון דמייתא כוותא - מתמעט, רטריי"ט, והוה ליה שלשה, ובטיל ליה לבוד, ואין כאן דופן.

What problem might arise with the wall described in the previous comment? What is the risk of building such a wall? Do you notice anything familiar in Rashi's medieval French translation?

ולאו אדעתיה - אינו נותן לב לתקנה דאינו ניכר

Why does Rabbi Meir, according to Abaye's understanding of him, still prohibit a sukkah wall composed of a hanging animal?

Technical Terminology in Rashi

Term	Translation
ליכא	

Hebrew Language in Rashi

	Root	Part of speech	Number	Verbs: person, tense	Translation of word as is
גדר	n/a			n/a	
רגליה	n/a			n/a	
דקל	n/a			n/a	
עָנְפֵי	n/a			n/a	
קורין					
רובצת					
חבלים	n/a			n/a	
מתמעט					

Aramaic Language in Rashi

	Root	Part of Speech	Number	Verbs: person, tense	Translation
למיחש			n/a		

33

כרעי	n/a			n/a	
פירצה	n/a			n/a	
קאי					
אמרינן					
בטיל					

Halakhic Concepts in Rashi

לבוד	(From *The Talmud, The Steinsaltz Edition: A Reference Guide*): *Joined, connected*. A law given to Moses on Mt. Sinai but not specifically mentioned in the Torah, stating that two solid surfaces are considered as connected if there is a gap of less than 3 *tefahim* between them. The law of *lavud* is used in reference to the laws of Sabbath boundaries and the laws of the construction of a sukkah.

CHAPTER 2
■ ■ ■

Looking for Problems: A Pedagogic Quest for Difficulties

Ethan M. Tucker

The Babylonian Talmud is a difficult text. This is obviously true for beginning students, for whom the language, the concepts, and the style of argument and presentation are simply foreign. Notably, this is equally true for the more advanced student. Even after clearing the hurdles of surface meaning and syntax, the logical assumptions and conclusions of the text can seem forced and incoherent. Talmud students are familiar with the experience of working hard to understand the text and at the end of that process may still feel puzzled and unsure if the text as a whole, in fact, holds together for them. In this sense, the Talmud is not merely a complex text in need of decoding; it seems to be rife with difficulties that are in inherent from its very creation.

As a result, when students complete their learning of a talmudic passage, or sugya, there is often a gap between what they understand the sugya to be saying and what "makes sense" to them. That gap usually translates into one of two outcomes. One is that the student emerges from the experience of learning as "alienated" from the text, perceiving the Talmud to be a foreign medium of expression that operates by different rules. The student may question the value of investing time in mastering something so foreign and may even eventually abandon Talmud study altogether. A second frequent outcome is that the student is so devoted to Talmud study—often for religious and cultural reasons—that he or she represses or dismisses the difficulties, chalking them up to some combination of the Talmud's lofty intellectual status and to his or her own intellectual deficiencies. This can lead to negation of self-worth as a learner.

I have been grappling with these issues for several years in the context of an advanced Talmud class at Mechon Hadar, an institution of higher Jewish learning based in New York City. At Mechon Hadar, students come from all over the country to study and learn Jewish texts intensively, at a variety of levels of textual competence and for anywhere from one week to several years. They do not receive any degrees; their motivations are primarily to study "in community," to experience a religiously oriented environment where men and women are equal citizens and leaders, and to acquire concrete skills for ongoing learning. My Talmud class is targeted to those with an extensive prior learning background, amassed through years of instruction and learning in North American Jewish day schools and in Israeli yeshivot. Students enter this class with the ability to read talmudic text and its commentaries independently, though few have had any real exposure to critical thinking skills or their application to talmudic text. I have observed many who suffer from the maladies described above: either an instinct to repress difficulties that they discover in the text or a feeling of alienation from its content (albeit with a concomitant desire to overcome those feelings).

In this chapter, I will explore a proactive, difficulty-seeking pedagogy—one deliberately seeking to identify and understand the problems in talmudic text—rather than an approach that sees problems as obstacles to overcome or as rough patches to smooth over as quickly as possible. My claim is that this *quest for difficulties* is key, both in order to honor the talmudic text itself and perhaps even more importantly, to honor students and their own self-confidence as they progress in Talmud study. While my fuller teaching method generally involves an attempt to reconstruct the history of the sugya in a way that addresses all of the difficulties we discover, I will focus in this chapter only on the first stage: teaching students how to identify problems in the text so that they can use those discoveries to leverage further learning.[1]

---

[1] One motivation for focusing on this first stage stems from simple issues of scope and length. But there is also something more fundamental here about separating the two phases. The first stage is primarily deconstructive. The method I will lay out in this chapter is focused on building up the learner and tearing down the text. The quest for problems takes a reader from engaging an ostensibly smooth text that the reader is meant to understand, to meditating on a collection of cruxes that affirm one's intellectual questions without clear answers. It is difficult—and one of my greatest challenges in teaching—to move from this first phase to a second phase focused on reconstruction. The process of reconstruction requires deep reverence for the text and its editors and a

Looking for Problems: A Pedagogic Quest for Difficulties | CHAPTER 2

I will begin with a general description of the method and then provide a concrete example of a sugya we studied together in class.

Step One: Developing a Coherent Surface Reading—*Daf Yomi*

The first step in engaging any text is attempting to understand it on its own terms. This critical initial step ought to be approached with respect for the author, but equally important is attaining a proper understanding of the genre of the text's content. All literary and artistic forms—in fact, all things meant to be heard, seen, or read—presume a basic type of interaction with the consumer or observer. Novels are designed to be read from their first to their last page in sequential order. Checklists are meant to be consulted repeatedly as their users plow through the tasks and items they list—but not necessarily in sequential order. Portraits are meant to be taken in all at once from a distance and to accurately convey the image of the person depicted. Symphonies, embodied in many distinct sheets of musical notation, are meant to be listened to when played by multiple instruments in synchronized time. Each embodies a unique form of interaction, an experience of absorption for human processing and fulfillment.

Talmudic sugyot, too, are designed to be absorbed in a particular way. All talmudic sugyot have a beginning, a middle, and an end. They are composed of a logical sequence of sources, statements, challenges, and questions meant to be narrated in order, with both literary and logical coherence. While a sugya may often appear difficult on initial viewing—either because of our own lack of comprehension or its inherent complexity—we must remember it is *intended* to have a coherent surface meaning that carries its readers from beginning to end.[2] The first step in analyzing any sugya (before one attempts to engage in a

---

willingness to admit that one's initial assumptions about the text, its genre, and its agenda may have been incomplete and wrong. While both the deconstructive and reconstructive elements are, in my view, critical to a deep Talmud learning experience, it is not simple to blend them together in the same classroom, much less in the same pedagogical writing. My goal here is to give full voice to this first stage of the process. I hope to revisit the second stage at a future time.

2   This point is virtually self-evident from the nature of the Talmud itself and its division into the logical-literary units we know as sugyot. The fact that the Talmud was originally

CHAPTER 2 | Ethan M. Tucker

deeper level of analysis and questioning) is to decide upon and engage with the coherent surface reading, which accounts for the sugya's basic data and makes sense of each and every one of the logical steps the sugya takes. I refer to this step as *daf yomi* reading, a practice well known to the global Jewish community but used here in a unique pedagogical context. This practice of the daily study of a folio of Talmud, in a relatively limited amount of time, presses the learner or teacher of a talmudic passage to work toward and achieve a viable surface reading of the text. Someone learning *daf yomi* has one task: to understand the basic content of the words of the sugya and to explicate the logic behind each and every step in the talmudic argument. This first phase of interpretation is nothing less than taking responsibility for the logical coherence of the sugya—owning it—so one can then coherently and comprehensively use it to dive into the sugya's deeper, layered meanings.

I always start my students with this basic task, which throws them into addressing any gaps in their knowledge by precisely defining words, identifying key legal terms, and sharpening the logic of the passage. This process collectively winnows, or blows away as chaff, the problems external to the text, ones that are mere products of a reader's incomplete knowledge or analytic sloppiness. Narrating and mapping out a coherent surface reading of a sugya forces the student to read precisely and correctly.

Opportunely, this step of basic "surface" understanding has an important secondary benefit: the student must confront the various assumptions that stand behind each logical segment of the text. These assumptions are, at this first stage, essential for a basic understanding of how the sugya works and how it coherently says what it says. These assumptions will often, however, also prove to be central tools for unlocking *deeper* issues. Highlighting and underscoring questions and problems in the sugya also constitute the core of the next second step of productive sugya analysis, discussed later.

---

transmitted orally also demonstrates that we are not dealing with haphazard notes on paper, but rather units that can be recited in a continuous flow. For a more general statement about the literary coherence of the Talmud, see Eliezer Lorne Segal, "The Use of the Formula *ki ha d*ʾ in the Citation of Cases in the Babylonian Talmud," *HUCA* 50 (1979): 199-218; Eliezer Lorne Segal, "Anthological Dimensions of the Babylonian Talmud," *Prooftexts* 17, no. 1 (1997): 33-61.

Contemporary translations and renditions of the Talmud—Steinsaltz's and Artscroll's are the most prominent of these—are primarily devoted to assisting learners in this first step of understanding. By spelling out assumptions, defining talmudic terms, and explicating logical leaps, aids that enable the reading of the sugya as a *logically ordered literary unit,* the essential form and function of any given sugya can be achieved. There is little doubt these tools are very useful in accomplishing this goal; however, any learner must accept that in seeking a deeper understanding of a sugya, they must devote considerable time to this first step, as the goal is *full comprehension* of the sugya's flow without any aids, to the point of being capable of fully explaining the sugya to someone else.

Step Two: Identifying Problems and Difficulties in the Sugya

As noted in the previous section, the practice of producing a coherent reading of a talmudic sugya almost always generates problems and difficulties, as well as answers and solutions. These problems and difficulties can come in many forms. One may realize that some of the assumptions learners arrive at, in order to make a sugya cohere, are far from obvious, or even, at times, only questionably sound. A sugya may claim that the sources it cites mean things that one would never, on a simple reading, have thought they meant. In addition, the implications of some of a sugya's logical turns may lead to surprising practical outcomes, or evidence from other familiar sugyot may contradict certain aspects of the sugya being learned.

A pedagogy of "looking for problems" turns the tables on these problems and prods students to locate and focus on finding each of the above difficulties, without, initially, trying to resolve them. To put it alternatively, while the first stage of analysis requires the discipline of respecting the sugya's integrity in order to narrate it from start to finish, this second stage requires a respect for one's own intellectual integrity. One must at this stage, flag all of the elements of the sugya that do not make sense and that seem difficult to accept or seem to stretch the interpretive imagination of the reader. This process of identifying and documenting difficulties forms the foundation for all subsequent analysis, and it is critical to engage in this process on one's own terms before turning to other sources and commentaries, which may or may not reinforce one's initial instincts and questions.

In the class I teach, this second stage is allotted a significant amount of time. During their independent preparation of the text, students are asked to make notes of the difficulties they encounter and to spend time identifying them *before* moving on to seeking other sources. We will often have an entire session solely devoted to naming these difficulties, without making any effort to resolve them. The active task of identifying difficulties is not merely a station on the way to resolution. It is a stage of learning with its own integrity, the key for understanding both the text and how we ourselves learn.

Step Three: Close Reading of Commentaries—Rishonim and Aharonim

Having identified difficulties on their own, students then turn to the rich literature of traditional commentary in order to forge and expand their own perspectives on the sugya. This literature contains a wealth of material that emerges from engagement with the talmudic text. At this stage, I ask students to focus primarily on using the commentaries of the rishonim (medieval) and aharonim (modern), in two ways: (1) They should mine this literature for new difficulties in the sugya, ones of which they were not previously aware. (2) They should find more precise and learned language for the difficulties they have already identified, since many, if not all of these, will have been flagged by earlier scholars. These commentators were master readers of the Talmud and came to the text armed with virtually flawless knowledge of its terminology and style, combined with massive stores of knowledge from a lifetime of learning Talmud and other rabbinic texts. These earlier sages, therefore, are ideally suited to highlight and formulate difficulties and raise questions regarding talmudic logic and language.

Vital, at this point, is a focus on the *questions* raised by these commentators, while avoiding any real engagement with their *answers*. Since my pedagogic frame seeks to focus students on difficulties, any efforts to resolve such problems will obscure the full force of the challenge of finding and naming them. It needs to be understood by learners that the centrality and certainty of these commentators is anchored in their role as *expert readers* of the text, as they convey to us their own struggles or dilemmas in helping to make sense of it themselves. In fact, I often point students to carefully selected excerpts of this commentarial literature, those portions that articulate the difficulties and problems I want them to spot in the sugya.

Taken in tandem, these three steps (developing a coherent surface reading, identifying difficulties in the sugya, doing a close read of the commentaries) accomplish at least three important goals. First, students are trained to hone their reading skills. Held accountable to the logical flow of the sugya, they demonstrate their skill by being able to explain its flow to themselves and to their study partner. Second, they are trained to trust their own instincts—if something seems difficult to them, it probably is. This builds self-esteem in learning and encourages further exploration. Third, they are taught reverence and appreciation for the text by engaging with its great commentators from the past. I cannot emphasize enough the potential for this process to help mitigate the students' sense of alienation from the text. By seeing that the discovery of difficulties in the talmudic text is old and was common during earlier eras, their own modern-day struggles become contextualized within a conversation of the ages. By realizing that great learners from the past also grappled with the Talmud, its assumptions, form, and logic, they can relate much more deeply with the larger enterprise of Talmud study.

What follows is a record of the engagement of my class with a mishnah and a subsection of a sugya from the second chapter of tractate Makkot in the Babylonian Talmud. My hope is that this example will make the method clearer to the reader.

A Case Study—Makkot 9a

Background

The second chapter of Makkot is focused on the issue of manslaughter in Jewish law. The Torah addresses this sort of unintentional killing in a number of places, prescribing that the Israelites set up special cities—*arei miklat*—that can serve as a sort of refuge and temporary exile for manslayers. One of the issues that arises in the Talmud's prolonged discussion of this topic is the relevance of the identities of the manslayer and the victim. The cities of refuge are clearly an Israelite/Jewish institution, and yet, there are other people—*gerim vetoshavim*/resident aliens—who live among the Israelites/Jews and who might be covered by this law. These resident aliens are not Israelites/Jews, and yet, the Torah, in a number of places, affords them equal protection under the law.[3] The whole system of manslaughter law and the cities of refuge clearly applies when one Israelite/Jew accidentally kills another. But what happens when others are involved? In rabbinic terminology, is a *ger toshav* (non-Jew in Israel) manslayer exiled (*goleh*) to the city? Does a *ger toshav* victim trigger exile (*galut*) for the killer? Indeed, Bemidbar 35:15 gives some guidance on this point:

לִבְנֵי יִשְׂרָאֵל וְלַגֵּר וְלַתּוֹשָׁב בְּתוֹכָם תִּהְיֶינָה שֵׁשׁ־הֶעָרִים הָאֵלֶּה לְמִקְלָט לָנוּס שָׁמָּה כָּל־מַכֵּה־נֶפֶשׁ בִּשְׁגָגָה:

> For the Israelites and for the resident aliens among them, these six cities shall be a refuge so that any manslayer can flee to them.

At a minimum, this verse clarifies that a *ger toshav* is among those who flee to this city when having accidentally killed someone. This law presumably certainly extends to a resident alien who accidentally kills another resident alien. But would exile to a city of refuge be appropriate even if a *ger toshav* killed a bona fide Israelite? Or would he, in that case, be subject to execution for causing the death of a full citizen? And what of the case of a *ger toshav* victim of manslaughter? Is such a person's death significant enough to require exile for the manslayer? Much of the content of the laws of manslaughter is responsive to a robust network of blood avengers who are woven into the fabric of Israelite kinship. Might it be that when someone kills a *ger toshav*, who is outside of this kinship structure, exile is neither necessary nor appropriate? The Mishnah and our sugya attempt to answer these questions.

Step One: *Daf Yomi*

Our sugya jumps off of a mishnah that appears as follows in Makkot 8b:

---

3   Exod 12:49, Num 15:15-16, 29 are a few examples.

Looking for Problems: A Pedagogic Quest for Difficulties | CHAPTER 2

הכל גולין על ידי ישראל וישראל גולין על ידיהן חוץ מגר תושב.
וגר תושב אינו גולה אלא על ידי גר תושב.

All go into exile for killing a Jew, and a Jew goes into exile for killing them, except for a resident alien (*ger toshav*).
And a resident alien only goes into exile for killing another resident alien.

The students' first step is to clarify the Mishnah's ruling. I ask them to consider the following chart, which they need to fill in (Figure 1).

I begin class by writing this empty chart on the board and asking the students to complete it, based on the minimal force of the verse in Bemidbar 35, combined with the Mishnah's ruling here. The students rapidly progress to the point seen in Figure 2.

Our class discussion that follows quickly settles a few points: When a Jew unintentionally kills another Jew, this is the classic, paradigmatic case the Torah discusses when dealing with manslaughter. Exile is clearly the procedure in such instances, as reflected in the upper-right box. In the second line of the mishnah, it is clear that a *ger toshav* does not go

	על ידי גר תושב (Resident alien victim)	על ידי ישראל (Jewish victim)	נהרג / הורג
			ישראל (Jewish killer)
			גר תושב (Resident alien killer)

Figure 1 Blank Chart Handed to Students.

	על ידי גר תושב (Resident alien victim)	על ידי ישראל (Jewish victim)	נהרג / הורג
	?	גולה	ישראל (Jewish killer)
	גולה	אינו גולה	גר תושב (Resident alien killer)

Figure 2 Initial Completion of Chart Based on the Mishnah.

| 43

into exile when killing a Jew, but does go into exile when killing one of his own.

Students quickly begin to disagree about the upper left box of the chart. What about the case of a Jew who kills a *ger toshav*? Does he go into exile? This hinges on how we construe the grammar of the phrase חוץ מגר תושב, "except for the *ger toshav*." Some students insist that this phrase in the Mishnah means to exclude the *ger toshav* only from those who go into exile for killing Jews (i.e., the first clause in the mishnah's first line). Others argue that it means to state that there is never exile in any sort of manslaughter case involving a Jew and a *ger toshav* (i.e., a comprehensive exclusion from the mishnah's first line). I point out that the first possibility seems grammatically stronger. If the Mishnah had wanted to exclude the *ger toshav* from both elements of the first line, it probably should have read: הכל גולין על ידי ישראל חוץ מגר תושב וישראל גולה על ידיהן חוץ מעל ידי גר תושב, "All go into exile for killing a Jew, except for a *ger toshav*, and a Jew goes into exile for killing them, except when killing a *ger toshav*." However, the second reading is stronger on account of the clause's placement. Why would a phrase intended to exclude only from the first clause of a line be placed at the end? (It is not plausible to say that this phrase חוץ מגר תושב, "except for the *ger toshav*," means *only* to exclude a Jew who kills a *ger toshav* from going into exile, but leaves intact the punishment of exile for a *ger toshav* who kills a Jew. Such a holding would have demanded the formulation חוץ מעל ידי גר תושב, "except *for killing* a *ger toshav*.)

We cannot really resolve this question based on our text of the Mishnah alone, so we leave a question mark in the upper left box. In fact, this lacuna in our chart is our first difficulty, our first sense that something may be off with our version of the mishnah, given that its legal holding on this key question is so unclear. Nonetheless, having mapped out the Mishnah together, albeit incompletely, I now move the students on to the talmudic sugya.

Below is a textual excerpt and translation of the part of the sugya on which I ask students to focus. For ease of following, I have underlined the core amoraic statement in question.

Looking for Problems: A Pedagogic Quest for Difficulties | CHAPTER 2

אלמא גר תושב עובד כוכבים הוא, אימא סיפא: גר תושב גולה ע"י גר תושב!

<u>אמר רב כהנא, לא קשיא: כאן בגר תושב שהרג גר תושב, כאן בגר תושב שהרג ישראל.</u>

איכא דרמי קראי אהדדי, כתיב: לבני ישראל ולגר ולתושב בתוכם תהיינה שש הערים, וכתיב: והיו לכם הערים למקלט, לכם - ולא לגרים!

<u>אמר רב כהנא, לא קשיא: כאן בגר תושב שהרג ישראל, כאן בגר תושב שהרג גר תושב.</u>

Therefore, a resident alien is considered a gentile! But that would contradict the end of the mishnah, which states that a resident alien goes into exile for killing a resident alien!

<u>Said Rav Kahana: There is no difficulty: here we are dealing with a resident alien who killed a resident alien, and here we are dealing with a resident alien who killed a Jew.</u>

Another tradition places two verses in tension with one another. It is written, "These six cities shall be for the Israelites and for the resident aliens among them," but it is also written, "These cities shall be a refuge for you"—[implying:] for you, and not for resident aliens!

<u>Said Rav Kahana: There is no difficulty: here we are dealing with a resident alien who killed a Jew, and here we are dealing with a resident alien who killed a resident alien.</u>

This sugya begins with a statement that the first part of the mishnah implies a *ger toshav* has the same status as a gentile—a foreigner who is not a local resident and is not subject to local law—who never goes into exile for killing someone and whose killing never triggers exile. The sugya then challenges this status equation from the second part of the mishnah, which states that exile does result when a resident alien kills a fellow resident alien. Rav Kahana resolves this tension between the first and second lines of the Mishnah. The Mishnah's first clause, he says, must refer to a case where a *ger toshav* has killed a Jew. Here, he is treated like a gentile and is killed, rather

| 45

than being exiled. The mishnah's second clause, he says, must refer to a case where one *ger toshav* kills another *ger toshav*. In that situation, the *ger toshav* is treated like a Jew; he goes into exile for this unintentional murder.

The sugya then proceeds to offer a second version of Rav Kahana, one in which he is responding to a tension between two verses, reflecting two case situations: the first verse suggests that the cities of refuge are for Jews and *gerim toshavim,* and the second verse suggests that they are only for Jews. Rav Kahana's statement clarifies that there is a difference between the case of a *ger toshav* who kills a Jew and a *ger toshav* who kills a *ger toshav*. The former case does not trigger exile, whereas the latter case does. This can account for the apparent conflict in each case.

The students spend their *havruta* time deciphering this basic structure of the sugya with the help of the staff. When we gather for class, I build on this knowledge and turn their attention to the first version of Rav Kahana, prodding them with inquiries and ending with a challenge. What exactly does the Gemara's opening line mean? In what sense does the first clause of the mishnah imply that a *ger toshav* has the status of a gentile? I ask the students to generate different possible meanings and write them on the board. Together, we generate three possible readings (A, B, C) of the line, אלמא גר תושב עובד כוכבים הוא:

A. The first line of the mishnah equates the *ger toshav* to a gentile by stating that a *ger toshav victim* does not trigger exile for the perpetrator.
B. The first line of the mishnah equates the *ger toshav* to a gentile by stating that a *ger toshav perpetrator* does not go into exile.
C. The first line of the mishnah equates the *ger toshav* to a gentile by stating that a *ger toshav neither* triggers exile *nor* goes into exile.

I ask the students to play out each possibility and to test it for logical coherence. I invite those who have not spoken until then to evaluate the suggestions made by their classmates. We begin by evaluating reading A. One student notes that, back in our discussion of the mishnah, the main point that was *uncertain* was whether a Jew goes into exile for having killed a *ger toshav*. This seems to preclude reading A, which presumes that our mishnah quite plainly eliminates exile in all cases involving a *ger toshav* victim. Another student points out that reading A is even more clearly excluded when we consider Rav Kahana's statement. Rav Kahana's entire point is to emphasize that a *ger toshav*'s status as a *perpetrator* is affected depending on who his victim is. His point is tailored to respond to a thought that a *ger toshav* perpetrator never goes into exile. This in no way responds to reading A of the mishnah's initial question, which is focused on the *ger toshav* as *victim*.

I then direct the class to move on to analyses of reading B and reading C. Our discussion in class confirms that each of these readings, or interpretations, is possible with the phrase חוץ מגר תושב, which might *refer back to the first clause of the first line*—thereby focusing on perpetrators—or *might refer to the entire first line*—thereby focusing on *both* perpetrators *and* victims. Rav Kahana, with his focus on the *ger toshav* perpetrator, seems a tighter fit with reading B, though reading C seems better suited to the Gemara's blanket claim that the Mishnah's opening line equates a *ger toshav* with a gentile, which would seem to be across the board. We leave this point open and table it for a later discussion. But this disciplined process of doing readings and analyses together in class has already begun to highlight a difficulty with the sugya: the best reading of the Talmud's initial line does not perfectly match the best reading of Rav Kahana, who is supposedly responding to it!

This first stage of approaching learning through "looking for difficulties"—what I have called *daf yomi*—forces the students to narrate the logical steps of the sugya, making it difficult to hide from its less than smooth features. With this basic reading of the sugya in hand, students now move methodically to focus intently on its difficulties.

Step Two: Identifying Problems

At this phase, students focus on issues that had risen for them in understanding the sugya. They do the first phase of this in *havruta,* the paired learning that takes up much of their morning study. Working with the text of the Talmud, a source sheet that guides them to pay attention to specific passages, and personal interaction with the *beit midrash* staff, they come into class ready to share what they have found. I begin the class by soliciting their findings, inviting them to share the difficulties they encountered. I clarify and restate each problem for the class. And then I write the problems on the board, one by one. Occasionally, there are problems that they have not noticed that I point out to them. In this sugya, the following issues arose:

1. As noted briefly above, there is a significant problem coherently reading both the sugya's opening line—אלמא גר תושב עובד כוכבים הוא—and Rav Kahana's response to it. A student explains that the best reading of the Gemara's opening line seems to be reading C, above. But Rav Kahana only seems to be responding to something along the lines of reading B. I suggest that this may indicate that something unusual has happened in the composition of the sugya.

2. If reading C is, in fact, correct, then what is the sugya's final opinion regarding the case of a Jew who kills a *ger toshav*? A student is bothered that the sugya would leave this point open.

3. When the Gemara says אימא סיפא, it proceeds to quote a version of the last line of the mishnah, one that lacks the words אינו and אלא. While this absence is not critical for the logical flow of the sugya, it is noteworthy that this is different than the version of the mishnah that appears on Makkot 8b, which has those words in the text. A student refers the class back to the printed text of this mishnah one page earlier and asks, "Why would the sugya have a different version of this mishnah?"

4. I point out that it is highly unusual to use the formulation כאן ... כאן to refer to two different *parts* of a text, as opposed to two *different texts*. This formulation is used broadly in the Talmud, and it is hardly, if ever, used to resolve a supposed contradiction between two lines of a single text.

5. Finally, I note that the second version of Rav Kahana, cast as a resolution of verses, is extremely suspicious. It is a very smooth reading by the class, making it seem like a later attempt to put Rav Kahana in another context that lacks the problems of the other version just detailed above. Moreover, I tell the students to search the term איכא דרמי קראי אהדדי in the Bar-Ilan electronic database of rabbinic texts. They discover that this is the *only* place in the entire Babylonian Talmud where this term is used! Aside from the fact that amoraim were not generally in the business of resolving scriptural contradictions, the form of using such a resolution as a replacement for an alternative is unparalleled elsewhere. This also "smacks" of something unusual in the development of the sugya.

Having completed this process, students now have a clearer understanding of why the sugya was challenging for them in the first place. Our classroom experience, with its combination of student sharing and teacher guidance, affirms the difficulties they have discovered were real. While it is tempting for the students to offer suggestions for resolving these problems, I do not let them do so at this stage. My goal is to keep them focused on the *difficulties* and to sit with those difficulties a bit longer. Since one of my central pedagogic aims is to help my students to distinguish between an insufficient ability to decode a text, on the one hand, and a cultivated sensitivity to textual cruxes on the other, it is essential that they *not* resolve the problems they have noticed too quickly. Remaining in a problem-seeking rather than problem-solving mindset provides further impetus to learning and facilitates our transition to examining commentaries that often flesh out these problems in further and deeper detail.

Step Three: Close Readings of Commentaries

I now direct students to turn to various commentators in order to sensitize themselves further to difficulties in the text. In general, I begin my first Talmud class by introducing students to a list of commentaries we will consult in the weeks ahead. I encourage them to explore these on their own, though I always select specific passages for each sugya that I want them to read carefully, closely.[4] In the case of this sugya, I directed them to study one particularly fruitful passage from the commentary of the Ritba, Rabbi Yom Tov b. Avraham Ishbili (thirteenth-fourteenth centuries):

ריטב"א ד"ה אמר רב כהנא
א"ר כהנא לא קשיא כאן בגר תושב שהרג ישראל כאן בגר תושב שהרג גר תושב.
פירש רבינו מאיר הלוי ז"ל דלאו דוקא דה"ה בישראל שהרג גר תושב שאינו

---

4 The degree of students' ability to discover such passages independently has generally varied widely in my classes. Some students are accustomed to picking up these commentaries on their own; my role is to teach them how to read them with an eye toward the difficulties that the texts raise. Other students have read such commentaries only when assigned them. For the latter group, while I try to encourage increased independent exploration, I maintain my focus on teaching them how to read, rather than how to independently locate commentaries.

CHAPTER 2 | Ethan M. Tucker

גולה וכדדייקא רישא כדאמרן אלא דנקט תלמודא לישנא קלילא, ותדע דהא לא קתני סיפא גלות אלא בגר תושב ע"י גר תושב, ולפ"ז לא חדש לנו רב כהנא כלום בתירוצו ולא יישב לנו הקושיא שלנו דאנן ידעינן דרישא מיירי בהכי וסיפא מיירי בהכי אלא דהוה קשיא לן רישא אסיפא, וי"ל דרב כהנא משמע ליה דלאו פירכא היא כלל דהא לא דמו כלל וזה דוחק, והנכון בעיני שיטת רש"י ז"ל דדוקא נקט רב כהנא דמתני' דקתני חוץ מן הגר תושב לאו אתרווייהו דיני דרישא קאי אלא בגר תושב שהרג את ישראל דוקא שאין לו כפרה בגלות ואולי הוא נהרג על שגגתו, אבל ישראל שהרג גר תושב ודאי גולה כי יש בשגגת הריגתו כפרה ע"י גלות (ש)(כיון שאנו אסורין להרגו במזיד ומצווין להחיותו, והא דלא קתני סיפא אלא דגר תושב גולה על ידי גר תושב לרבותא נקט דאפילו גר תושב שהרגו צריך כפרה כל שכן ישראל שמוזהר עליו להחיותו שהקב"ה רוצה בכפרתו, ויש סיוע לפירוש זה לשון הגמרא שבכאן וכן מדלקמן דתריצנא הכי כאן בגר תושב שהרג את ישראל וההוא בדוקא נקיט ליה לדברי הכל, כנ"ל.

Ritba s.v. "Amar Rav Kahana"

"Said Rav Kahana: There is no difficulty—here we are dealing with a resident alien who kill a Jew, and here we are dealing with a resident alien who killed a resident alien."

Rabbi Meir Halevi [Abulafia of Toledo, thirteenth century] of blessed memory explained: Not only [does a resident alien who kills a Jew not go into exile], but it is also the case that a Jew who kills a resident alien does not go into exile, as is deduced from the first line of the Mishnah. But the Talmud simply chose to use smooth [and imprecise] language. This reading must be correct, because the end of the Mishnah only prescribed exile for when a resident alien kills a resident alien [implying that this is the only case where a resident alien victim triggers exile for the perpetrator].

[Ritba responds:] But according to this reading, Rav Kahana has taught us nothing new with his resolution and did not resolve our question! We know that the first line deals with [a case of a resident alien killing a Jew] and that the second line deals with [a case of a resident alien killing a resident alien]! We were bothered by the contradiction between the two parts of the Mishnah! Perhaps we could say that Rav Kahana's point is that there is no problem here, since the cases of the first and second clauses of the Mishnah are so dissimilar. But this is extremely forced.

It seems to me that the correct approach is that of Rashi, who held that Rav Kahana was very specific [and thought that a resident alien victim only triggers exile for another resident alien]. When the Mishnah says חוץ מגר תושב, is it only referring to the first clause of the first line, stating that when a resident alien kills a Jew, he cannot get atonement through exile and may be killed for his error. But when a Jew kills a resident alien, he is clearly exiled: [the Jew] *can* receive atonement through exile [and the Jew deserves exile] because we are forbidden to kill a resident alien and must make efforts to preserve his life. The second line of the Mishnah only teaches that a resident alien goes into exile for killing another resident alien to make the point that *even* a resident alien perpetrator goes into exile and receives atonement for killing a resident alien. All the more so does a Jew go into exile for killing a resident alien, since the Jew is obligated to preserve his life, and the Holy One desires the Jew's atonement. There is support for this explanation in the Talmud's language here, which specifically says that a resident alien who kills a Jew does not go into exile [implying that in the reverse case, the Jew does go into exile]. So it seems to me.

The first thing the students discovered in this passage is that the problems they discovered are not new. The question of what happens to a Jew who kills a *ger toshav*—the box we had to leave with a question mark when analyzing the Mishnah—was indeed a matter of dispute among the medieval commentators. In this case, Ritba and Rabbi Meir Halevi disagree as to whether the Jew is exiled, confirming that the Mishnah does not obviously address it. We also see that Ritba's reading *depends* on having the Gemara's version of the Mishnah text: וגר תושב גולה על ידי גר תושב, confirming our feeling that the gap between this version and that of the earlier citation of the mishnah—וגר תושב אינו גולה אלא על ידי גר תושב—is significant. Finally, we also see confirmed the tension between a smooth reading of the Talmud's opening line—אלמא גר תושב עובד כוכבים הוא—and a smooth reading of Rav Kahana, who only seems focused on the *ger toshav* as perpetrator. Rabbi Meir Halevi argues for reading C of the opening line of the Gemara—a *ger toshav neither* triggers exile *nor* goes into exile—whereas Ritba pushes for a reading of Rav Kahana that precisely responds to reading B—a *ger toshav perpetrator* does not go into exile, but a *ger toshav victim* would trigger exile for a Jew. These were all problems the students noted on their own.

But this close reading of Rabbi Meir Halevi's interpretation and Ritba's response yielded further insights during our class discussion as well. We engaged Ritba's response. Ritba notes a major problem with having Rav Kahana respond fully to reading C of the opening line. Rav Kahana has then told us nothing new! When the students had discussed reading C, they were bothered by the fact that the opening line of the mishnah says that a *ger toshav* does not go into exile when killing a Jew (just like a gentile would not), given that the second line *does* talk about the *ger toshav* going into exile when killing a *ger toshav*. But then Rav Kahana just resolves our problem by telling us a distinction we could have seen in the Mishnah's text ourselves! Would not he then be simply telling us that the seeming confusing contradiction between the first and second parts of the mishnah, in fact, is nothing to be bothered about? How can he say that? If the problem is so insignificant, why did the Gemara ask it in the first place? If, on the other hand, there is some sort of conceptual contradiction between the Mishnah's two holdings, Rav Kahana's statement does not address it!

At this point in the discussion, a number of students are ready to dismiss Rabbi Meir Halevi's opinion as insufficiently thorough and to favor Ritba's reading as superior. I stop the discussion and pull the students back from that conclusion—surely Rabbi Meir Halevi was aware of this weakness and yet he *did* adopt reading C. I asked the students, "What bothered *him*? What problem was Rabbi Meir Halevi attempting to avoid with *his* interpretation of the sugya? Here, they do not generate an answer, and I must guide them. Ritba's solution suffers from a serious problem as well. In his reading, Rav Kahana offers something indeed new: clarification that when a Jew kills a resident alien, he *does* go into exile. While this explanation of Rav Kahana does the kind of work we would expect his לא קשיא statement to be doing—adding new information that was not previously obvious—it suffers from one obvious problem: there is no indication that this is what Rav Kahana is saying! He is focused on the *ger toshav* as a perpetrator and says nothing about him as a victim!

This passage is an excellent example of how an interpretational dispute can help students see a fundamental, unavoidable problem in the sugya. Both Rabbi Meir Halevi and Ritba are able to smooth out one aspect of the sugya, but only by distorting another. Once my lesson has emphasized this point, the students express frustration; so what did Rav Kahana actually mean? They begin to sense that perhaps something about Rav Kahana's statement—at least as it is presented in the final form of our sugya—is amiss. Between the opening question that he does not seem to fully respond to, the potential superfluity of his contribution to the conversation, and the replacement version of his statement that seems to be an attempt to run away from these problems entirely, we can see that something happened to Rav Kahana's statement in the course of the editing of our sugya. At this stage in our analysis, I do not endeavor to provide any answers.[5] At the end of this phase of the process, my goals are more tailored to the students and their sense of themselves as learners. I want them to feel fully and deeply intellectually engaged by the sugya and its commentators, while also feeling validated and affirmed that the issues that had vexed them in their reading were real, shared by great minds that came before them. While they are anxious for resolutions to the difficulties we have noticed, I direct them at this stage to appreciate how both they and earlier commentators were joined in grappling with fundamental problems of the text. Although this is not meant to suggest an intellectual equilibrium of students and the ancient masters, students do often express excitement and gratitude that they are not the first to sense these difficulties, which are not merely nor wholly attributable to a lack of reading skill on their part.

As I mentioned at the beginning of this article, my classes proceed from this point to try to resolve the problems we have raised, primarily through investigation of parallel sources and the possible historical developments they may suggest to us. That stage, beyond the scope of what we

---

5   In this particular case, the presence of variants in the text of the Mishnah is a key element in reconstructing what happened to Rav Kahana's statement "when and why." In most cases, there is no textual variant, and we must look to parallel sugyot and materials from Palestinian collections in order to reconstruct the history and account for the problems.

are examining in this text, aims to leave students with a deeper reverence for the editorial processes and voices that have bequeathed the Talmud to us. In this specific example, explicated in my class and in this chapter, we explored the notion that textual shifts in the mishnah (alluded to above) made it impossible for later editors to read the mishnah as had Rav Kahana. This led to a crisis in interpretation and even inspired the creation of a new context for his statement.

Conclusion

In this chapter, I have laid out the first stage of a pedagogy of "looking for problems," a strategy that aims to connect students to the talmudic text by specifically highlighting the points of greatest difficulty. Even the most advanced students have not been trained to look for enduring problems in the text, which remain even after they have successfully decoded both language and syntax.

I have seen strong results from using this teaching method approach. At the end of the semester, students filled out a survey reflecting on their learning process. All students agreed or strongly agreed that they had improved their ability to read medieval commentaries accurately, and two-thirds felt they could independently use the difficulties found in the commentaries of the rishonim to identify underlying problems in the sugya. Training students to diligently identify and interpret these difficulties can lead to specific positive benefits, beyond that of improved Talmud reading:

1. I have a strong informal sense that students using this method learn to distinguish between complexity and difficulty, thereby becoming both sharper readers and thinkers. Complexity includes all of the challenges of decoding language and keeping track of logical thought. Difficulty encompasses the aspects of a text that challenge even the most knowledgeable and astute readers, usually because those aspects are inherent elements of the text that trace back to the dynamics of its creation.

2. Students gain confidence in their own voice and in their own instincts. Time and again, my students are delighted and astonished to discover that their problems with the text are not due solely to their ignorance. This builds long-term interest in and commitment to Talmud study. One student wrote on the survey, "The honesty of this method struck me, as well as the deep appreciation for the tannaim, the amoraim, and the rishonim, along with the appreciation for the learner's intelligence and the quest for satisfying and true answers. I feel that this method was the deepest and most correct of the ways I have learned Talmud until now."
3. Students learn that they are not alone. When they see their own challenges refracted through the language of revered talmudic sages from the past, they begin to understand themselves as part of a storied history of talmudic interpretation. Perhaps most important, their difficulties are situated "inside" this discourse as opposed to being the observations of those frustrated with the enterprise from the outside. This emerges in self-evident fashion in our classroom discussions, as students express satisfaction in discovering that experienced masters of the past were bothered by the same textual and logical issues that bother them.
4. Students build reverence for the different voices in the talmudic text. By refusing to blindly accept editorial analysis of the earlier words of the tannaim and the amoraim, students learn to take these early sages seriously. When we refuse to gloss over the difficult interpretations and assumption proffered by Talmud sugyot, we manifest a deeper commitment to the notion that mishnayot, baraitot, and *meimrot* ought to mean what they seem to say they mean. This encourages students to treat the language of these earlier texts with reverence, as opposed to viewing them as mere verbiage to be manipulated at will. One student commented on the post-class survey as follows: "[This method] posed an innovative model for engaging with our texts in a religious setting. We do so not to prove [the rabbinic sages wrong, but to better understand [them]. A truly wonderful and exciting project. I really feel like

I have a grasp of the rabbinic project more than I ever have." [A fuller explication of how I engender reverence for the craft of the talmudic editors is tied to the phase of my method focused on the reconstruction of the sugya, which is beyond the scope of this article.⁶]

Teaching with this method of "looking for problems" takes the talmudic form seriously and on its own terms. The talmudic sugya is a work of literature, even an art form, that is meant to be read in sequence from beginning to end. Reading the sugya carefully in this way reveals its complexity and sharpens our textual insights as learners. This method has deepened my own appreciation for how the Talmud is replete with difficulties that are not easily solved. Teaching this approach has strengthened my respect for my students and myself as learners. Challenging texts, such as the talmudic texts, approached properly, enrich our life and future investment in Judaic studies and help us grow in our own self-worth. For such a complex and difficult text as the Talmud, confronting its problems head on is thus an essential part of the larger pedagogic picture and has the potential to mirror growth in ourselves.

---

6   For an example of all aspects of the method applied to a single sugya, see my chapter, Ethan Tucker, "The Stammaitic Impact on Halakhah: Two Sanctifications, Two Cups of Wine", in *Reconstructing the Talmud: An Introduction to the Academic Study of Rabbinic Literature*, ed. J. Kulp and J. Rogoff. (New York: Mechon Hadar 2014).

CHAPTER 3

■ ■ ■

What Others Have to Say: Secondary Readings in Learning to Read Talmud

Jane L. Kanarek

It is commonplace to consider that simply reading more on a particular topic will increase a person's understanding of that topic. Yet, an additive vision that more exposure to information will increase our knowledge is too simplistic. Such a model masks a more complex reality—that learning to read one text in order to better read and better understand another text is, in fact, a complicated, refined, and cultivated process. That process is exquisitely true of reading the Bavli, the Babylonian Talmud, a complex and multi-tiered work. Indeed, understanding the rich labyrinth of the Bavli means knowing *how* to read the Bavli's many layers of meaning. The focused integration of academic secondary readings into a Talmud course that also emphasizes the skills for decoding talmudic text from its original language—combined with beginning to learn the Bavli's extensive medieval commentary tradition—enables students to learn how to access the richness of the Bavli's multiple layers. Secondary readings contribute to this process by helping students to commit and engage with an approach that embraces (1) being alert to ambiguity; (2) seeing ways in which one sugya connects with another; (3) raising multiple possibilities for a diversity of meanings, both on the micro-level of a word and on the macro-level of the sugya as a whole; (4) finding subtexts that are latent in the sugya; (5) connecting a sugya to a wider world of ideas; and finally (6) bringing one's own concerns and questions to that reading.

The careful integration of secondary source material into a course that also aims to build the important skills of translation and parsing an argument enables the Bavli's textual complexities to emerge in a fuller manner. The skill of learning to understand the thesis of an academic reading and relate that thesis back to the Bavli gives students the opportunity to build on others' ideas and research, to question their own conceptions, and to integrate different theoretical frameworks into their own learning. As students build their skills in decoding a sugya through translation and commentary, the range of questions raised in the secondary readings encourages students to expand even further their own readings. They discover issues in these secondary sources that they would not have considered on their own, realize that they have similar questions as the authors, and ultimately, generate their own inquiries. Because students must learn how to read these articles in and of themselves, and then learn how to "turn around" and apply those ideas to the sugyot, they come to see their search for meaning in the text as another reading skill that needs to be built—much as does their ability to translate and parse a sugya's argument. The complexity of the articles helps students to understand that reading richly is not a simple endeavor. Reading secondary articles in order to better read talmudic sugyot is a skill: reading one in order to read the other.

In this chapter, I articulate four different teaching practices that I utilize to help students learn how to read secondary articles with the Bavli, provide concrete examples of these practices, and then show how they come together in the final exam. Combining the components of translation, commentary, and secondary articles enables a multi-directional conversation: the Bavli speaks to students from its ancient context as they, in turn, speak to the Bavli from their contemporary one.

Course Background

The course that forms the basis for this chapter is a one-semester Talmud class that I taught at the Rabbinical School of Hebrew College in the spring of 2014.[1] The course was designated as an intermediate level class that met twice-a-week for a total of three hours. Students were required to participate

---

[1] During the class, I kept a teaching journal and made audio recordings of many of the sessions. In addition, I kept copies of all written student work. This article relies on reflection guided by investigating those records, written and spoken.

What Others Have to Say: Secondary Readings in Learning to Read Talmud | CHAPTER 3

in four-and-a-half hours of *havruta* study in Hebrew College's *beit midrash* (study hall). There were nine students in the class, who were in their second, third, or fourth years of rabbinical school. Thus, all of my students had studied Talmud in prior settings; some had been my students in former classes that had included utilizing medieval commentaries, particularly those of Rashi and Tosafot. In this class, our base talmudic text was the eighth chapter of tractate Bava Kamma, known as *perek ha-hovel* (the chapter of "one who damages"), and from which we studied selected sugyot. These sugyot are all based on the five financial penalties that Mishnah Bava Kamma 8:1 lists as an assailant's liability to an injured party: depreciation (*nezek*), pain (*tzaar*), healing (*ripui*), idleness (*shevet*), and shame (*boshet*).[2] By the course's conclusion, students had considered not only the tannaitic framing[3] of each of these five penalties, but more centrally, how the Bavli conceptualizes each of these categories separately and how they join together into what I call a compensatory package.

For each sugya, I gave students a study sheet that included a list of technical terminology, questions that acted as guides to following a sugya or a commentator's argument, and questions that were meant to act as triggers to thinking about the sugya's meaning (beyond that of literal translation and explanation). These study sheets were meant to be used during the above-mentioned *beit midrash* time. In addition, students were also required to read one article or book chapter each week and email me a 300-500 word write-up of the assigned reading. I will describe this writing assignment in more detail later in this chapter.

The course also included three other assignments: an outline of a sugya, a midterm, and a final. For the outline, students had to punctuate and divide a sugya into its chronological layers. For the midterm, they had to translate and explicate a sugya's argument and define its technical terms. For the final, they had to repeat the exercise of the midterm with another sugya and then write an essay that utilized the secondary readings to analyze a sugya we had not studied in class. The outline and essay were both take-home and

---

2 Chosen sugyot also explicated M. Bava Kamma 8:6.
3 I chose the word "considered" to indicate that students are not expected to develop a full conceptual picture of tannaitic literature. We studied Mishnah and Tosefta and a very limited amount of tannaitic/halakhic midrashim.

open-book assignments. The translation exercises were in-class and closed-book assignments. In all of these cases, students could prepare with a *havruta*, a study partner, as long as the final work was theirs alone. The outline, midterm, and first part of the final all aimed to train and reinforce the more technical skills of sense-making: translation, parsing of sentences, use of technical terminology, and explanation of the argument. The second part of the final, the essay, aimed to encourage students to pull together the disparate study materials used in class—the sugyot, medieval commentary, and secondary articles—into a broader scope, in which they had to articulate their ideas about the new sugya, there utilizing the materials that we had previously studied. From the outset of the class, I knew which sugya I would assign for the essay portion of the final. Thus, as we studied the course material, I was conscious of building toward the components of the final.[4] Because the essay portion asked students to integrate the three skills (decoding, translating, parsing an argument) we had worked on in the course, it was the strongest marker of whether my students had learned to read the Bavli in ways I was seeking for them to understand.

Pedagogical Components of Reading Secondary Articles

In teaching students to read secondary articles in conversation with the Bavli, I used four pedagogical techniques: (1) topical division of the secondary articles on the syllabus; (2) weekly writing assignment on an article; (3) focused discussion of an assigned article or group of articles; and (4) weaving an author's points into a discussion about a sugya or commentator. In what follows, I describe each of these techniques in greater detail and provide concrete examples from the course. With the exception of the first technique, topical division, these examples are taken from student writing and from transcriptions of recorded class discussions. I have taken care to utilize a variety of student voices and their writings, with a majority of the class students represented.[5]

---

4   On teaching toward the final exam within seminary classes, see Jane Kanarek, and Marjorie Lehman, "Assigning Integration: A Framework for Intellectual, Personal, and Professional Development in Seminary Courses," *Teaching Theology and Religion* 16, no. 1 (2013): 18-32.

5   I have given all students pseudonyms.

Several criteria guided my choice of class material to present in this chapter: (1) having excerpts from the beginning, middle, and end of class; (2) representing a range of writing abilities; and (3) representing a range of verbal analytical abilities. I have not always chosen the most polished writing or speaking. Thus, I do not claim to be training my students to read (or write) as precisely as academicians or that all of my students learn to read to the same level of expertise. But the class material illustrates that due to their reading of and reflection on secondary reading, my students, as a group, did learn to read the Bavli more richly than they had been able to at the beginning of the course. They read in order to learn how to read.

Helping Students Organize the Articles

The first pedagogical method, dividing the secondary articles by topic within the syllabus, is organizational and took place prior to the course. Within the syllabus, I divided the assigned articles into four categories: (1) biblical literature and rabbinic exegesis, (2) comparative scholarship on rabbinic culture and its Greco-Roman context, (3) contemporary legal theory, and (4) scholarship on rabbinic conceptions of shame.[6] On the first day of the course, I described these categories to the students and explained to them that by dividing the articles by topic, the aim was to facilitate their ability to focus on one model for studying rabbinic literature at a time and then, by the end of the course, to have built a repertoire of "different sub-approaches" that

---

6 To give some examples, in category 1, students read Moshe Greenberg, "Some Postulates of Biblical Criminal Law," in *Yehezkel Kaufmann Jubilee Volume: Studies in Bible and Jewish Religion Dedicated to Yehezkel Kaufmann on the Occasion of His Seventieth Birthday*, ed. Menahem Haran (Jerusalem: Magnes Press, 1960), 5-28; David Kraemer, *Reading the Rabbis: The Talmud as Literature* (New York: Oxford University Press, 1996), 33-48; in category 2, Catherine Hezser, *Jewish Slavery in Antiquity* (New York: Oxford University Press, 2005), 247-74; Yael Richardson, "Legal Shame: Shame as a Legal Concept of Damage in Roman and Rabbinic Law" (Honors thesis, Brown University, 2007), 7-32, 69-86; in category 3, Robert M. Cover, "Violence and the Word," *Yale Law Journal* 95, no. 8 (1986): 1601-29; Robert Goodin, "Theories of Compensation," in *Liability and Responsibility: Essays in Law and Morals*, ed. R. G. Frey and Christopher W. Morris (Cambridge: Cambridge University Press, 1991), 257-89; in category 4, Jonathan Crane, "Shameful Ambivalences: Dimensions of Rabbinic Shame," *AJS Review* 35, no. 1 (2011): 61-84; Jeffrey L. Rubenstein, *The Culture of the Babylonian Talmud* (Baltimore: The Johns Hopkins University Press, 2003), 67-79.

they could then utilize together. Articles contextualized rabbinic literature in its cultural world as well as provided theoretical tools for thinking about law and its functions—both in the more local context of punishment and compensation and in the larger context of law as a cultural phenomenon. By organizing secondary sources in this way, I hoped to encourage students to focus on smaller details within the sugyot as well as to abstract those details to larger generalizations.

How Writing Helps Students Learn How to Read

Each week, students had to complete a writing assignment on an assigned article. This weekly writing assignment challenged each student to articulate the central aspects of an author's argument and then to write an almost equivalent length piece on how they thought that argument related to some of the studied sugyot. In asking students first to articulate an author's argument, I wanted them to become stronger interpreters of academic articles in and of themselves. By asking students to tie the argument back to the Bavli, I wanted them to learn how to take an argument that might not (and often did not) explicitly discuss our sugyot, yet nonetheless, use that argument to pull out ideas implicit in the Bavli. The sequence of the assignment steps was important: only after a student could state an author's argument did I want her to move onto the second step of tying the article to class sugyot. As can be seen below, I limited the length from 300-500 words, wanting to make the assignment doable and not overwhelming.[7] I find writing assignments to be useful as a (not too) subtle tool that encourages students to complete reading articles before class and to think more deeply on their own about that article before we engage in class discussion. The weekly assignment was as follows on the next page (Figure 1).

To illustrate the assignment and this aspect of the learning to read process, I have chosen writing samples from four different students.[8] They

---

7 As this course is what we term a core-text course in the Rabbinical School curriculum, the primary focus of preparation for assignments is meant to be time in the *beit midrash*. These at-home reading assignments are meant to complement but not to overwhelm or subsume that preparation time.

8 Writing excerpts have been corrected only lightly for spelling and grammar. Because I taught this class as part of a rabbinical school curriculum and not a doctoral one, I did not emphasize the craft of academic writing and even allowed (and expected) the students

What Others Have to Say: Secondary Readings in Learning to Read Talmud | CHAPTER 3

> **For each article, please write the following:***
>
> A. Description of the author's main argument. Your description should include the author's thesis and the main points that the author uses to build his or her argument.
> B. Reflection on how the ideas in this article might better help you to read our rabbinic material.
>
> The articles will not always correspond exactly to the topic of the day's sugya, so your reflection can be on the sugya we are discussing or on other sugyot that we have read in the course.
>
> **These pieces should be 300-500 words.*

Figure 1 Weekly Writing Assignment.

are based on articles from the beginning, middle, and end of the course. The first example is from the first writing assignment, an article by Moshe Greenberg titled, "Some Postulates of Biblical Criminal Law." Because this article was the initial reading assignment, Miriam, our student, does not yet have a repertoire of sugyot from the Bavli chapter we are studying to which she can connect her reflections, which follow below:

> Greenberg builds his argument by comparing law codes of the Near East to law systems in the Bible. He compares the values of the biblical societies to the values of the Near Eastern societies. The law codes of the Near East embody a human authority, but the ultimate authority of biblical law is God. By looking at these other law codes, we notice that the Bible is much more harsh when it comes to crimes against other human beings, and that the ancient Near East law is much more strict when it comes to crimes against property. ... Law is being studied as its own entity and not through other sociological and literary lenses.
>
> Thus far, we have studied many of the biblical passages referred to in the article as well as Hammurabi's code. What is interesting for me in light of

---

to take associative leaps in their writing that might not be as acceptable in a doctoral program. Writing passages thus reflect a range of writing skills.

reading this article are the different value systems at play in each body of law. It is interesting to think about the power of authority in each (man vs. God) and the values of each society (human vs. property). The biblical law reflects many of the values of Israelite society, as the body of cuneiform also reveals values of a society. Moving forward in our study, this framework will be key to understanding the values at play in our rabbinic texts.

In this passage, Miriam accomplishes a number of important tasks. First, she articulates the central points of Greenberg's article: law should be studied as a framework that reveals a culture's values, and in this case, one of those values is that the ultimate authority of biblical law is God.[9] She then continues on to name that values play an important role in different bodies of law and that law reveals a society's values—and most importantly, that this framework should encourage us to see how rabbinic texts might reflect rabbinic culture's values. Miriam's articulation of this idea about text and law reflecting values and not simply prohibitions and imperatives may be intuitive to scholars of rabbinic literature and law. However, for this student, Greenberg's article enables her to articulate this concept, see it applied to one text of literature (Bible) and then wonder about how that same framework might apply to the Bavli. It gives her a theme through which to approach the class material. She has begun to wonder about the wider world of ideas that our suygot may broach.

The second student's writing passage stems from an article read at the midpoint of the semester, the conclusion of Kevin M. Crotty's *Law's Interior: Legal and Literary Constructions of the Self*.[10] While Greenberg's article discusses biblical law and at least mentions rabbinic law, Crotty's book is not connected with the study of rabbinic literature. Instead, it is part of the field of general legal theory and, in particular, that of law and literature. This student, Gilah, ties Crotty's more general reflections about law to a specific sugya about the rabbinic move from the biblical model of punishment for

---

9   There are other aspects of Greenberg's argument that she does not name, such as his explanation for why biblical law does not allow ransom for murder, whereas Near Eastern law does. See Greenberg, "Some Postulates," 13-20.
10 Kevin M. Crotty, *Law's Interior: Legal and Literary Constructions of the Self* (Ithaca: Cornell University Press, 2001), 225-28.

What Others Have to Say: Secondary Readings in Learning to Read Talmud | CHAPTER 3

physical assault through *lex talionis* (an eye-for-an-eye) to the rabbinic model of punishment through financial penalties (B. Bava Kamma 83b-84a):

> In this conclusion, Crotty defines "law" in three respects, all of which reflect law as something carried out by humans. First, law is not a system, but a practice. Whereas a system is understood as something that could function autonomously according to specific guiding principles, law is an attempt by people to contain the complexities of life, so that life can function. But law doesn't happen, really, outside of human life, which is complicated, so it can't just simply follow guidelines.
>
> This framing of law is helpful in particular when thinking back to the sugya about *lex talionis*. As we noticed that the rabbis struggled mightily between *lex talionis* and financial compensation, we can see the rabbis managing their recognition of the complexities of life (namely, that *lex talionis* doesn't necessarily make sense for a variety of reasons in a variety of scenarios). They are trying to work within the standing legal tradition, while the social/religious understanding of what is right is broadening.
>
> This article is also interesting when thinking about the project of reading Gemara as a whole, as opposed to studying halakhah [law]. At this point, I understand the Gemara both as a legal text and as literature. As such, it seems like a perfect document for proving Crotty's point that law and literature are working in the same field, with the same materials but different priorities. While usually we see literature and law separately, by weaving together legal arguments with narrative, the Gemara text highlights how law and literature are working from the same material, and how the complexity of human life is incredible (possibly even celebrated), and it makes the creation of rules very challenging.

In this excerpt, Gilah makes three significant reading moves. First, she articulates Crotty's point that law is a practice, something engaged in by people, and it is not an autonomous and abstract entity that exists independently from the human realm. She engages with Crotty's academic argument about law independently of a talmudic context. Second, she ties this understanding of law back to the first sugya studied in the class, one that discusses the validity of financial

CHAPTER 3 | Jane L. Kanarek

compensation for physical assault. She connects the transition from a biblical model of eye-for-an-eye punishment to a rabbinic financial one to Crotty's understanding of law as a practice that is located within the complexities of human life and to the internal constraints of the rabbinic legal tradition. Gilah thus uses Crotty's understandings about law in general in order to better understand the specifics of rabbinic punishment in a particular sugya. However, this student also makes another move: she connects Crotty's ideas not just to the texts we have been directly studying in this class but also to larger questions about the nature of the Bavli as a whole. Crotty helps Gilah to broaden her understanding of the Bavli as a document that weaves together law and literature and as an example of human complexity. In her eyes, the Bavli becomes a document that illustrates the difficulty of forming prescriptive rules and how law and literature, although often considered opposing entities, are working from the same basis and through the same cultural problem—law and its interaction with the complexities of human existence. Crotty's article helps Gilah to locate the Bavli within a field of wider questions asked by the humanities in general and to interrogate more subtle issues that this sugya about *lex talionis* explores. In other words, Gilah is learning to read on the micro-level of the sugya and the macro-level of the Bavli as a whole. She has met the reading challenge of this assignment: to take an argument that does not discuss our talmudic topic, yet nonetheless, use that argument to expose ideas implicit in our sugyot.

The third student piece stems from a section of the course where we read a series of articles about the concept of shame within rabbinic literature. These articles were connected with a group of sugyot that explore the financial penalty for shame caused by physical assault (*boshet*, B. Bava Kamma 86a-86b). The extent of liability for shame depends on factors such as the relative social status of the involved parties and whether or not the injured person is conscious of having been shamed. The student below, Rebekah, responds to two chapters from an honors thesis by Yael Richardson,[11] which compares rabbinic notions of shame with contemporaneous Roman ones:

> What can we learn about both cultures' understanding of the experience of shame by reading our sugyot in relationship with these chapters? Why, for the rabbis, can *boshet* only be triggered when a physical assault has

---

11   Richardson, "Legal Shame," 7-32, 69-86.

What Others Have to Say: Secondary Readings in Learning to Read Talmud | CHAPTER 3

taken place? What is the relationship between *boshet* as an internal experience and *boshet* payments? What do they actually seek to redress? Who is covered under *boshet* payments? What does it mean that for both the rabbis and the Romans, there were certain people (demarcated by gender, national origin, internal capacity, experience, etc.) who were outside protection? And how do we read these sugyot in our times? Do we, inheritors both of the rabbis' tradition and of Roman jurisprudence, understand shame to be more in the paradigm of the rabbis or of the Romans?

The thesis chapters enable Rebekah to place rabbinic and Roman sources in conversation with one another. For this student, such a comparison sharpens certain elements of the texts we studied, such as the relationship between shame and physical assault, internal and external pain, and outsiders and insiders. It also prompts her to take the sugyot about shame that we have studied in class and ask about their relevance to a contemporary paradigm. In other words, this passage reveals that the student is learning to read Talmud as a document located within a wider cultural world and as a document whose concerns and values may need to be reinterpreted for a contemporary context. She understands what Richardson articulates in her writing and then uses Richardson's ideas to read our sugyot about shame with an enriched perception.

The last student passage I quote from the writing assignments stems from the final article of the class, "Pricing Persons: Consecration, Compensation, and Individuality in the Mishnah." The article's author, Mira Balberg, proposes two models for rabbinic conceptions of personhood: unity and multiplicity. In the unity model, people are understood as essentially replicas of one another—while in the multiplicity model, people are understood as essentially different.[12] These two models also can be seen in the ways in which rabbinic texts assign

---

[12] Balberg's article is, of course, more extensive and complex than the brief description I have presented. Balberg connects the unity and multiplicity perspectives with the monetary valuation of human beings (including for damages) and suggests that in evaluating the worth of persons, the rabbis of the Mishnah move between recognition of individual disparities (multiplicity) and a commitment to their parity (unity). She locates this move both within rabbinic interpretive culture as well as within wider cultural currents within the Hellenistic and Roman world. Mira Balberg, "Pricing Persons: Consecration, Compensation, and Individuality in the Mishnah," *Jewish Quarterly Review* 103, no. 2 (2013): 169-95.

CHAPTER 3 | Jane L. Kanarek

monetary value to people in evaluating their worth. The student's comments refer to material studied earlier in the class: the first Mishnah in this chapter and a sugya that tries to understand how to calculate payment for pain alongside a payment for physical damage (B. Bava Kamma 85a):

> If humans are made in the image of God, how can any humans be valued or priced? How does unity and multiplicity play into biblical and rabbinic theology? Where do slaves fit into this conversation? Are slaves human, too? What good does multiplicity do if we revert back to "*ka-yotzeh ba-zeh*" [like this one] when legislating liability and damages? Is this not a function of unity?

This brief excerpt illustrates a number of elements of how James, the author of these comments, is learning to read. First, he articulates his points in the form of questions. He is not searching for definitive answers about the material we have studied; instead, the article prompts him to articulate questions that are either new or remain unanswered. Second, these questions link to a number of different rabbinic texts we have studied over the course of the semester, from calculating compensation for physical damage through a person's worth on the slave market (*nezek*) to calculating compensation for pain using what I term "the reasonable person" (*adam ka-yotzeh ba-zeh*; M. Bava Kamma 8:1) standard. This mention of the slave may also connect the article by Mira Balberg to one we had read earlier about the realia of slavery in the ancient world.[13] Third, while some of the questions are very broad, others are exceptionally focused. James wonders both about biblical and rabbinic theology writ large as well as a particular legal detail in compensation for pain. In order to read in this way, he had to be able to understand both the article's argument on its own terms as well as recall a number of sugyot. The article has prompted him to weave together a number of shorter sugyot into questions about the worth of the individual versus a collective paradigm, the Divine-human relationship, and liability for injuring another human being—something that would not have been possible at the outset of the course. James has learned to read on the micro-level of a phrase (*adam ka-yotzeh ba-zeh*) and the macro-level of a number of sugyot and then to connect these to a wider world of theological inquiry.

---

13   Hezser, *Jewish Slavery*, 247-74.

What Others Have to Say: Secondary Readings in Learning to Read Talmud | CHAPTER 3

These four writing samples represent one important aspect of how I wanted the students to learn how to read the Bavli: to understand an author's argument and then to connect that argument back to the text of the Bavli, in this case, material from *perek ha-hovel*. Secondary articles should help students to see that they can find more ideas to explore and more questions to ask when they utilize the work of others than if they simply read the text of the Bavli only. These articles have enabled students to read these sugyot as engaging questions—not only about financial compensation for physical assault but also about theology, human worth, and law's societal role.

How Talking Helps Students Learn to Read Secondary Literature

As a complement to student writing about secondary literature, I also used focused discussion of an assigned article or group of articles. I would ask one student to articulate a particular author's thesis, and then ask other students to build on and critique that student's statement. Afterwards, I would ask students to articulate what interested them in the article. These questions are meant to serve a number of purposes: to help students refine what they had previously written, to listen to one another, to build on one another's words, and to trigger additional connections between the article and the sugyot. In other words, they enable the students to draw out more from the sugyot than they would have by only writing about the article. As articles were assigned weekly, my initial goal was to have a weekly discussion about each individual paper. In practice, I was inconsistent about meeting this goal. At times, I would initiate a class discussion about one article in particular. At other times, I would wait until we had read a few articles on one topic and then discuss the group together. Nevertheless, when I did initiate these conversations, I consistently did so at the beginning of class, before we had begun to read the day's assigned suyga. I did this for two reasons: first, since it was easy to spend the entire class period reading a sugya and commentaries, I wanted to ensure we would have time to talk about the relevant article. Second, by placing the article at the beginning of class, I hoped that the ideas we discussed would remain relevant for the class that day.

The following excerpts from class discussion all focus on the topic of shame (*boshet*) and the previously mentioned assigned reading from Yael Richardson.

The transcriptions stem from the same class period.[14] I began the class by asking students to define Richardson's methodology of analyzing shame:

> Jane Kanarek: Think back to Richardson, what's she doing? What's her approach?
> Sam: She says she wants to do a survey of how *boshet* shows up in a legal context in the Talmud and try to understand something about what *boshet* is from those legal contexts.
> JK: Great. And it's not only in the Talmud that she's doing this.
> Sam: In the rabbinical [works] in general, because she also did Tosefta …
> JK: Right, but I mean not just in rabbinic literature. She's also doing Roman law. It's a comparative approach. … What's useful about taking a comparative approach and putting rabbinic law in conversation with Roman law? Why might someone want to do that instead of just looking at the Talmud?

Sam answers my question about Richardson's methodology by naming only the talmudic context of her work. I then challenge him to widen that lens, and he does so by naming an earlier rabbinic work, the Tosefta. I articulate that Richardson's approach is a comparative one and ask a further question: why is the comparative approach useful? While students have written about Richardson's approach before class, and I have read their work, I still think it is useful for them to restate her approach to one another in class. This act enables them to refine verbally what they have written and to build on their writing through conversation with one another. Thus, as the conversation continues, another student says:

> Rebekah: It's easier then to see what's missing. If you just look inside tradition, it's not as clear what is being left out or added to.

And yet another student adds the following:

> Dan: I think that the word innovation has to be brought in. That's really what you're seeing—you're seeing things that were just kind of general throughout society and what innovation the rabbis had—not just where

---

14 May 5, 2014. Some of the language in the transcriptions has been made smoother in order to make them easier to read.

What Others Have to Say: Secondary Readings in Learning to Read Talmud | CHAPTER 3

they differed, but I think that's kind of about the timeline, where they have added on or where they felt they needed to add on.

Finally, building on the students' comments and summarizing the discussion on Richardson's piece, I name some additional elements of which I would like them to be cognizant:

> JK: By looking at other cultures, you can also look at the kind of questions that other people have asked about non-rabbinic cultures and then ask those questions as well about rabbinic culture. ... [Richardson] brings a scholar who divides Roman shame into different categories, different types of shame, and then does that same typology for rabbinic shame. Shame caused by verbal or physical aggression, feelings of embarrassment, which can lead to withdrawal or passivity. Shame by association—"*boshet panim*" ["shame of the face"]—a sense of shame. So it pushes us. We did this instinctively in class. But her approach emphasizes that of not looking at all shame as the same and asking questions about gradations and change.

My approach in this part of our exchange relies on the students' own insights as well as my explicitly naming for them details about which I would like them to be attentive. In this case, I ask students to pay attention to the ways in which Richardson's writing articulates different categories of shame and then how the students themselves began to do this in class, even before reading Richardson's work. By making this point explicit, I want them to see how her reading methodology enhances what they have already begun to do on their own. Consequently, later in the same class, Dan comments:

> Dan: I've been reading the two sugyot [on shame][15] together and with the other stuff on *boshet*. It's become a question for me of: Are we always talking about there being all sorts of different types of *boshet*, or is it that, normally, there's just *boshet*, and then, in certain situations, we really have to tease it apart and say there's *kisufa* [shame that a person

---

15 The student is referring to two of the assigned sugyot on shame, in this case, ones found on B. Bava Kamma 86a-b (*man tana le-ha de-tanu rabanan – de-mikhlemu leh de-mikhlam*) and on B. Bava Kamma 86b (*bae rabi abba bar memel – de-mikhlemu leh ve-lamikhlam*). I assign four different sugyot on shame.

feels internally]¹⁶—whatever it is? Or should we now be looking back into all the *boshet* stuff we've read and saying what *boshet* were they actually talking about?

Although Dan does not explicitly name Richardson's article, he does allude to it in his comment about "the other stuff" and in his observation that we may need to pay closer attention to the word "*boshet*" and interrogate its range of meanings. Dan utilizes both what he has read in the Bavli itself ("all the *boshet* stuff we've read") and what he has read in the articles on shame,¹⁷ to question his earlier reading assumptions about a base meaning for shame ("normally, there's just *boshet*"). His answer utilizes the Hebrew and Aramaic terminology of the Bavli, alerting us to the fact that his questions also depend on a close reading of the text in its original language. Weaving together the material he has encountered, the student now wonders whether we need to consider each case of *boshet* individually, to ask about specific meaning each time the word "shame" appears in a sugya. The engagement with secondary articles through reading and then discussion, as well as the primary text of the Bavli, leads Dan to articulate a goal of reading more closely for specific meaning and not making assumptions about one word having the same meaning whenever it appears. The class discussion has pushed him to refine his ideas and questions past that of the writing alone and to link his ideas even more closely to the actual text of the Bavli.

How Weaving Secondary Literature into Conversation about a Sugya Helps Reading

The method of weaving a particular author's points into a discussion about a sugya or commentator was not a teaching methodology that I articulated to myself at the outset of the course. My original plan had been simply to concentrate discussions on an article or group of articles at the beginning of most

---

16 The Bavli here contrasts *kisufa* (shame experienced internally by a person) with *ziluta* (shame that degrades a person in the eyes of others) and *boshet mishpachah* (shame that degrades a person's family). See B. Bava Kamma 86b and Rashi s.v. *kisufa*.
17 I assigned three different pieces on shame: Crane, "Shameful Ambivalences," 61-84; Richardson, "Legal Shame," 7-32, 69-86; Rubenstein, *Culture of the Babylonian Talmud*, 67-79.

classes, using these discussions to help students better understand the articles themselves and then apply them to reading the sugyot. However, because of inadequate time in class for discussion of the primary talmudic texts and students' lack of reliability in completing their written assignments on time,[18] I found myself compensating (after the fact) for that lack of a consistent, focused discussion by choosing select, important points from secondary articles and weaving those points into conversations about specific sugyot—a short-cut to achieving what more classtime might have fulfilled. Yet, in reviewing class audio transcripts, I realized this was actually an effective method of asking students to be attentive to the ways in which a particular article could sharpen their understanding of a sugya and enable them to connect contemporary ideas and concerns to the talmudic material.

The examples below concentrate on compensation for *shevet*, idleness from work caused by injury (B. Bava Kamma 85b-86a). The Bavli discusses two different methods of compensation for *shevet*. One compensates for permanent injury at a fixed rate and the other for temporary injury at a rate that changes according to occupation:

> JK: [I]f we think back to [Catherine] Hezser's article, she really did differentiate between day laborers and slave laborers, who were sometimes hired for specific skills.
>
> Dan: We might map onto this by splitting up the sugya and saying the top part of the sugya is talking about day laborers, where you're just going to say, "I don't care what you're doing day-to-day and how much you're getting paid. There's a standard rate—that's what you get paid." And

---

18 I had also hoped that students would divide their pieces relatively evenly between articulating an author's argument and connecting that argument to the rabbinic passages. While I consider 300-500 words to be a relatively short assignment, the students often handed in pieces that were much longer than that word count. In addition, they would devote much more space to the author's argument than to connecting that argument to the rabbinic material. My assessment is that students found the word count number itself to be intimidating and responded by either handing in the piece late or writing something that was too long. They also may not have had a clear idea of the length of 300-500 words and so compensated by writing longer and with less focus. In the future, I plan to return to a model I have used in other courses, which asks for a specific number of sentences for each segment of the assignment. I also hypothesize that summarizing an existing argument is easier than creating a new one and connecting the articles to the sugyot, a tendency that can be addressed by telling students how many sentences to write on each part of the assignment.

people for *omanut* [occupation or craft], that's our second one, where whatever craft you have and a specific injury and how it affects your craft. That's going to work into our *shevet* [idleness] payment. As Leah was saying earlier, it's like day laborer equals time.[19]

Into the class discussion, I bring one point from Catherine Hezser's article on Jewish slavery in antiquity and remind the students of Hezser's historical point about the differentiation between types of workers. Dividing laborers into different groups and having different systems of compensation was not foreign to the ancient world. Dan then takes this idea and maps it onto the sugya itself, a passage where the first part describes a fixed rate of compensation for idleness, while the second describes a variable amount (B. Bava Kamma 85b). He also connects this idea with a point raised earlier in the class by another student. Dan's words demonstrate that he is thinking with the article, using the information there in order to try and explain the complex content and composition of a puzzling sugya. Again, my concern here is not with whether or not Dan has accurately read the sugya. Instead, I want him to make connections from the secondary article to the sugya—and even to the comments of other students. Dan is learning to read the Bavli using the research and the ideas of others, connecting the Bavli to a wider world of ideas.

The second example is also concerned with compensation for idleness in regard to permanent and temporary injury. In this sugya (B. Bava Kamma 85b-86a), the sage Abaye proposes that an identical method of compensation be utilized for permanent and temporary injury, a combination of a variable payment for the extent of physical injury (here, called *shevet gedolah*) and a fixed one for idleness that is calculated according to a minimum wage (here, called *shevet ketanah*). The sage Rava on the other hand proposes that there be two methods of compensation. Permanent injury should be compensated as described above by Abaye, while temporary injury is assessed according to wages lost:

> Leah: I wonder if Abaye just doesn't want there to be two systems. Just like there's a thing that we do when people get injured and that's the slave market evaluation [*nezek*] and *shomer kishuin* [a cucumber guardian] and

---

19 Class transcription, March 24, 2014.

What Others Have to Say: Secondary Readings in Learning to Read Talmud | CHAPTER 3

for reasons of fairness or reasons of speed or for any sorts of reasons or just reasons of simplicity of the legal system. [He] just doesn't want there to be two different rubrics operational—just, this is what we do every time.

JK: Right. In other words, it could be really complicated to try and determine whether this is "*sofah lahzor*" [in the end it (the injury) will heal], a temporary injury? Amputation [permanent injury] [is] obvious. It's not going to [heal]. But anything else, it seems like …
Leah: Totally unclear.
JK: It's unclear.

A number of elements are present here. Leah opens by trying to make sense of Abaye's position that there should be identical methods of compensation for permanent and temporary injury. She proposes a number of different ideas: fairness, speed, simplicity, and consistency. I then rephrase her words to emphasize her idea of simplicity. Since it is difficult to know with certainty whether an injury will completely heal, perhaps the best course is one method of compensation for any injury. Both Leah's proposition and my answer reference terminology from the sugyot we have studied: *shomer kishuin* and *sofah lahzor*. More importantly, she has rephrased the terminology used by Abaye in this sugya (*shevet gedolah* and *shevet ketanah*) into terminology used elsewhere in this chapter, that of the slave market[20] and a cucumber guardian.[21] This move by Leah illustrates her ability to read beyond the local sugya and to make connections to other rabbinic material we have studied. While she does not explicitly mention any of the secondary articles, her mention of "simplicity of the legal system" may hint at Crotty's idea that, while one of the main functions of literature is to explore human complexity, one of the functions of law is to simplify.[22]

Leah continues by pushing back at my suggestion that the complications entailed in determining whether an injury is permanent or temporary

---

20 See M. Bava Kamma 8:1 and Rashi's allusion s.v. *shevet gedolah*. See also the sugya on *shevet* on B. Bava Kamma 85a.
21 See M. Bava Kamma 8:1, T. Bava Kamma 9:2, B. Bava Kamma 85b, and Rashi s.v. *ve-shevet ketanah*.
22 Crotty, *Law's Interior*, 227-28.

may drive Abaye's suggestion. She wants to emphasize timing in making the legal decision. At this point, I bring in an idea from Crotty:

> JK: But, if we go back to Crotty's claim in the article that one of the functions in law is to simplify, perhaps Abaye is leaning in that direction and trying to say, "Look, I can simplify this law a little bit for you. It doesn't actually have to be so complex." And Rava's paradigm is putting the complexity back in the law as well.[23]

For Crotty, one of the main functions of literature is to explore human complexity, but one of the functions of law also is to simplify. Both law and literature are complementary and represent different aspects of human life.[24] It seems self-evident that the Talmud, as a work that is both law and literature,[25] may include both perspectives. It is possible to see Abaye's one solution as an attempt to simplify and Rava's as an attempt to recognize the complexity of the legal situation. Equally important, by introducing Crotty's ideas into this conversation about compensation for physical injury, I was able to model for the students a way in which general legal theory can be useful for thinking about rabbinic literature and, as well, speak specifically about conflicting legal opinions in a particular sugya. I made subtexts in the sugya explicit.

Weaving comments from different articles into the conversation about a sugya began as a compensatory technique for a lack of time to dedicate exclusively to discussing secondary readings. To the positive, it *became* a technique for reminding students of the secondary literature we had read and for encouraging them to consider how they might use these articles in their own thinking about sugyot. I provided them with suggestions of how a particular thinker might help them as well—this to foster them to begin to think on their own about what an article might offer in the way of a richer reading.[26]

---

23 Class transcription, April 9, 2014.
24 Crotty, *Law's Interior*, 227-28.
25 See Jane L. Kanarek, *Biblical Narrative and the Formation of Rabbinic Law* (New York: Cambridge University Press, 2014); Jeffrey L. Rubenstein, *Stories of the Babylonian Talmud* (Baltimore: The Johns Hopkins University Press, 2010); Barry Scott Wimpfheimer, *Narrating the Law: A Poetics of Talmudic Legal Stories* (Philadelphia: University of Pennsylvania Press, 2011).
26 Writing on what Jewish scholarship can offer Jewish education, Barry Holtz comments that a teacher's task is "to create pedagogic situations that allow students to uncover for

What Others Have to Say: Secondary Readings in Learning to Read Talmud | CHAPTER 3

Becoming Their Own Readers: The Final Exam

As mentioned earlier in my description of the course, the final exam is designed to tie together the different elements of the course, to be able to explain the technical elements of a sugya, to connect the ideas in one sugya with those in another, to engage medieval commentary, and to utilize secondary articles. I concentrate here on describing and analyzing student writings from the essay portion of the exam, the section that most reflects this chapter's focus: the use of secondary scholarship in reading a sugya.[27] I focus primarily on students' use of these readings but also illustrate a few of the ways in which these readings are tied to some of the technical skills of translation and parsing an argument. The examples in this section stem from the final essay papers of two students, Dan and James.

For the final essay, I asked students to examine a sugya from B. Bava Kamma 84a that we had not previously studied. I instructed them that their reading of the sugya needed to integrate one specific Tosafot,[28] any sugyot and medieval commentaries from class assignments that they had found relevant, and at least four of the secondary articles. The articles they chose needed to represent both the general reading we did on law as well as those specific to rabbinic literature. While I did not require that they translate the sugya word-for-word, their essays needed to demonstrate a full understanding of the base sugya itself.

The following description of this sugya on B. Bava Kamma 84a intentionally glosses over most of the interpretive difficulties and ambiguities; it is meant as a guide to help the reader of this chapter better understand some of the excerpts from the final essays and not by any means to portray a full depiction of the sugya. The sugya opens by describing a case where a donkey cuts off the hand of a child of indeterminate age (*yanuka*).[29] A conflict between

---

themselves what he [the article's author] has uncovered for us [the teachers]." Barry W. Holtz, "Across the Divide: What Might Jewish Educators Learn from Jewish Scholars," *Journal of Jewish Education* 72 (2006): 19.

27 For reasons of space, I have only included excerpts from two of the exams. As a group, the essays had many overlapping and fascinating themes. I regret I was not able to quote from more, even all, of my students; their learning achievements deserve recognition.

28 Tosafot s.v. *zilu shomo leh arbaah devarim*.

29 *Yanuka* can refer to a suckling infant, child, or schoolboy. See Jastrow s.v. *yanuka*. The semantic range of *yanuka* will be an important interpretive point in some of the student essays.

three sages (Rav Pappa, Rava, and Abaye) ensues about the nature of compensation the child is owed by the assailant. They eventually reach the conclusion that the child is owed payment for *nezek*, or physical injury, something that, as I have remarked earlier, is evaluated by the child's worth on the slave market. The father states that he does not want this money, because it will degrade the child. He is challenged about this decision and, in turn, informs his challengers (likely Rav Pappa, Abaye, and Rava) that when the child grows up, he will compensate the child from his own funds. The sugya concludes with the father's declaration; whether his declaration is accepted remains unanswered. This legal narrative[30] is short, complex, and full of ambiguity. With plenty of openings for interpretation, the passage serves as a fitting final assignment.[31]

I begin with text from Dan's exam that addresses the meaning of the word previously translated as "child" but that the student below translated as "infant," *yanuka*:

> The word I have translated here as infant, *yanuka,* has meanings that could allow for readings of this child's age being anywhere from that of a nursing infant to a child who has already started their studies in school. Though this detail of age might not seem to matter much, it allows for very different readings of the father's response to the court's process of estimation. I will discuss this at length later in my commentary. Before moving on from here though, let us note that one should pay heed to the use of *yanuka* instead of the word *katan* (minor) which is certainly present throughout the rest of the chapter.

Dan correctly identifies that the sugya opens with a problem of meaning: what age exactly is this *yanuka* whose hand is severed? He also states that this problem of translation has implications for the legal process described in the continuation of the sugya. In addition, Dan notes that the vocabulary of *yanuka* differs from the terminology used for a child (*katan*, or minor) in the other sugyot we studied. Dan has made two significant advances in his reading: first, he demonstrates he knows translation is significant, and that he must pay attention to the range of meanings a word can have. Second, he shows us

---

30 On the genre of legal narratives in the Bavli, see Wimpfheimer, *Narrating the Law*.
31 I also chose this sugya because of one other element: its mention of both *nezek* and degradation (*ziluta*). Since the first sugya we study deals with *nezek* and the last sugyot shame or degradation, this sugya contains within it the themes that bookend the course.

that attention to the technicalities of translation also has ramifications for the possible different understandings of a sugya's content. Dan then goes on to observe that this question of age is raised by Tosafot in their comment on this same passage.[32]

Later in the essay, Dan ties the question of the age of the *yanuka'* to information he learned about slavery from the article by Catherine Hezser. He questions why Rav Pappa states that this injured infant or child should not be paid *nezek*, when he has clearly suffered irreversible damage. Among the possible explanations Dan provides is one that explores the relationship of a child's age and fiscal value on the slave market:

> [I]f we extrapolate from Hezser's claims in *Jewish Slavery in Antiquity*, where she writes, "Children were obviously cheaper than mature slaves, since the possibilities for their employment were limited, and they had to be nourished until they had reached their full labour capacities" (Heszer, 248). Hezser speaks here of children, perhaps on the older end of our reading of *yanuka* from before. If we read our child to be an infant, it is possible that their value on the slave market is either not part of the realia of slavery for the rabbis or that the price of baby slaves is so low as to make the estimation of the baby's value useless for the calculation of *nezek* payments.

Dan extrapolates from Hezser's writing on children put into the slave market in order to explain a puzzling aspect of the sugya. Why does a sage, who should know that this infant or child would receive the *nezek* payment, say that he should not? Dan uses knowledge from this secondary source to construct one possible reading of this puzzle.[33]

James' exam takes a different contextual view and utilizes this sugya as a framework for addressing large questions about justice and the construction of the rabbinic legal system. These questions, however, are also embedded in

---

32   While the student does realize that Tosafot addresses the question of age, he mistranslates the passage. Mistranslation of Tosafot was a common problem in these finals. Thus, while students brought Tosafot into their comments, their use of Tosafot was not as strong as the other essay components. They simply were not as prepared to utilize medieval commentaries.

33   The student provides three other possible readings. Since these other readings of the sugya do not reference secondary readings, I have not included them.

close readings of the sugya itself, along with ideas raised by the secondary readings. James' essay opens with inquiries that question the nature of repayment:

> What is at stake when it comes to ensuring that justice is served? Who is repayment, at its core, supposed to appease? Is retribution and compensation reparative for the individual, or is it to maintain a more objective and interdependent communal and societal system or both? Is that system in danger of collapsing if repayment is not made? What are the potential dangers that come with opting out of the system?

Although the sugya itself never names these questions in its legal narrative, by identifying them as central issues, James demonstrates his ability to transform a rabbinic text into a dialogue about the nature of justice and the stability of law as a communal institution. Equally important, his opening questions allude to issues raised in secondary readings, in this case, one piece on compensatory justice[34] and another on retributive and restorative justice.[35] Both of these articles stem from the more general field of jurisprudence; however, neither mentions nor alludes to rabbinic literature or even to the broader field of Jewish legal thought. Nevertheless, James finds the

---

34 The role that a compensatory system plays in punishment within a judicial system is raised by Goodin. He argues that compensation's function is "to right what would otherwise count as wrongful injuries to persons or their property." Goodin, "Compensation," 257. He delineates two types of compensation, means-replacing compensation and ends-replacing compensation. Means-replacing compensation aims to provide people with the equivalent means for pursuing the same ends as before the loss (i.e., giving someone an artificial leg who loses a leg). Ends-replacing compensation aims to replace the loss by helping people to pursue another end in a way that leaves them subjectively as well-off as they would have been before the loss (i.e., giving someone who has experienced bereavement an "all-expense paid Mediterranean cruise"). I am skeptical of the example Goodin provides for ends-replacing compensation as meeting the characteristics he himself outlines for this form of compensation, but it should nonetheless help illustrate the difference between the two compensatory frameworks. Goodin argues for the superiority of means-replacing compensation *over* ends-replacing compensation. Goodin, "Compensation," 257-89.

35 Retributive and restorative justice are discussed in Michael Wenzel, et al., "Retributive and Restorative Justice," *Law and Human Behavior* 32, no. 5 (2008): 375-89. Retributive justice as a response to rule violation describes a unilateral imposition of punishment. Restorative justice is a two-sided process that involves the creation of a shared-value consensus. Offenses are viewed as a conflict between victim, offender, and community. Both retributive and restorative justice can include financial compensation to the victim as well as punishment to the offender in an attempt to repair the breach in justice. The key difference is whether the process is one-sided or two.

What Others Have to Say: Secondary Readings in Learning to Read Talmud | CHAPTER 3

vocabulary and ideas introduced by these articles useful in helping him to frame his reading of the final sugya. He has learned that concepts developed outside the world of rabbinic literature can aid in bringing to the surface issues latent in the text of the Bavli itself, such as the nature of justice, the function of punishment, and the role of both in sustaining a legal system.

As James moves through an explication of the sugya, these questions of justice continue to loom large. The following passage focuses on the portion of the sugya where the father objects to having his baby's/child's worth assessed by his estimated value on the slave market:

> Here, the baby's father speaks up: "No! I don't want to degrade my baby in this way! I don't want to go through with this. I say no!" There are a number of important things that happen here. First, we have a non-rabbi speaking. When in our text do we hear the voice of a lay-person … ? Here we have a commoner, not just a rabbinic objector, but a real, live, messy human deeply impacted by and invested in the matter at hand. … And perhaps most importantly at this point, for the first time, it is more than law that is being questioned. With the father's statement, justice itself is being destabilized. It would be one thing for the *perpetrator* to demand out of the justice system. It is another thing for the *victim* to decline what's owed to him. This turns it all on its head. This makes us ask deeply about justice's role in that society.

James notices some important differences between this sugya and others we studied this semester. First, we hear the voice of a layperson, the father. Second, this non-rabbinic voice introduces a complexity or "messiness" into what had been, until this point, presented as a question of legal categorization: From which of the different categories of compensation should the injured party be compensated? Earlier in this essay, James mentioned the ideas of Crotty about literature making the simple complicated and law simplifying what is messy. He thus utilizes Crotty's ideas to read the specific ways in which this story stands at the nexus of law and literature—and even the nature of justice itself. James reads the sugya not simply as a question about the correct method of payment but about justice writ large.

Indeed, as James continues, he integrates these ideas about compensation, retribution, and restoration more deeply into his reading of the sugya:

> Why doesn't he [the father] want their justice? Perhaps the damage done is so severe that going through any process other than grief and caring is too much for the father right now. Maybe the process of evaluating the baby as if he were a slave was particularly triggering or complicated or sad for the father. Perhaps there was a recognition that, like Goodin spoke of, there is no means-replacing[36] compensation for losing a hand (at least in the days before prosthetics, and I would argue, even in our time), so why even try. Whatever the reason, the father makes known clearly his desire for a particular justice. And yet, the rabbis won't listen. They are blinded by their own definition.

In wondering about why the father refuses compensation for *nezek*, James directly mentions the ideas of the author Robert Goodin on means-replacing compensation. He does not state that Goodin's ideas categorically explain the father's actions; he does not seek an exact identity between the author's ideas on compensation and those presented in the sugya. Instead, he utilizes them as a way to explore a plausible reading of the story's plot. James continues with further interrogation of the father's position and that of the rabbis:

> Is this the difference between restorative and retributive justice?[37] The father is demanding a say. The rabbis are, on their own, meting out punishment and pushing for its conclusion, seeking some abstract or objective sense of the ideal, detached from the parties involved. In contrast to that, Wenzel tells us that in restorative justice "all the parties with a stake in a particular offence come together to resolve collectively how to deal with the aftermath of the offence and the implications for the future." Restorative justice also takes on an overarching value of healing, rather than punishing. While it's hard to know what the father is feeling, we might surmise that it is healing he is after. Otherwise, why would he be asking for what he asks for? It also seems clear, given their words and actions, that the rabbis care little about what he's feeling and what he wants. This is a far cry from restorative justice.

Here, James does two things: he uses the ideas of restorative and retributive justice as a framework for explaining the opposing positions of the

---

36 See footnote 35 on means-replacing compensation.
37 See footnote 36 on restorative vs. retributive compensation.

rabbis and the father. But he also uses the sugya to help him refine the differences between retributive and restorative justice. In other words, the article on retributive and restorative justice both helps him to read the sugya and to propose another explanation for the rabbinic and parental responses, and the sugya helps him to better understand these two types of justice. In order to propose these readings of the sugya, James has not only had to track the father's response but the chain of argument that precedes it. He has had to be attentive to ambiguities in language, shifts in voice between named rabbis, an anonymous interlocutor, and the father, as well as be sensitive to a range of possibilities for narrating the legal story itself. James has decoded the sugya and used the article to help him read the sugya insightfully.

The final passage I cite from James' essay reveals this sensitivity to language as tied to his questions about justice:

> In what ways is justice personal (akin to *kisufa* [shame that a person feels internally], B. Bava Kamma 86b), where what matters most is the individual's experience of it? And in what ways is justice a societal and objective truth (more like *ziluta* [shame that degrades a person in the eyes of others], B. Bava Kamma 86b)? When viewed as the former, restoration, listening, healing, remains a possibility. When assumed to be the latter, what is lost? Can one opt out? What are the repercussions? Does opting out stunt or disrupt the foundations of justice? What kind of abuse does a system leave itself open to if opting out is a possibility? To what extent do we owe it to each other to buy into the same system? Where is our responsibility to navigate the individual complexities of humans?

Here, James links two different concepts of shame (personal vs. communally experienced shame) that have appeared in our sugyot to his larger questions about justice. He utilizes these two concepts as ways for thinking about the costs and benefits of a justice that is tailored toward individuals and one that is oriented more toward an overarching societal standard. Exploring the possible motivations of the characters in this brief sugya, by using the lenses provided by a number of secondary readings,[38] enables James to read

---

38 The student cites secondary readings in addition to the ones I have presented here. He also utilizes Cover, "Violence and the Word," 1601-29; Crane, "Shameful Ambivalences," 61-84; Hezser, *Jewish Slavery*, 247-74; and Rubenstein, *Culture of the Babylonian Talmud*, 67-79.

this Bavli passage as an exploration of modes of justice. These secondary readings permit him to proactively explore motivations for the characters' behaviors, to open possibilities for the many ambiguities in the narrative, and to connect these with much larger questions from the world of jurisprudence. Learning to read through the lens of secondary readings has enabled James to understand the rabbinic sugya in question not only as a specific legal case history but also as a meditation on justice in general. The articles have empowered him to read the range of interpretive possibilities latent in the sugya and then to connect these readings to a wider world of thinking about law as one mode through which humans express their visions for constructing society.

Conclusion

In the opening of this chapter, I describe my goal as enabling students to have a richer understanding of the Bavli itself through the integration of secondary readings into a one-semester course. Three primary methods were used to target my learning objectives: weekly writing assignments, class discussion, and producing a final essay. Collectively, all three were meant to teach students how to read with a greatly enriched approach. And indeed, students did learn how to read more richly. Grounded in the specific language of different sugyot, they became alert to ambiguity, able to connect one sugya with another, raise multiple possibilities for meaning, locate subtexts, connect sugyot to wider ideas in the humanities, and bring their own concerns and questions to their readings.

Asking students to seriously engage with the ideas of others through writing and discussion, ideas that are directly linked and those that are less obviously linked to the topic at hand, challenges them to expand their current reading capabilities. Students must "step out" of their own minds and into the intellectual worlds of others. As they do so while closely reading the words of the Bavli, the Bavli begins to reveal its ambiguities and questions to them. In turn, the experience of immersing themselves in the ideas of others encourages them to engage with their own ideas and bring them back to the world of the Bavli. Through such a circle, students expand what they are able to say about and see in a sugya—and begin to discover the extraordinary over the already known.

CHAPTER 4

And No One Gave the Torah to the Priests: Reading the Mishnah's References to the Priests and the Temple

Marjorie Lehman

This past fall, I taught an undergraduate Mishnah course at the Jewish Theological Seminary, one that is required for students majoring in Talmud and is as well a course for non-majors who wish to fulfill a requirement of one of two Talmud courses. I had ten students in my class, ideal for a seminar focused on teaching students how to read the Mishnah closely. About a third of these students were graduates of Jewish high schools and had studied Mishnah before; a third were students who knew little or no Hebrew and had never seen the Mishnah before last fall; and a third were upperclassman, who had experience studying all types of Jewish texts. Although my goals in teaching students to read Mishnah are many, during this semester, I wanted to teach the students to read the material about the priests and the Temple critically. It occurred to me early in the semester that the students seemed entirely comfortable reading the Mishnah with the idea that the rabbis swiftly took over to lead the Jewish people when the Temple was destroyed in 70 CE, and that the rabbis also had made every effort to incorporate vestiges of this "Temple past" into their present—preparing for a future with a rebuilt Temple. The Mishnah, my students all thought, was a positive testament to the rabbis, whom they believed had to create a type of Judaism that could function without the Temple. In other words, they believed rabbinic Judaism was a natural outgrowth of Temple Judaism in response to the crisis of the destruction, and references to the Temple in the Mishnah offered evidence of an actual Temple that would be rebuilt one day.

I was struck by how tightly the students held onto this narrative, using it to read the Mishnah. As their teacher, I questioned if I had paid enough attention to how powerfully embedded this understanding of the Temple was in the Jewish upbringing of our students, in this class and perhaps in others as well. Most of my students had been making reference to the Temple in their prayers and had been directed to read about and construct images of the Temple in school and in camp. Many had even visited the outside wall of the Temple in Jerusalem with various youth groups and participated in teen programs, where they were taught to think about this site as the holiest of Judaism's shrines.[1]

I determined that teaching my students how to read the Mishnah, therefore, needed to include an objective that incorporated teaching them how to read the Mishnah's references to the Temple critically, and, more specifically regarding the priests, analytically. My objective became for them to leave class more suspicious of the rabbis' references to the Temple and to enrich, if not complicate, their sense of the relationship of the rabbis to the priests and the Temple. Rather than approaching the material with a set of installed pre-set conclusions about the rabbis and the Temple and asking students to answer my questions by drawing from what they had learned prior to entering my classroom, I wanted them to *read for the questions that the rabbis were asking themselves* regarding the priests and the Temple.[2] These

---

1   Since teaching this Mishnah class, I have thought a lot about Eli Gottlieb and Sam Wineburg's question, "Is the hallmark of mature historical thinking [even academic thinking] the understanding that knowledge is constructed and fallible? Or is it the ability to remain firmly committed to one's heritage despite this knowledge?" As a professor teaching in an academic institution that is also a seminary, should I be teaching my students to undo what they know? Indeed, I need to think more about the balance between developing critical thinking skills and the importance of recognizing the commitment of many of my students to a particular sense of the past. See Eli Gottlieb and Sam Wineburg, "Between Veritas and Communitas: Epistemic Switching in the Reading of Academic and Sacred History," *Journal of the Learning Sciences* 21 no. 1 (2012): 87.

2   See Robert B. Bain, "Rounding Up Unusual Suspects: Facing the Authority Hidden in the History Classroom," *Teachers College Record* 108, no. 10 (2006): 2080-81, where he makes reference to Richard H. Brown, "Learning How to Learn: The Amherst Project and History Education in the Schools," *The Social Studies* 87, no. 6 (1996): 267, and notes the following: "School history appears to be shaped by the assumption that 'students learn best and most usefully … [when] being asked to master the conclusions of scholars about questions the students only dimly comprehend.' In reversing the

issues solidified that I did not want my students to approach the Mishnah as a finished and closed book that simply described a group of early rabbis and their laws, nor did I want them to presume there was only one perspective on the Temple communicated within the Mishnah. I wanted them, instead, to see the many different ways that the rabbis describe, discuss, and think about the Temple, from the legislative dicta to the well-orchestrated narratives, examining what each could possibly mean. When their analyses began to problematize their initial conception of the link between the Temple and the rabbis, I would know they had learned to read Mishnah.

Overall Structure of the Class

My Mishnah class met once a week for two hours, with the goal of reading one chapter of Mishnah each week from the twentieth-century Hebrew edition, edited by Pinhas Kehati. This particular edition provides the students with a clear vocalized Hebrew text and an easy-to-read modern Hebrew commentary, summarizing classical commentators.[3] Most mishnayot we read closely, word-for-word, translating, while others we merely referred to, so as to cultivate a sense of the development of ideas within one entire chapter and then, ultimately, to compare chapters from different tractates of the Mishnah, one to the other. I intended for the students to compare one chapter on holiday ritual, for example, to another on capital punishment, in the name of giving them a sense of the Mishnah as a whole document. This approach supported a pedagogical decision to root my course in an approach that presumed an intentional reworking of source materials by a strong redactional hand with an ideological agenda, albeit while making students aware of other text-critical approaches via secondary readings we discussed in class—rather than teaching my students

---

historian's logic of questions and answers, teachers *first* definitively and confidently provide answers and *then* pose the questions. Suspicions are rarely raised, except the suspicion that the students have not yet mastered the facts found in the texts and classroom materials."

3   Although Pinhas Kehati's edition of the Mishnah (Jerusalem: Mekhon ha-mikdash, 1997) has been translated into English, I discouraged the students from using it, and we never used it in class. We also did not do any manuscript work, as this was an undergraduate survey course of the Mishnah.

to read mishnayot through the lens of other tannaitic sources available to them in the Tosefta, Palestinian, and Babylonian Talmuds.[4] I did this for the sake of teaching my students to read *the* Mishnah alone, that is, to focus their attention on what is included in this one collection only. I knew that most entered my classroom with a sense that the Mishnah was one book, and I felt that looking at too many other parallel sources would make learning to read the Mishnah daunting and overwhelming. I also did not feel that in a thirteen-week course we would cover much ground if I did not approach the Mishnah synchronically—I wanted my students to experience as many mishnaic texts as possible—or at least as many complete chapters as possible.

Before reading each mishnah, we began with several questions of inquiry, such as "What is the underlying issue with which the mishnah is grappling?" This enabled us to give each mishnah an introductory organizing title that we inserted into an ongoing outline that I prepared with the students in class. After class, I would update the printed copy and send a new, revised version to them. Following a few introductory set-up inquiry questions related to the main topic of the chapter, I turned to the fundamentals of translation, asking students to tell me which words do not make sense to them, which concepts are confusing, what seems contradictory, and what continues to confound them. The terse mishnaic Hebrew, the students soon learn, is not easy to translate. Relying on their knowledge of modern Hebrew often draws them off course. Many are fooled by what looks on the surface like easy Hebrew, guessing at the meaning of various words and phrases. When I observed the students struggling with my instructions to draw diagrams of what was occurring in a mishnah or arguing over how to dramatize a mishnah, I knew that

---

4   Students read sections of Jacob Neusner's *Evidence of the Mishnah* (Chicago: University of Chicago Press, 1981); Seth Schwartz's "The Political Geography of Rabbinic Texts," *Cambridge Companion to the Talmud and Rabbinic Literature* (Cambridge: Cambridge University Press, 2007), 75-98; and Shaye J. D. Cohen's critique of Neusner's *Evidence of the Mishnah*, "Jacob Neusner, Mishnah and Counter-Rabbinics: A Review Essay, *Conservative Judaism* 37, no. 1 (1983): 49-53. Also note Christine Hayes, "What is (The) Mishnah? Concluding Observations," *AJS Review* 32, no. 2 (2008): 291-97, for a brief overview of more recent studies of the Mishnah and Mira Balberg's comments on reading the Mishnah in her book, *Purity, Body, and Self in Early Rabbinic Literature* (Berkeley: University of California Press, 2014), 12-13.

the difficulties with translating these texts had become apparent to them. Part of learning to read was about learning how to work through their confusion, and so together, as a class, we worked on translations, evaluating which worked better than others.[5] Students were required to defend their preferences, and sometimes, we were left with no choice but to adopt two opposing translations. Through these practices, students began to realize that learning to read Mishnah was about recognizing that the texts could support more than one translation and learning to defend the best reading, an accomplishment of critical skill.

Where are the Priests? Encountering the Problem and Developing a Teaching Strategy

I began my Mishnah course with a simple but direct prompt to my students to think about what the Mishnah had to say about itself, before we began our reading of full chapters. For this exercise, I had the students read M. Eduyot 1:4-6; 5:6-7, M. Hagigah 1:8, and M. Avot 1:1. Our discussion of M. Avot 1:1, which presents the chain of transmission suggesting that Moshe received the Torah from Sinai and then passed it down, served as an important classroom moment, sensitizing me upfront to my students' prior assumptions. M. Avot 1:1 states:

> Moshe received the Torah from Sinai and transmitted it to Joshua and Joshua to the elders and the elders to the prophets and the prophets transmitted it to the men of the Great Assembly.

After a long struggle in class over how to define the meaning of the word Torah and whether the Mishnah was considered by the rabbis as "Torah," I recall we entered into a lengthy discussion over what the students viewed as a surprising omission. They wanted to know, "Where were the *kohanim*, the priests, in this chain of transmission?" They seemed to expect a reference to the priesthood and were bothered by the fact that this mishnah failed to make reference to them. Did the priests not receive the Torah and the laws of the cultic system? Did they not need to pass this part of Torah

---

5 See Sam Wineburg, "Reading Abraham Lincoln: An Expert/Expert Study in the Interpretation of Historical Texts," *Cognitive Science* 22, no. 3 (1998): 321.

down to the next generation if the Temple was to be operative?[6] It had not occurred to me that this omission of the priests would create a stumbling block. I had never thought about the priests as proto-rabbis or as transmitters of what developed into a rabbinic tradition. The image the rabbis had constructed for me, whether it was historically true or not, was of a priesthood that performed ritual and passed it down to the next priest. Put simply, the rabbis represented to me a different line of individuals, who transmitted ideas that were not necessarily present in the written Torah to their rabbinic disciples. For the rabbis of M. Avot, as I perceived them, the priests were not relevant to the history of Torah transmission through oral Torah study, and this took the students by surprise. But, this was also a wake-up call for me. I made a note in my teaching journal that same afternoon, reminding myself to pay careful attention to how my students, current and future, read texts that mentioned the Temple and the priests (10/2/13). I had to recognize linearity was important to them and how much they wished to fit what they knew about Judaism (quite a bit for some of them) into a coherent if not linear system. Would I be able to dissect the rabbis' references to the Temple in such a way as to represent them as men struggling in their relationship with the priests, rather than simply as men inheriting all that the priests represented and moving forward with as many pieces of this priestly legacy as they could, without a Temple? Would the students be able to resist reading the Mishnah as simply a collection of historical records of a past Temple reality, and, instead, be open to reading the texts of the Mishnah as attempts by the rabbis, not to describe their own world as it was, but to construct it as they wished it to be?[7] Would they be able to see that the rabbis of the Mishnah were a group of Jews grappling with self-identity and legitimacy at a time when they had little authority? Would they be able to read the Mishnah and see a group of men who were asking the question, "Who are we and who do we want to become?" Would they be able to integrate

---

[6] See Peter Schäfer, "Rabbis and Priests, or: How to Do Away with the Glorious Past of the Sons of Aaron," *Antiquity in Antiquity: Jewish and Christian Pasts in the Greco-Roman World*, ed. Gregg Gardner and Kevin Osterloh (Tübingen: Mohr Siebeck, 2008), 166-72, for discussion of this omission of any reference to the priests.

[7] Samuel S. Wineberg, "On the Reading of Historical Texts: Notes on the Breach between School and Academy," *American Educational Research Journal* 28, no. 3 (1991): 499.

references to the Temple into their understanding of the answer to this question without falling back on their prior assumptions? If the students demonstrated those levels of complex inquiry, I noted in my journal, I would feel confident that they had learned to "read" the Mishnah (10/2/13). As the next class session began, I was silent about my concerns and held back from revealing my own views. I wanted them to react to the texts in such a way as to begin laying the groundwork for reading the material about the priests, the sacrifices, and the Temple critically. The question remained, "How would I lead my students to this end, this more subtle but complex understanding?" The texts themselves were very complex and referred to the Temple in so many different ways.

The strategy that I began that day and continue to develop involves making certain that students take note of the array of ways that the mishnayot describe Temple-related issues. It is key to my strategy that the students grapple with the various ways the Mishnah approaches the Temple, even within one chapter. I want them to confront both narrative and legislative references, differentiating between the types of ideas the rabbis wished to convey via each genre and topic. I intended to present to them the same set of questions over and over again, beginning always with what they thought the issue was that the rabbis were struggling with.[8] I wanted them to articulate a question or describe an issue upon which the rabbis constructed the Mishnah. While some students answered my questions, many more posed questions to my questions—indeed, they were a participatory group. In truth, I saw this asking of questions as part of reading well. I was hoping that they would feel troubled and perplexed, if not confused. Their questions meant that they were trying to juggle multiple variables in order to work through their confusion. All of this, I hoped, would help them to challenge the very clear-cut impressions they had of the Talmud when the semester began.

---

8   The collective nature of the Mishnah compiled by different people over a long period of time means that there is no one narrating voice, and we cannot speak of an author in the way that we imagine an author today. I used the term "the rabbis" often throughout the semester, even though I did not wish to convey to my students that they should think of the Mishnah's early rabbis as one monolithic group. See also Balberg, who discusses the difficulties of describing this multi-layered document and its ideas in *Purity, Body, and Self,* 12-13.

Becoming Comfortable with the Strategy of Questioning: Our Classroom Study of Tractate Yoma

In doing a quick read for an overview of tractate Yoma, my students were immediately struck by a lengthy narrative regarding the observance of Yom Kippur in the Temple. When we began our close reading of M. Yoma 1:1, the students soon learned that preparing the high priest for the central Yom Kippur rite involved separating him from his household a week before the holiday.[9] After examining this mishnah very closely and then reading the remainder of the chapter, they observed that tractate Yoma began with an utterly detailed account of the Yom Kippur Temple rite, one that bore no resemblance to anything they recognized about Yom Kippur today. They were convinced that the Mishnah was entirely descriptive, and that the purpose of preserving such a detailed record emerged from a rabbinic belief that the Temple would be rebuilt, and the priests would resume cultic worship. They found no signs of psychological struggle and no conflict over the rebuilding of the Temple, just an accurate historical record of what was and what would eventually be. Some correctly called it nostalgia, but none could make sense of why Mishnah Avot failed to mention the priests and why, in contrast, so much of Mishnah Yoma focused on them. A level of confusion was percolating in our classroom, generating questions about the tension created by this comparison. That, for me, was an important step in the process of learning to read the Mishnah.[10]

Matters became more complicated when the students read, translated, and outlined M. Yoma, chapter 8, the last chapter in the tractate. The prohibitions associated with this holiday, which included fasting, made the

---

9   Once one reads this mishnah fully, it appears that the reference to "household" is actually a reference to the priest's wife. In rabbinic literature, a man's wife is referred to in an idealized way as "his house." See also B. Shabbat 118b; and B. Gittin 52a. See Tamara Or, *Massekhet Betsah: A Feminist Commentary on the Babylonian Talmud* (Tübingen: Mohr Siebeck, 2010), 20; Tal Ilan, *Massekhet Ta'anit: A Feminist Commentary on the Babylonian Talmud* (Tübingen: Mohr Siebeck, 2008), 26-28; Cynthia Baker, *Rebuilding the House of Israel* (Stanford: Stanford University Press, 2002), 35; and see Charlotte Fonrobert, *Menstrual Purity: Rabbinic and Christian Reconstructions of Biblical Gender* (Stanford: Stanford University Press, 2000), 40-67.

10 See Wineburg, "Reading Abraham Lincoln," 340, where he summarizes the approach of a teacher to reading and interpreting texts unfamiliar to him.

And No One Gave the Torah to the Priests | CHAPTER 4

portrayal of Yom Kippur in this chapter more similar to what the students knew of their present-day observance. The students, however, were taken by surprise when they confronted references to the Temple cult even in this final chapter which described the post-Temple Yom Kippur. As we read, I reminded them to take careful note of when anything Temple related was mentioned and to pay careful attention to the issue with regard to which Temple-related material appeared. I reminded them to think about what was at issue for the rabbis, that is, "What did they think was bothering the rabbis?" Hoping that at some point in the lesson the students would articulate their questions, I prompted them with my own. I wanted them to begin to unravel the texts by asking, "Why is the Mishnah making reference to something Temple-related in this context? How does the Mishnah speak about the Temple?" And, finally, "How does this reference compare to others that we have seen?" I cautioned them to read slowly and not to skip passages that seemed foreign to them.

We began with fasting and the prohibitions listed in M. Yoma 8:1 that defined Yom Kippur as a day of affliction in keeping with the biblical commandment in Leviticus 16:29, "In the seventh month, on the tenth day of the month, you shall practice self-denial."[11] By M. Yoma 8:3, the mishnah reveals that a person who forgets that the day is Yom Kippur and eats inadvertently is required to offer one *hatat*, a sin offering. One of my students then asked, "If the Mishnah was redacted after the Temple was destroyed, how could the rabbis legislate for bringing sacrifices?"[12] By challenging the text, she was absolutely on the right track. But then I asked her, trying to refocus the entire class toward what questions to ask first when they read the Mishnah, "So what issue are the rabbis grappling with here? What is bothering them about the Temple and the cult? What questions do you think they were asking themselves?" M. Yoma 8:8 also presented the idea that not

---

11 See also Lev 16:31, 23:29; Num 29:7.
12 I have left out the names of my students to protect their privacy, but have noted the date a comment was made. As I was not able to teach and write down their comments word-for-word during class, and an audio-recording presented too many complexities in altering the class atmosphere, I wrote the students' and my comments/questions from memory immediately after class into my journal. For this reason, what I have placed in quotes are how I remembered an exchange between students and myself and are not exact quotes, except those from tests or submitted writings.

only could Yom Kippur atone for one's sins, but so too could sin offerings and guilt offerings. "Sin offerings and guilt offerings again?!" a student asked, surprised. The student conveyed that she was not even sure that the reference to sin offerings and guilt offerings in M. Yoma 8:8 referred to Yom Kippur. The chapter seemed to shift focus from Yom Kippur to other related and unrelated issues, and this unnerved her. At that point, I went back to my questions about the Temple, asking, "What issues are the rabbis grappling with here? What is bothering the rabbis? Why is the mishnah making reference to something related to the Temple cult in this context?"

Most students argued that the rabbis were trying to remember the past, believing that someday they would reintroduce rituals like the sin and guilt offerings. To "write out" offerings would mean that they were discrediting the priests and the cult. Surely, the rabbis would not have intended that. On the surface, my students seemed to be reading well. Their attempt to make sense of the material by placing it into familiar rubrics was a good sign. However, drawing such conclusions as they did only convinced me that their reading skills were not sufficiently honed. They were holding on too tightly to their past understandings. They were not looking for what was implicit in the text; they were not assuming there might be polemical impulses at work on the part of the authors of the texts they were reading. The students seemed only to be summarizing what they read in the Mishnah, relying on *familiar answers* to questions about the Temple after its destruction. It occurred to me that my students were accustomed politically and religiously to the idea of communal pluralism and so, in their minds, the rabbis were bringing a priestly ritual past into their present. In addition, I realized that some of the students were simply outside of their comfort zone. Because the Mishnah was unlike anything that they had ever read, it was unfamiliar territory. Indeed, they were trying to make the strange familiar and the impenetrable penetrable by falling back on what they knew.[13] The students did not consider that the rabbis were

---

13 See Samuel S. Wineburg, "Historical Problem Solving: A Study of the Cognitive Processes Used in the Evaluation of Documentary and Pictorial Evidence," *Journal of Educational Psychology* 83 (1991): 73-87. See also Wineberg, "Reading Abraham Lincoln," 322. In the end, while I was trying to make the strange familiar so that the students would feel more comfortable reading the Mishnah, I was more intent on making their familiar notions

placing themselves in a position of knowledge about the cult so that they could assert rabbinic authority over all legal matters, including those matters that had once been relegated only to the priests.[14] This power dynamic was on my mind, as I noted in my journal at the end of class, but not on the minds of the students (10/9/14).

Recognizing the way the students were answering the question regarding what was at issue for the rabbis, I needed to suggest to students that they think about the texts as less descriptive and more constructive—less as historical artifacts and more as the product of people imagining a different future. I asked them to consider the question, "Did the rabbis really want to return to Temple Judaism?" "Possibly," I argued in return, and continued, "The rabbis mentioned the Temple cultic rites in M. Yoma 8 in order to think through the difference between Temple Judaism and rabbinic Judaism. Possibly, the rabbis wanted to present their own rituals as doable and observable, something sacrifices had never been." A few of the students began to challenge me with their reading of the final mishnah in M. Yoma, chapter 8, describing it as nothing other than a nostalgic text. Even though I disagreed with their reading, I was comforted by their ability to oppose me, which, in my mind, displayed evidence of reading skills that were developing. Below is a summary of what transpired that day during the remainder of class.

Reaching the final mishnah, the students noted that M. Yoma 8:9 used the metaphor of a *mikveh* (a ritual bath used to clear a person of ritual impurities). They were well aware that the priests could not offer sacrifices and perform their priestly duties unless they were ritually pure. They knew that purity and impurity were central to the running of the Temple, and, therefore, they correctly argued that a *mikveh* was a central part of the priests' institutional life.

---

about the Temple strange. See Jonathan Z. Smith, introduction to *Imagining Religion: From Babylon to Jonestown* (Chicago: University of Chicago Press, 1982), xiii; Jonathan Z. Smith, *Relating Religion: Essays in the Study of Religion* (Chicago: University of Chicago Press, 2004), 383, 389, where he argues in his essay, "God Save this Honorable Court: Religion and Civic Discourse," 382-89, that making the familiar strange enhances a person's perception of what they have always held to be familiar, readying them to see it in a new way. See Smith's, *Relating Religion*, 382-89.

14 At that moment, I was thinking of Naftali Cohn's argument; see Naftali S. Cohn, *The Memory of the Temple and the Making of the Rabbis* (Philadelphia: University of Pennsylvania Press, 2013), 2.

M. Yoma 8:9 compared the *mikveh* to God, stating that "just as a *mikveh* cleanses impure ones, so too does God cleanse Israel."[15] Formulating the notion of spiritual forgiveness for sinning by using the image of transitioning from impurity to purity in a *mikveh* conjured up, for the students, a reference to the priesthood and the Temple, not to mention of a cult that cleared the people of their sins. "The notion of repentance, mentioned for the first time in M. Yoma 8:8 and then here in M. Yoma 8:9, was brilliantly intertwined with a Temple metaphor," a student argued, supporting the case of most of the students that the rabbis were amalgamating their past and their present comfortably.

Rather than rushing to offer my own view, I tried to focus the students to read the mishnah differently. I said, "Do you all agree? Is this the only way to read M. Yoma 8:9? How does it fit together with the material regarding the sacrifices that you read about earlier in the chapter? How does it align with offering a sin or a guilt offering? Reading Mishnah means that you need to recognize ambiguities, places where things do not fit together, and to raise questions about them." I also pointed out that the rabbis probably picked the *mikveh* as an image because a ritual bath could be built and was used even in the absence of the Temple. And then one student rebutted, weaving together disparate elements:

> In this case, though, God poured the water. God did the cleansing and not the actual bath. This is different from the sin and guilt offerings that were proffered by individuals via a priest-intermediary and which were mentioned in the same chapter. Why place both of these images side-by-side in the same chapter, if not to convey something through that juxtaposition? Maybe, offering sacrifices is not the same as fasting or of going through a personal process of repentance, as a result of which God cleansed a person directly in the image of the waters of a ritual bath.

I felt like this student was reading all of the pieces of the chapter together quite successfully because she was trying to synthesize the pieces of the chapter that did not cohere with one another on the surface. She was trying

---

15 Note that we discussed in detail how the verses Ezek 36:25 and Jer 17:13 worked within the development of the point made in M. Yoma 8:9. Indeed, this mishnah is more complicated than I mention here.

to make sense of an apparent tension in the text and use it to see the rabbis as men struggling to differentiate themselves from the priests.

In response, I first acknowledged the perspective put forth by the students earlier in the class, claiming that, indeed, they were correct to some degree, "The rabbis were men searching on some level for continuity." But, the rabbis of the Mishnah also made a strong argument for discontinuity as well. They were developing a different theology of sin and repentance by the end of tractate Yoma that was distinct from the way the priests approached atonement during the Temple era. The pomp and circumstance associated with the Temple rite of Yom Kippur, which centered on a high priest who cleared an entire community of their sins, ended up by the final mishnah in the tractate as an individual quest for repentance from God. And then a student interrupted, "And these are not the same. I am not sure that one could develop naturally from the other. Offering sacrifices to clear one of sin through a priest *is* spiritually and religiously different from individual repentance." I concurred, saying, "The rabbis may have been trying to construct something different and not an ideology that was exactly continuous with what had preceded it, an ideology that could develop without the Temple and one's reliance on the priests." This was what I wanted the students to consider as they learned to read the Mishnah's references to the Temple.

Reframing the Same Questions: Reading Mishnah Pesachim Chapters 8 and 10

The week that we studied tractate Pesachim, we compared two chapters (date of class: 10/16/13). I told the students in advance that we would do a close reading of chapter 10, which would appear quite familiar to them, as it outlines the Passover Seder ritual. At the same time, I told them we would peruse chapter 8, highlighting only a few specific mishnayot, in order to think about how and why the rabbis discuss the Passover sacrifice in the way they do.[16] I asked the students, again, to tell me what they

---

16 After the cultic centralization of King Josiah, the celebration of Passover was transferred to the central Sanctuary in Jerusalem (2 Kgs 23:21-23). After the Exile, the requirement that the slaughtering, preparing, and eating of the paschal animals was to take place in the Temple continued (2 Chr 30:1-5; 35:13-14; Jub 49:16, 20). Later, because of the large

thought was at issue for the rabbis with regard to each of the mishnayot that mentioned the Temple. I was intent on making sure there was a pattern to my questions—a reading objective that I kept repeating. But, instead of moving on and asking—"Why is the Mishnah making reference to something Temple-related in this context? How does it speak about the Temple?"—I tried to make my questions more pointed, asking—"How does the Mishnah talk specifically about the Passover sacrifice in chapter 8, and how does this differ from the way it is discussed in chapter 10? And, when the rabbis refer to the Temple in chapter 10, do they always do so in the same way each time?" I was looking for the students to read by comparing and contrasting the mishnayot one to the other, as well as to do the same with the two chapters overall.[17] I wanted them to be able to recognize that the Mishnah makes different types of references to the Temple and the cult.

As we began to discuss M. Pesachim, chapter 8, one student reflected his surprise over how complicated it was to offer the Passover sacrifice. At that moment, I felt as though the student was reading closely and critically. He was trying to make sense of why the Mishnah chooses to present the Passover sacrifice as it does. I let the point dangle, and we moved on to discuss how one not only needed to be registered for the sacrifice by the one performing it, signifying a person's inclusion in the offering, but, in many cases, it was imperative that a person consented to his/her inclusion. Without proper registration and consent, one could not eat from the Passover offering at all. "According to the Mishnah, when do problems arise in terms of fulfilling this commandment?" I asked them. While none of the students had linked this question to describing what they thought was at issue for the rabbis, I felt that prompting them would help them to locate what might be lying beneath the

---

numbers of participants, the paschal animal was killed at the Temple, but boiled and eaten in the houses of Jerusalem (M. Pesachim 5:10; 7:12). See Ernst Kutsch, "Passover," in *Encyclopaedia Judaica*, 2nd ed., ed. Michael Berenbaum and Fred Skolnik (Detroit: Macmillan Reference USA, 2007), 15:680.

17 I agree with Sam Wineberg, who writes of the importance of creating intertextual connections across multiple sources; in my case, it was across mishnayot, rather than processing each mishnah as an independent text, "On the Reading of Historical Texts," 515.

surface of the mishnah's words. To answer my question, we made a list of possibilities on the board:

1. When a woman's husband and her father slaughtered the Passover offering for her, and it was unclear in which sacrifice she was to be included.
2. When two guardians sacrificed the Passover offering for one orphan, it was unclear in which sacrifice he/she was to be included.
3. When a person was half-slave and half-free.
4. When a master was not specific with the instructions given to his slave in a case where he had asked him to slaughter the Passover sacrifice in his stead.

A student sounded shocked when she looked at the board, "Did they not know how to communicate with one another? Are you trying to tell me that husbands and fathers did not speak to one another before Passover and that orphans' guardians ignored one another regarding a ritual about which the Bible clearly states is punishable with *karet* (the punishment of being cut off from the people of Israel)?"[18] I responded, "*I* am not telling *you* that; the Mishnah has made it its business to describe some sort of breakdown in communication when, indeed, communication happened to be necessary for performing this ritual. What do you make of that?" They had no answer. I was not sure I had one either, but I liked where the discussion had led us. I felt that the student was asking questions indicating that she was not simply translating or reporting on what the Mishnah said. Indeed, she was uncovering issues that were more implicit. This gave me a clue to her ability to read Mishnah better than she had the week prior. I wanted the meaning of the mishnayot to develop in each student as they questioned the texts. I wanted them to feel "productively" confused and to recognize that to feel confusion can be a component of reading well, precisely because it generated the kind of questions that helped to unravel ideas implicit in a mishnaic passage.[19]

---

18   See Lev 23:29.
19   See Robert Scholes, *Textual Power: Literary Theory and the Teaching of English* (New Haven: Yale University Press, 1985), 14, as quoted and discussed by Wineberg, "On the Reading of Historical Texts," 519.

Our discussion also brought to light that what made the Passover sacrifice complicated and threatened the inclusion of the entire community was the status of ritual impurity. Menstruating women (*niddot*) as well as men and women who had discharges that were not seminal or menstrual (*zavim* and *zavot*) were not fit to partake of the offering if they were still impure when the time arrived to eat. Women, together with slaves and minors, could not sacrifice the Passover offering (M. Pesachim 8:7). Performing the ritual for only one person also emerged as a concern (M. Pesachim 8:7). When I asked, "What do you make of this?" the student who was taken by surprise earlier, wondering why individuals did not communicate with one another around the Passover sacrifice, said, "I think the rabbis are trying to tell us that the rite of the Passover offering did not work smoothly. It did not unite families. It called attention to the impure and it excluded people. Something about the rite does not feel positive." I quickly transitioned us to M. Pesachim 10 with the question, "And what led you to believe in M. Pesachim 10:1 that the Passover Seder was entirely different in flavor and feel?" I was pushing them to read texts alongside one another. I did not want them to complete chapter 8 and "file it away." I wanted them to keep it active in their mind so as to think more about it via a comparison to other texts found in M. Pesachim 10 that would also make reference to the Temple and the Passover sacrifice.

Together we began to read the first mishnah of chapter 10. The students quickly noted that "even the poorest man in Israel was not to eat until he reclined." One student then quickly described reclining as a symbol of free men and gravitated to the social implications, not only of making everyone recline, but of equating all people one with the other, whether poor or rich. "Such a democratic concept," he said excitedly. The students also noted that a person had to make sure that all people had four cups of wine, even if he was feeding himself from the charity plate two meals a day,[20] and one student highlighted how a father taught all of his sons, the smart and the ignorant, about the rituals of Passover (M. Pesachim 10:4). The contrast to M. Pesachim 8

---

20   There are several ways to read this part of the mishnah. See Rashi, Rashbam, and Tosafot on B. Pesachim 99b, regarding four cups of wine and the word *"tamhui."*

was striking. In chapter 10, no one seemed left out. The ritual was constructed to be inclusive.

We then talked about whether there was a Seder leader, like a high priest, or someone similar to a head-of-household who had once sacrificed the Passover offering. M. Pesachim 10:3, which begins, "They brought before him הֵבִיאוּ לְפָנָיו [vegetables to perform the rite of *karpas* ...]," left us wondering—"who" brought the vegetables before "whom." We talked about how vague the Mishnah can be in omitting subjects and objects of phrases. Many of the students were convinced that there was a leader of the Seder and the word "him" referred to that person. They appeared to draw from images of parents leading their own Seders, and certainly, the words הֵבִיאוּ לְפָנָיו could be translated to reflect that. But some were willing to argue that all of the people at the Seder were responsible for bringing vegetables before "him," that is, before each individual sitting at the table so that everyone participated equally. Indeed, the more we read and talked about the tenth chapter, the more the difficulties and exclusions presented in the eighth chapter emerged. "Did the rabbis really want to bring back the Passover sacrifice?" one student queried and then asked further, "Why bring back a rite that excludes and that is difficult to execute? And, by the way, how do we know that all Jews could have even made it to the Temple? Was it even feasible for very many Jews to be in the Temple at the same time? Were not some excluded by virtue of being sick, feeble, too old, or too young?" Another student then piped in, "You know that father in M. Pesachim 8:3 that we read about, who engaged his sons in a competition to see who could get to the Temple first? Where was he living? How far was it from the Temple?" And another asked, "Why did the Passover sacrifice need to become a matter of competition? The Passover Seder, as narrated in M. Pesachim 10, did not pit one son against another." "On the other hand," she continued, "Why include the Passover sacrifice in the Mishnah at all and write about it in such detail?" The questions were getting better. This last student had begun to show that she was not simply accepting what the Mishnah said. She could do more than report on its contents. She could also challenge it with the "why" question—an important aspect of reading analytically. Even if she had no answers, I was satisfied, because learning to read did not necessarily require that she find the answer. It was about learning to ask questions that opened up the text for further introspection. After class that day, I wrote in my teaching journal that I was feeling hopeful (10/16/13). Maybe some of the students were beginning to detect that the Mishnah's objective in including the details of the Passover sacrifice was not merely for the purposes of preservation, although I did not dismiss that argument as a possibility. What had come to light was that the Mishnah seemed to be displaying the complexities of the cult in light of a developing rabbinic ritual.

The following week, we took another look at M. Pesachim 10; that is, we focused on its references to the Temple, leaving chapter 8 aside (10/23/13). Chapter 10 also made references to the sacrificial cult and to the Temple, both of which we highlighted on our class outline in yellow. We then plowed through the chapter for a second time, paying careful attention to when and why anything related to the Temple was mentioned within the context of narrating the Passover Seder rite. At M. Pesachim 10:3, one student yelled out, completely convinced his sense was correct that the rabbis wished to preserve a very clear memory of the Passover sacrifice, in the hope, he argued, of restoring the ritual:

> They brought before him matzah and lettuce and haroset and two cooked dishes [one to remember the Passover sacrifice and one to remember the hagigah sacrifice], even though the haroset is not an obligation. Rabbi Eliezer in the name of Rabbi Tzadok says: It [the haroset] is an obligation. And in [the time of the] Temple, they would bring before him the body of the Passover sacrifice.

For the student grappling with M. Pesachim 10:3, the opinion of Rabbi Eliezer, who spoke in the name of Rabbi Tzadok,[21] represented the importance of memory. He argued that the phrase הֵבִיאוּ לְפָנָיו (they brought before him) made a direct reference to the vegetables and cooked meat being brought to a person at the Seder after the destruction of the Temple as a reminder of a time when the Passover sacrifice was slaughtered in the Temple, and the roasted meat was prepared and "brought" to the people. Another student saw this ritual as merely a placeholder of sorts, readying an individual for the

---

21 See B. Yoma 23a and my article, "Imagining the Priesthood in Tractate *Yoma*: Mishnah *Yoma* 2:1-2 and BT Yoma 23a," *Nashim: A Journal of Jewish Women's Studies and Gender Issues*, no. 28, Spring 2015: 88-105.

And No One Gave the Torah to the Priests | CHAPTER 4

symbolic associations of various rites with what had once been done in the Temple. M. Pesachim 10:4, which included a version of the four questions that mentioned eating only roasted meat at the Seder, seemed also a similar reference. "Rather than being required to eat the roasted meat," the student argued, "we needed to recite a question that conjured up a memory of it. In this way, the rabbis transformed a ritual practice into a liturgical one, all for the sake of remembering."

"Memory, yes," I agreed, as the mishnaic text supported the idea. "But what did the rabbis want to remember? What is really at issue here for the rabbis? What does M. Pesachim 10:5, quoted below, add to this discussion?"

> Rabban Gamaliel used to say: Whoever has not said these three things on Passover, has not fulfilled his obligation and they are: Pesach, Matzah, and Maror. Pesach—because God passed over the houses of our ancestors in Egypt.

My students were beginning to think about the different ways in which one chapter of Mishnah referred to the Temple. In pressing that learning to read very closely meant continuing to ask questions, I said to them (again), "How did the rabbis refer to the Passover offering here?" This, so that these differences would emerge more clearly in class, and they could try to uncover what was at issue for the rabbis. A student keenly recognized that in M. Pesachim 10:5 the rabbis choose not to connect the familiar term for the Passover offering "Pesach" explicitly to the Temple cult. Instead, M. Pesachim 10:5 makes a direct link between the offering and the events leading up to the Exodus from Egypt. Memory was wedded to a historical narrative. It was important to remember God's salvific powers and, of course, redemption. And so, I said to them, "Is M. Pesachim 10:5 simply about referencing the Passover sacrifice, the "Pesach," or are the rabbis struggling with the definition of memory?" Again, I left the question dangling. It was more important to me that I modeled for them the need to keep returning to the question of what was at issue for the rabbis.

When the students turned to the liturgical discussion about the integration of the Hallel prayer into the Passover Seder, they were quick to recognize that M. Pesachim 10:6 referred to the Temple in yet another way, by specifically expressing a desire to return to the practice of celebrating holidays and offering sacrifices in the Temple. When the mishnah asked the question, "Until where does one recite [Hallel] at the Seder?" Rabbi Akiva (d. 137 CE) pointed out that one begins with, "So may the Lord our God of our ancestors bring us to future festivals and pilgrimages which approach us in peace, rejoicing in the building of Your city and joyful in Your service, and may we eat there from offerings and from the Passover sacrifices … " and ends with, "Blessed are You, the Redeemer of Israel." This meant that M. Pesachim 10:5 and 10:6, taken together, connected both the event of the past Exodus and a hope for a rebuilt Temple in the future to redemption. One student remarked, "Wow, so the Mishnah presents here a distant past defined by redemption and a distant future also defined by redemption—the rabbis *remember* in a very controlled way, as if they are carving out a space in their present for something else, something different, to develop." At that moment, I felt that the student was trying to synthesize the mishnayot and to make sense of the chapter as a whole.[22] More importantly, he had tried to figure out what was at issue for the rabbis and had brought us back to the rabbis' struggle with memory.

However, the final mishnah in the chapter and of the entire tractate posed another challenge to this student's theory. Steeped as it was in detailed references to matters of impurity and the cult that were foreign to my students, they were confronted with Temple ritual recorded as if the Temple was still standing. M. Pesachim 10:9 sounded as though the members of the rabbis' community were eating the Passover sacrifice itself:

> The Passover sacrifice if eaten after midnight imparts uncleanness to the hands. The *pigul* and *notar* impart uncleanness to the hands. If a person recited the blessing over the Passover sacrifice, he is exempt from saying a blessing over any other sacrificial meat that he eats. If he recited a blessing over any other sacrificial meat, he is not exempt from saying the blessing over the Passover sacrifice. This is the opinion of Rabbi Yishmael. Rabbi Akiva says: Neither of them exempts the other from a blessing.

---

22 Personally, I had not even thought of the chapter quite like he had; however, he had made an interesting point, something I had not thought of before. He had taught me. He had shifted my perception of a text and, to me, that was a sign of reading well.

And No One Gave the Torah to the Priests | CHAPTER 4

After defining the terms and noting yet another way of making references to the Temple cult, I asked the students to think about why the rabbis imagined themselves eating the Passover sacrifice in the present? Why end tractate Pesachim this way? Maybe this was a source about keeping the rituals of the cult alive so that there would be a record for some future time?" And then, one student observed, "So, why did tractate Yoma end with a metaphorical reference to purification, whereas, here, we are made to feel as though the Temple is still standing, and its rituals are still observable?" The student was comparing tractate to tractate—precisely what I had wanted to occur. I argued for the possibility that the Mishnah communicated different perspectives and that one could not generalize about what it says. I noted that the rabbis were, indeed, struggling and did not have all of the answers to their own questions.

Several students remained convinced that the rabbis were committed to establishing a sense of continuity in a seamless way between their past, present, and their future. I was disappointed that some of their prior assumptions had not begun to unravel. They continued to hang on to the notion that the rabbis preferred the cult and longingly wished to bring back the Passover sacrifice—hence, ending the tractate with the sacrifice itself. But then, one student's comment captured everyone's attention. He felt that the final mishnah, which included an opinion by Rabbi Akiva, robbed the priests of their authority. "Where were the priests' voices? Why were the rabbis—and not the priests—legislating for ways to offer and eat the Passover sacrifice? Rabbi Akiva lived alongside priests, so why record his opinion as if he was not in conversation with them?" This student recognized in the rabbis of the Mishnah a desire for authority as a way of legitimizing themselves over and above the priests. The student continued, "I have a feeling that the rabbis did not see themselves as provisional leaders, ready to step aside when the Temple was standing once again. Therefore, didn't the rabbis need to present themselves as men knowledgeable about the cult?"[23] Another student, recalling material she had read in

---

23 While not relevant to the discussion of the Passover sacrifice, I did make a mental note about teaching mishnayot from tractates Nega'im and Niddah. I wanted to push the point further that the rabbis cultivated an image of themselves in the Mishnah as the ultimate interpreters of biblical texts as well as the most knowledgeable arbiters of purity law. See Mira Balberg, "Rabbinic Authority, Medical Rhetoric, and Body Hermeneutics

| 105

an article describing the perspective of Jacob Neusner,[24] raised the following point: "The Mishnah, as Neusner has argued, is a document that reflects rabbinic self-interest, their ideology, their ideas—so isn't it arguable that the rabbis were interested in how they could claim authority? Knowing about the cult, teaching about the cult, and speaking about the cult as if it was happening was to speak in their own self-interest. Maybe they would be able to convince priests to join their ranks. Maybe they would look like they knew about all matters of law, including sacrificial law. Maybe they were savvier than we think. The fact is, the voices in the Mishnah, at least here in M. Pesachim 10:9, belong to the rabbis alone."[25]

I felt like these students had gotten somewhere. They had let go of prior assumptions and had begun to understand that reading the Mishnah was intimately connected to being suspicious of their prior views. Reading the Mishnah was also dependent on asking question after question. While I told my students that all of the pieces might not ever fit together smoothly, it was clear that some of them were beginning to detect that the relationship between the rabbis and the priests was far more complicated than they had

---

in Mishnah Nega'im, *AJS Review* 33, no. 2 (2011): 326. See also Charlotte E. Fonrobert, *Menstrual Purity: Rabbinic and Christian Reconstructions*, 126-27, where she discusses how the rabbis construct a rabbinic system of knowledge about women's bodies, despite the problems that arose for them in doing so.

24 I was probably smiling at that moment, as this student managed to draw from secondary material in order to read primary source material. I always assign various articles in any given semester, hoping that the students will learn how to integrate the points made within them into their study of rabbinic texts. This, in my mind, is part of learning how to read, and I spend time at the beginning of each new unit talking about how to "read" these articles as well as summarizing the questions the authors ask and the answers they offer. I noted these questions and answers on the outlines I sent to the student each time we completed a unit of texts, hoping that doing so would help the students in their understanding of the articles' usefulness.

25 Although we did not read Naftali Cohn's scholarship, his work informed the way that I responded to the student. Cohn argues that the rabbis fully intended to assert their authority over all of Jewish ritual, even ritual that was no longer practiced. They wanted to present themselves as the legal experts over all matters. Indeed, they wanted others to seek them out with respect to their legal opinions. The rabbis may have lacked real authority, but they wished to convey that their role was critical to the preservation of true tradition and practice. See Naftali S. Cohn, "The Ritual Narrative Genre in the Mishnah: The Invention of the Rabbinic Past in the Presentation of Temple Ritual," (PhD diss., University of Pennsylvania, 2008), 225, and Cohn, *Memory of the Temple*, 2.

originally thought. "Ambiguities and contradictions mean something in the Mishnah," I noted to them.

I then added, "Neusner believed that the Mishnah did not contain archives of raw data, but texts seeking to create a fictive sense of reality for polemical purposes. So, were the rabbis polemicizing against the priests? Was the student right? Did he have a point?"[26] I then raised the idea that epigraphic and archeological remains, in addition to Jewish literature from this period, reveal that priests continued to identify as priests and that the rabbis did not win them all over in the first generations after the Temple was destroyed. The priests maintained their economic standing by continuing to receive tithes, to observe purity and impurity laws, and to play a role in the religious and political affairs affecting the Jewish community, even after the destruction of the Temple.[27] I suggested that the rabbis may have represented a small community of Jews at the time who were feeling a sense of insecurity, even threatened by the continuing, stable presence of the priests. The Mishnah was a way in which they could "write" themselves into authority.

Two students held to their original ideas about the rabbis and claimed that they were trying to follow in the footsteps of the priests. The rabbis were not trying to reject the priesthood or critique it. The rabbis were merely dealing with the crisis of the destruction of the Temple, struggling for continuity. They brought passages from M. Pesachim 10 that reemphasized the rabbinic commitment to symbolically remembering the Passover sacrifice, and, indeed, they were making a good case. I wrote in my journal that day after class that the students were reading very differently from one another (10/23/13),

---

26 See Seth Schwartz's, "Political Geography of Rabbinic Texts," 85-87 for an overview of Neusner and other scholars on the reading of rabbinic texts. My students were assigned this article and asked to comment on which scholarly approach to the study of rabbinic texts they most preferred and why.

27 While my students had not read this material, I was referring to Matthew Grey, "Jewish Priests and the Social History of Post-70 Palestine," (PhD diss., University of North Carolina, 2011), 6-12, 84. See also Grey's more extensive discussion, where he makes note of the fact that some priests were active in the rabbinic movement, p. 44. For a larger discussion, see Seth Schwartz, *Josephus and Judean Politics* (Leiden, Neth.: E. J. Brill, 1990), 58-109; and Stuart A. Cohen, *The Three Crowns: Structure of Communal Politics in Early Rabbinic Jewry* (Cambridge: Cambridge University Press, 1990), 158-71; Catherine Hezser, *The Social Structure of the Rabbinic Movement* (Tübingen: Mohr Siebeck, 1997), 487.

virtually each displaying her or his own individual view. However, what I really wanted was for them to see that the Mishnah conveyed *more* than one perspective and for them to hold two or more perspectives simultaneously. I wanted them to see evidence in the Mishnah of nostalgia for the Passover sacrifice, but also recognize that the rabbis were engaged in a struggle with that very past. They were wrestling with how to assert their own sense of legitimacy and authority and to differentiate themselves from the priests.

The Case of Bikkurim: Thinking about Temple Narratives

M. Bikkurim enabled my students to think more about the Mishnah's inclusion of detailed narratives describing Temple rites. M. Bikkurim 3 contained a description of the well-orchestrated ceremony of bringing first fruits to the Temple. For now, I will put aside a discussion of the complex relationship between this rite and the pilgrimage holiday of Shavuot and focus on how the students began to think about why the rabbis would have preserved such a detailed description of rites they no longer performed, vestiges of which were never incorporated into any future observance. As we all noted in class, even the symbols that might have been used to remember the rite of bikkurim seemed somehow lost entirely, unlike anything we had seen with respect to the Passover sacrifice. I framed our study of M. Bikkurim both within readings of the biblical material on bringing first fruits (Exod 23: 14-17, 19; Exod 34:22-26; Deut 16:9-12 and 26:1-11) and Jonathan Smith's secondary source article on the purpose of ritual.[28] The students had to prepare M. Bikkurim 1:1-2 as well.

In reading M. Bikkurim 1:1-2, the students were immediately struck by the fact that, like the Passover sacrifice, some individuals were included in the rite and others were excluded. That part was familiar to them. They pointed to the fact that M. Bikkurim 1:1 noted: "There are some who bring bikkurim and recite [Deut 26, which serves as the central liturgical component accompanying the offering], and there are those who may only bring [the bikkurim] but do not recite [Deut 26] as well as those who may not bring [bikkurim] or recite [Deut 26]." The Mishnah went on to provide a

---

28 Jonathan Z. Smith, "The Bare Facts of Ritual," *Imagining Religion*, 53-65.

definition of those excluded from the rite of bringing bikkurim, and they included not only those who did not own land, such as tenant farmers, lessees, occupiers of confiscated property, or robbers, but also those whose produce grew partially on their own land and partially on someone else's land (M. Bikkurim 1:1-2). What was less familiar was the point made in M. Bikkurim 1:2 that the key to the rite of bringing bikkurim was fulfilling Exodus 23:19, which states that one must bring "the fruits of *your* [own] land" and that land had to be located in the Land of Israel. Additionally, all of the produce brought needed to be crops that were listed in Deuteronomy 8:8, including wheat, barley, and pomegranates.

"What an exclusivist rite!" remarked one student. She was thrown by the need to own land and land in Israel in order to perform this rite. "Diasporic Jews could not participate!? Didn't Jews live outside of Israel at the time of the Mishnah!" she exclaimed. And then, the questions began to roll in. After we read M. Bikkurim 3:1, which states, "How does one separate the bikkurim?" and the students confronted the very straightforward answer of the mishnah, "When a man goes down to his field and sees a ripe fig, a ripe cluster of grapes, or a ripe pomegranate, he ties reed-grass around it, saying, 'Let these be bikkurim'"—there were many disgruntled students. "How can the mishnah speak as though everyone "sees" a ripe fruit? We just learned that some Jews did not even own land!" And another student pointed out quite astutely, "What about droughts and an overabundance of rain that diminished crop yield or blights that destroyed crops altogether?" They were beginning to recognize the difficulties in observing this rite as the rabbis described it. And one more student said, "If the rabbis wanted us to preserve this rite, why not make allowances for a procession with any type of produce, whether grown from one's own land or not, as a way of recognizing the power of God in having enough to eat. Surely, the rabbis were trying to "write" bikkurim out of existence. This is what was at issue for them here. It makes sense to me." And one more student was able to point to the complicated relationship the rabbis may have had with ownership of land in the Land of Israel. "By the time of the redaction of the Mishnah," she noted, "were the rabbis in control of the Land of Israel? Is this why the rabbis wanted to orchestrate a beautiful imaginary procession in the remainder of M. Bikkurim 3 that could never be performed by everyone?" The students were posing questions that reflected their ability to challenge what they were reading, and I felt that the class had begun to read critically. They were asking and answering why it was that the rabbis chose to depict the ritual of bikkurim as they did. They seemed to feel that the rabbis were constructing the ideal rite while couching it within rhetoric that questioned its ability to be observed. The students were asking better questions and making better observations. When I thought about why, I recalled that the students had also read a seminal article about ritual written by Jonathan Smith, "The Bare Facts of Ritual." Prior to our class, they had written two-page papers that asked them to respond to the following prompt, whereby I expected them to read the mishnayot through the lens of Smith:

> Essay Assignment No. 4: The bringing of first fruits to the Temple celebrates the perfect harvest. The complex interaction between God, nature, farmer, priest, the need for food, one's gratitude for food, and the gracious act of gift-giving are intertwined in a manner that presumes perfection. Invariably, the system does not always work in real life, because droughts occur, people falter in their farming abilities, and people question their beliefs in God and His role in the process of food production. However, in a utopian way, in the ritual performance of bringing bikkurim, all of the pieces are present and perfectly integrated. All of the variables are controlled so that the ritual is not like real-life. Contingency, variability, and accidentally have been factored out, generating a ritual that allows a person to have an ideal experience. Ritual acts as a human labor, struggling with matters of incongruity. To what extent do you think the statement made here, based on Jonathan Smith's article, "The Bare Facts of Ritual" (*Imagining Religion*), describes or does not describe the ritual of bringing bikkurim? Why do you think the rite completely fell by the wayside? Please make sure to refer to specific mishnayot.

I believe that this assignment, based as it was on writing an essay that revolved around the reading of primary sources alongside a secondary source, contributed to the students' ability to read the Mishnah more deeply.[29] The

---

29 Teaching my students how to read the Mishnah was also about guiding them toward secondary sources and teaching them how to read them as well. I wanted the students to learn to move from primary to secondary sources and back to primary sources. I hoped

fact that the students needed to refer to the mishnayot themselves while thinking about Smith's argument, which had nothing to do with Jewish ritual, the Mishnah, or the Temple, seemed to "productively" slow the students down.[30] It made them think harder about what they were reading. It seemed also that they had begun to take my question of what was at issue for the rabbis more seriously. As such, I received papers that included the following comments, attesting to my students' reading skills:

> Student 1: The rabbis in M. Bikkurim 3 make the ritual of bringing bikkurim to the Temple seem like a ritual designed for an ideal world as Smith describes—but, they also admit that not everyone could participate (M. Bikkurim 1:1-2). The rabbis describe a well-orchestrated procession that could not be performed, because they recognized how imperfect this rite actually was. It was not feasible for everyone to perform it.

> Student 2: Bikkurim had to be specific types of crops brought from specific areas. What if I did not grow those crops? What if these crops were ruined? The ritual would not happen at all. I think the rabbis wanted to see this rite abandoned, because it could never be perfectly executed. There were just

---

that reading Ishay Rosen-Zvi's article, "Orality, Narrative, Rhetoric: New Directions in Mishnah Research," would open my students' eyes to more recent contributions to scholarship on the Mishnah and help them to understand why some scholars wish to undermine what they see as a naïve conception of mishnaic texts dealing with the Temple. Rosen-Zvi argues that the Mishnah's detailed expositions, narratives, and references to the Temple made the Temple imaginatively and perpetually present through the *study* of the Mishnah. A newer ritual could be seen emerging whereby rabbis "performed" these texts in their minds and imagined them in their daily conversations, studying about the Temple together with one another, rather than actually performing these rites. We read this article in conjunction with M. Pesachim, chapters 8 and 10, in order to think about the Mishnah's references to the Temple. See Ishay Rosen-Zvi, "Orality, Narrative, Rhetoric: New Directions in Mishnah Research," *AJS Review* 32, no. 2 (2008): 242-49. Also see Jane Kanarek's chapter "What Others Have to Say" in this volume.

30 Regarding the importance of slowing down see this case study: Jane Kanarek, "The Pedagogy of Slowing Down: Teaching Talmud in a Summer Kollel," *Teaching Theology and Religion* 13, no. 1 (2010): 15-34; reprinted as "The Pedagogy of Slowing Down: Teaching Talmud in a Summer Kollel," in *Turn It and Turn It Again: Studies in the Teaching and Learning of Classical Jewish Texts*, ed. Jon A. Levisohn and Susan P. Fendrick (Boston: Academic Studies Press, 2013).

too many variables that "could not be factored out." This was not a rite that would stabilize the authority of the rabbis; it would only undermine it.

Student 3: The bikkurim rite fell by the wayside because it was inherently a futile attempt to subdue the natural imperfections behind the harvest.

Student 4 (quoting Smith, p. 57): I believe that we must "perceive ritual as a human labor, struggling with matters of incongruity." By attempting to institute the ritual of offering bikkurim as an ideal ritual that overcomes variability and accidentally, the authors of the Mishnah consciously instituted its downfall.

This was the point at which I felt as though the students had read and understood how to use Smith to understand the Mishnah. In their minds, Smith's version of "what ritual is" simply did not work for bikkurim. One could labor hard to offer up the perfect harvest, but perfection was unachievable. There would always be those who could never participate in this rite, challenging its communal nature. Then one student remarked, "The narrative of bringing bikkurim to Jerusalem (M. Bikkurim 3) makes it sound like everyone was involved, but that is not possible. The third chapter makes this rite sound like it worked perfectly each year. In contrast, the first perek, M. Bikkurim 1:1-2, offers us a different impression when it excludes certain individuals from this rite. I almost feel as though the rabbis included such a discussion about bikkurim in M. Bikkurim 1 and 3 to convince themselves that their observances were more inclusive, even more democratic, than those of the Temple."

And yet, there was still another student who, after offering an excellent analysis of the Mishnah through the lens of Smith, pulled back with the following view, "Perhaps the rabbis wanted to keep the people yearning for the restoration of the Temple. By leaving the people who would one day read the Mishnah with Temple rituals unfulfilled, the rabbis may have hoped to instill a never-ending drive toward reestablishing the home of the Jewish people in Israel and reestablishing a home for God in Jerusalem." I could not argue that the student was incorrect, and I did not want to deny the hopeful tone that seemed to emanate from M. Bikkurim 3, but it proved to me how important the image of rebuilding

And No One Gave the Torah to the Priests | CHAPTER 4

a past Temple was for some students. They seemed not to want to overlook this reading lens, even when they had evidence of another perspective.

Additionally, I had wanted the students to consider that the mishnaic discussion about bikkurim was a way for the rabbis to think through their attitudes toward ritual more generally. "How would rabbinic ritual differ from Temple ritual?" I asked the students. One student responded, "Possibly, for the rabbis of the Mishnah, rituals were eliminated precisely when they did not work effectively, when they could not factor out 'incongruity' [referring back to Smith] and when any human labor exerted to perform them did not generate an ideal experience." "Is this why," one student argued, "Shavuot became dissociated with bikkurim, and the notion of receiving the Torah became the reason for its observance? Everyone received the Torah." And then one student chimed in, remembering our first class on M. Avot 1:1, "except the priests."

At that moment, we had come full circle, and I felt that the students were ready for the final. However, in reading the finals, I was soon to learn that I had not brought everyone to the point where they were questioning the rabbis' references to the Temple.

The Final Exam—Mixed Results

Prior to the final, the students were in possession of outlines from our classes, their own notes, a list generated by us as a class of the many ways we could characterize the Mishnah, and a review sheet. I believed that I had provided what was necessary for all of my students to succeed on the final exam and that each had learned to read the sources that mentioned the Temple critically. I believed that I had taught them to ask the right questions of the texts and to propose answers that made sense, taking into careful consideration the words of each mishnah they read. And yet, when I gave them a question about references to the Temple in the final chapter of Pesachim (10) and asked them to discuss the significance of including such passages in the Mishnah's outline of the Passover Seder, despite the fact that by the time of the redaction of the Mishnah the Temple had been destroyed; I got a wide array of responses on the final. This was another reminder to me of how firmly some students held onto their prior assumptions about the

Temple, the priests, and the cult. Here were two responses to my question on the final about M. Pesachim 10, inasmuch as I quoted the relevant mishnayot referring to the cult for them:

> Student 1: The rabbis of the Mishnah were hoping that one day the Temple would be rebuilt, and the Passover sacrifice would become, yet again, part of the Passover celebration. The rabbis were trying to maintain a relationship with their history. The Mishnah depends on the previous legitimacy of the Temple and hopes for its resurrection.

> Student 2: The inclusion of references to the Passover sacrifice and the Temple in M. Pesachim 10 shows that even though there was no Temple, it remained an ideal. David Kraemer [whose article we read][31] states that the Mishnah can be read as a document that presents an idea for a messianic future where there are sacrifices and, therefore, the references to the Temple and the cult in these mishnayot are spoken in a positive voice. This presents an attitude that the Temple cult is to be viewed favorably and that everything must be explained in order to keep the idea of the Temple alive.

These two students each fell back on arguments that the class had made earlier in the semester and seemed not to distinguish between the four different types of references to the Temple and the Passover sacrifice that appeared in M. Pesachim 10. One student had referred to David Kraemer's perspective in his article on the Mishnah, and, therefore, I felt the student had done his homework. And yet, messianism played such a small role in our discussions. I was even surprised that this student, in particular, embraced the messianic era as a way to explain the Mishnah, knowing him as I did by the end of the semester.

I was perplexed. Why had these students fallen back on presumptions that they had made as the semester began? Why hadn't they, at least, offered a more balanced view, arguing that they could see a nostalgic group of rabbis who were also struggling with the cult? There were more students, however,

---

31 David Kraemer, "The Mishnah," in *The Cambridge Guide to Ancient Judaism: The Late Roman Rabbinic Period*, ed. Steven T. Katz, vol. 4 (Cambridge: Cambridge University Press, 2006): 219-315.

who grasped the deep issue of how the rabbis used the Mishnah to negotiate their own future vis-a-vis the priests in a post-Temple Judiasm, writing finals that reflected the perspective of the student below:

> The rabbis' description of the Passover ritual is not history, but historical fiction. The sacrifices had long ceased to have been offered by the time the Mishnah was redacted, and I am not sure they were offered exactly as the rabbis of the Mishnah describe them. But that is not what is significant here. Instead, the rabbis are engaging in an imaginative exercise intended to present signs of struggle as they attempt to create something rabbinic. How much of priestly ritual can they move to the side and how much must they embrace in order to appear legitimate and include the priests in their new order? Passages such as these depict the rabbis' nostalgia and their efforts to appropriate the best parts of the Temple for the non-Temple religion which they were molding.

When I thought back on the semester, I felt that learning to read was about more than acquiring the knowledge to translate the texts in order to understand the rabbis, to define their legal concepts, and to profess their ideas. It was also about engaging in a type of thinking that involved considering the rabbis as men constructing a future, rather than merely describing a past.[32] Some of my students had a difficult time letting go of prior presumptions about the Temple, because they were reading the Mishnah as one organic book while looking for historical clues to a past era. It was comforting for them to think about the Mishnah as democratic and ethical in the way that it preserved much of the Temple rite while, at the same time, charting a provisional Judaism in a time of crisis. It was much harder to think about the Mishnah as a "thought experiment," reflecting the struggles of several generations of rabbis who were imagining themselves with the authority to create something new and different from Temple Judaism. I also feel that for some students their insecurities around taking tests, especially those that require reading and translating material in Hebrew without the help of notes, got the best of them. Possibly, for this reason, they relied on previous ideas that were well known to them.

---

32 Wineberg, "On the Reading of Historical Texts," 515.

Looking to the Future

Looking back on the semester, I thought that I could have been clearer with my students. Along with our outlines of the chapters of mishnayot, our lists, our highlighted references to the Temple, our questions, and our proposed answers, I should have had each of them create one additional chart. This would be a worksheet of three columns for focused references; in the first column would be every mention of the Temple they found; in a second column, they would record all of their questions regarding each reference and proposed answers; and finally, in a third column, they would have to answer the question as to why they thought the mishnah referred to the Temple as it did and to answer—"What was bothering the rabbis here?" If I had asked them to create such a chart and had they looked back over it after an entire semester, they might have seen instances where it looked like the rabbis were holding onto the past, cases where the rabbis seemed to be differentiating themselves from the past, or even instances where the rabbis were critiquing the past. They would have more readily been able to detect contradictory strands and ambiguities. They would have felt that it was impossible to fall-out on one side of the issue of why the rabbis spoke about the Temple as they did. The chart would have slowed their pace as they tried to review for the final,[33] preventing them from drawing any swift conclusions and hopefully detecting evidence of a complex relationship between the priests and the rabbis. In the end, I wanted them to understand that the Mishnah refused to erase its own struggle and the students to be able to chart that struggle. The next time I teach this course, I intend to add this strategy.

---

33 Kanarek, "Pedagogy of Slowing Down," 15-34.

CHAPTER 5

■ ■ ■

Talmud for Non-Rabbis: Teaching Graduate Students in the Academy

Gregg E. Gardner

There is an adage in Hebrew, *ha-mevin yavin*, "those who understand will understand."[1] In order to understand something, you will have had to have already understood it or something very close to it. It implies elite knowledge, insularity, and high barriers to entry for those who are not already in the know. The underlying premise of insularity embedded in this aphorism contrasts sharply with the openness and expansiveness that characterizes Jonathan Z. Smith's two central tasks in the academic study of religion: to make the familiar strange and the strange familiar. The first task, he says, is to make the familiar appear to be strange in order to enhance our perception of the familiar, to see it afresh.[2] This, Smith writes, is what distinguishes and "prevents the study of religion from being an exercise in the transmission of a religious tradition."[3] For the academic study of rabbinic literature, this requires an audience of students with knowledge of Hebrew and Aramaic, as well as experience in reading rabbinic texts–which is usually gained through traditional venues of Jewish education. These students would

---

1   I thank the workshop participants, Carey A. Brown and Jordan D. Rosenblum for their helpful feedback on this chapter. I also thank my students for their willingness to participate in this project and I dedicate this study to them. I alone am responsible for all remaining errors.
2   Jonathan Z. Smith, introduction to *Imagining Religion: From Babylon to Jonestown* (Chicago: University of Chicago Press, 1982), xiii; Jonathan Z. Smith, "God Save This Honourable Court: Religion and Civic Discourse," *Relating Religion: Essays in the Study of Religion* (Chicago: University of Chicago Press, 2004), 383, 389.
3   Smith, "God Save This Honourable Court," 383.

then be challenged to read the Talmud through an academic lens, which would be strange and new to them in light of their traditional background. Despite this increased interest in Judaic studies and rabbinic literature in particular, very few colleges and universities in North America could regularly fill a classroom with students who possess the background needed to read these texts in their original languages.[4]

The focus for many (if not most) instructors of classical rabbinic literature at colleges and universities is on Smith's second task: to make the strange familiar. Late antique or classical rabbinic texts are indeed strange. They were written by rabbis and for rabbis who lived centuries ago and far away. Their interests (e.g., laws of purity and tithing) and contexts (Roman Palestine and Sasanian Mesopotamia) are very distant and foreign from those of students in North America today. Any single rabbinic discussion, moreover, presumes that the reader has extensive background, not only in the Hebrew Bible but also in all other rabbinic texts. Left to its own device, the field of Talmud study could maintain, reinforce, and perpetuate its own insularity. Needless to say, this would be a great loss to religious studies and the broader liberal arts, as these texts are key to understanding many areas of Jewish studies, and their unique style and features make them especially apt for developing students' critical thinking and analytical skills.[5] As such, instructors of rabbinics at secular universities are faced with the task of making these strange texts accessible, relevant, and meaningful to students of diverse backgrounds.[6] They teach Talmud by making the strange familiar

---

4 On the flourishing of the study of rabbinics at secular universities, see David Stern, "Rabbinics and Jewish Identity: An American Perspective," in *Jewish Thought and Jewish Belief [Hebrew]*, ed. Daniel J. Lasker (Beer-Sheva, Israel: Ben-Gurion University of the Negev Press, 2012), 10.

5 Elizabeth Shanks Alexander, "Why Study Talmud in the 21st Century: The View from a Large Public University or Studying Talmud as a Critical Thinker," in *Why Study Talmud in the Twenty-First Century? The Relevance of the Ancient Jewish Text to Our World*, ed. Paul Socken (Lanham, MD: Lexington Press, 2009), 11-24; Michael Chernick, "Neusner, Brisk, and the *Stam*: Significant Methdologies for Meaningful Talmud Teaching and Study," in *Turn It and Turn It Again, Studies in the Teaching and Learning of Classical Jewish Texts*, ed. Jon A. Levisohn and Susan P. Fendrick (Boston: Academic Studies Press, 2013), 105-07.

6 Ethan Tucker calls this the "democratization" of the Talmud in his forward to *Reconstructing the Talmud: An Introduction to the Academic Study of Rabbinic Literature*, ed. Joshua Kulp and Jason Rogoff (New York: Mechon Hadar, 2014), 9.

to those with little or no prior exposure to rabbinics, Jewish studies, and—very often—religious studies in general.

Little has been written to date on teaching rabbinics at secular universities.[7] This chapter contributes to our understanding of this issue by exploring the teaching of Talmud to graduate students who have little or no background in rabbinics or late-antique Judaism. The students in this study specialize in classics, archaeology, early Christianity, or other areas of research into the ancient world. Embracing this context, I define learning to read and attaining proficiency in Talmud as the acquisition of the background and skills needed to access and read the texts on one's own for the purpose of integrating rabbinic literature into one's own research project. This broad goal can be broken down into the following subgoals:

1. Relevance and motivation. To students without background in rabbinic literature, it is not always clear what these texts are and how they can be useful for research in classics, ancient history, and early Christianity. The instructor, therefore, needs to provide sufficient background and motivation for students to engage with these texts.

2. Reading and understanding texts in translation. While there are a number of English translations of the Talmud, reading and understanding them is far from straightforward. Guidance by experts is often required in order to gain an understanding of the text's content, structure, and genre. Here, the goal is for students to understand the basic meaning of the text (i.e., *peshat*), as well as to achieve a deeper appreciation of the text's literary features, structure, historical contexts, etc.[8] The features that lie beneath the surface can be

---

7 Notable exceptions include Alexander, "Why Study Talmud," 11-24; Michael L. Satlow, "Narratives or Sources? Active Learning and the Teaching of Ancient Jewish History and Texts," *Teaching Theology and Religion* 15, no. 1 (2012): 48-60; Michael L. Satlow, "Teaching Ancient Jewish History: An Experiment in Engaged Learning," in *Turn It and Turn It Again,* Michael L. Satlow, "Teaching Ancient Jewish History," in Levisohn and Fendrick, *Turn It and Turn It Again,* 212-35. Most scholarship, however, has focused on teaching at rabbinic seminaries and Jewish day schools; see the collection of papers in Levisohn and Fendrick, *Turn It and Turn It Again.*

8 This aligns with the "contextual orientation" to teaching rabbinics as discussed by Jon A. Levisohn, "A Menu of Orientations to the Teaching of Rabbinic Literature," *Journal of Jewish Education* 76, no. 1 (2010): 19-21; Jon A. Levisohn, "What Are the Orientations to

illuminated by connecting the text to the broader study of ancient Judaism and the history of religions.[9]
3. Identification and access. Students should be able to identify primary sources relevant to their interests and access them, even in English translation. Regrettably, the citation methods rabbinic texts are inconsistent and opaque, as systems of transliteration, abbreviation, and citation differ from one scholarly publication to another.
4. Integration into an independent research project. Having accessed, read, and analyzed the texts, I seek to provide students with the skills necessary to integrate classical rabbinic texts into their own research projects. Underlying and motivating this goal is that students would acquire the background needed to navigate and understand these texts, as well as recognize and appreciate the Talmud's significance for the study of religion and the ancient world.

This chapter will explore these goals and issues through a multifaceted and integrative approach to teaching that combines lectures, in-class readings of texts, and student research projects.[10] In reflecting upon and analyzing the students' work and feedback, I find that focusing on rabbinic narratives (*aggadah*; plural: *aggadot*) and texts related to material culture are particularly effective to teach students with little or no background in Jewish studies to learn to read Talmud.

Teaching Context

This study draws upon my experience teaching classical rabbinic literature to graduate students in classics, archaeology, and religious studies at a large public university. Most of these students have training in Greek, Latin, and classical studies. Perhaps two or three had some prior exposure to biblical Hebrew or had read some rabbinic texts in translation in a previous

---

the Teaching of Rabbinic Literature?" in Levisohn and Fendrick, *Turn It and Turn It Again*, 61-63.
9 Alexander, "Why Study Talmud," 11.
10 Jane Kanarek and Marjorie Lehman, "Assigning Integration: A Framework for Intellectual, Personal, and Professional Development in Seminary Courses," *Teaching Theology and Religion* 16, no. 1 (2013): 18-32.

university course. To be sure, the majority had little or no prior exposure to Jewish studies, let alone rabbinic literature.

In many ways, my teaching context is similar to that described by Elizabeth Shanks Alexander, where Talmud is taught to students of diverse backgrounds within the framework of a broad liberal arts education.[11] The intended student audience, moreover, dictates certain requirements and restrictions. Whereas rabbinic seminaries may offer Talmud over the course of multiple years of study, opportunities for learning to read Talmud are more limited at secular universities. There may be a single one-semester upper level undergraduate course that focuses primarily on rabbinic literature or one graduate seminar offered every few years in which rabbinic texts play a significant role. That is, the intricacies of rabbinic literature must often be condensed into a single semester. Very often, Talmud is taught within the context of broader courses in Jewish studies, further limiting the amount of time that can be spent guiding students through the material.[12] While these scenarios pose a number of challenges, they also represent important opportunities to introduce students to the rich corpus that is rabbinic literature. Indeed, this class may be a student's first and only exposure to the Talmud in an academic context. However brief and limited, exposing the students to the material helps address lacunae in an essential area of religious studies.

Relevance and Motivation

Before teaching Talmud, it is first necessary to teach *about* Talmud.[13] Why study rabbinic literature? What is its use for us as students, scholars, and researchers? Alexander likewise notes the imperative to build students' investment in the material from the outset, "I can't be subtle," she writes, "I need to be very transparent about what they stand to gain."[14] Like Alexander, I do not presume that these students have personal, cultural, or religious motivations

---

11   Alexander, "Why Study Talmud," 11-19.
12   It is common to have a short unit on rabbinics in a survey class (ibid., 11); Jordan D. Rosenblum, "The Tofu Model: Using Tofu to Teach Introduction to Judaism." *Syllabus* 1, no. 1 (2012): 1-8, accessed July 3, 2015, http://www.syllabusjournal.org/article/view/9981.
13   Alexander, "Why Study Talmud," 14.
14   Ibid., 14.

for learning to read Talmud.¹⁵ Thus, I endeavor to demonstrate the importance of the Talmud from a number of perspectives. One approach, as outlined by Chernick, is to emphasize the importance of Talmud for the diachronic study of Judaism, articulating that it is "the historical victor in the narrative of the Jewish people."¹⁶ In this respect, I discuss the Talmud's centrality to Jewish life from the middle ages to today, touching upon its preeminent status in Jewish law and traditional Jewish education. The popularity of *daf yomi*, the Talmud's digitization and its accessibility on all types of electronic devices, and the proliferation of translations and commentaries all attest to rabbinic literature's continued importance to Jews and Judaism today. Having provided this background to students, I next discuss the relevance of classical rabbinic texts specifically for the study of the ancient world, as these texts constitute an important set of primary sources on life in the later Roman Empire and Sasanian Babylonia. As such, rabbinic texts can be useful to scholars of the Near East, classics, early Christianity, and the ancient world.

During my course, I provided the background and motivation for studying rabbinic texts through a lecture that also introduced students to the history of the rabbinic movement. The lecture also gives an overview of the classical rabbinic corpus, discussing dates, genres, and areas of focus. Based on their reactions in class, the students seem to have gained a firm understanding of the significance and background of classical rabbinic texts. It also clarified and sorted out some confusion and misconceptions that they had carried. One student mentioned that after the introductory lecture she was now more aware that there was little agreement on what comprises the rabbinic corpus. "This was confusing at first. I thought I made a mistake in reading things," she said, referring to the readings assigned for class. Rather, she now sees that there can be variety and multiple understandings of even the basic question of what constitutes the rabbinic corpus.

Reading the Talmud in Translation

In selecting texts for introducing students to rabbinic literature, I gave careful consideration to genre. Even in English translation, legal *sugyot*

---

15   Cf. the described in Tucker, forward, 9.
16   Chernick, "Neusner, Brisk, and the *Stam*," 107.

may easily overwhelm first-time readers of rabbinics for a number of reasons. First, the subject matter is often very foreign to modern-day interests. Substantial portions of rabbinic texts are devoted to esoteric topics, such as levirate marriage, offerings to the Temple, and other subjects for which students possess little background.[17] Even seemingly familiar topics, such as support for the poor, are often embedded in contexts (e.g., premodern agrarian societies) that are very distant to North American university students.[18] Second, while all rabbinic texts presume background and fluency in the Hebrew Bible (which non-specialists cannot be expected to have), the high concentration of prooftexts in legal *sugyot* can overwhelm a non-specialist trying to work through the text. Third, the method of legal argumentation is serpentine, with phrasing that is often elliptical and filled with questions, retorts, and unstated assumptions that can be difficult for neophytes to penetrate.[19] Even in translation, rabbinic texts can be sufficiently foreign that students may wonder if it is worthwhile to invest the time and effort needed to understand them.[20]

Midrash can be equally intimidating. It often makes exegetical assumptions that would be unfamiliar to non-specialists. Midrash also requires a detailed knowledge of Hebrew to understand not only the exegesis but also the underlying textual and linguistic tensions that the exegesis is meant to address.[21]

---

17 Notably, in his effort to teach rabbinics in ways that make the material applicable to modern life and interests, Jonah C. Steinberg, "Academic Study of the Talmud as a Spiritual Endeavor in Rabbinic Training: Delights and Dangers," in Levisohn and Fendrick, *Turn It and Turn It Again,* 380, is compelled to "liberally reinterpret" the material in tractates Kodashim and Taharot to concentrate on theology. See also Elie Holzer and Orit Kent, *A Philosophy of Havruta: Understanding and Teaching the Art of Text Study in Pairs* (Boston: Academic Studies Press, 2013), 208.
18 See, for example, M. Pe'ah 4:10, where provisions for the poor are determined by the precise method by which one reaps a field.
19 Chernick, "Neusner, Brisk, and the *Stam*," 106; Martin Goodman, introduction to *Rabbinic Texts and the History of Late-Roman Palestine,* ed. Martin Goodman and Philip Alexander (Oxford and New York: Oxford University Press for the British Academy, 2010), 1-3.
20 For a similar challenge in liberal seminaries, see Chernick, "Neusner, Brisk, and the *Stam,*" 106–07; Steinberg, "Academic Study," 377-85.
21 Jeffrey L. Rubenstein, "From History to Literature: The Pedagogical Implications of Shifting Paradigms in the Study of Rabbinic Narratives," *The Initiative on Bridging Scholarship and Pedagogy in Jewish Studies Working Paper No. 26* (2010): 6, accessed April

Holzer, Kent, and Rubenstein have found that narrative texts (*aggadot*) provide a more gradual entry into rabbinics.[22] Narratives require less prior knowledge of complex legal concepts and modes of argumentation. Some narratives are relatively short and, therefore, can be studied in full within a limited class period. Holzer and Kent also note the evocative nature of narratives, in that they seem relatively straightforward but also invite closer and repeated examination that reveal new intricacies. As "literary-artistic creations," *aggadot* allow students to apply methods of literary analysis that they may have acquired or been exposed to from other courses, building their investment in the text and their sense of authority as legitimate interpreters of the text.[23] Narratives are also relatively self-contained and make sense on their own, as the frame of reference can be limited to the text at hand.[24] While deeper layers of meaning are surely revealed when one connects a particular *aggadic* text to other rabbinic texts and broader rabbinic concerns, the basic meaning of a narrative and its didactic purpose can often be uncovered without specialized or comprehensive knowledge of the rabbinic corpus.[25]

Holzer and Kent discuss choosing narratives that address specific themes. For their study of *havruta*, they chose *aggadot* based on the theme of learning.[26] For my ancient studies-oriented graduate students, I chose a text containing imagery and themes that might be familiar to them—a siege by the Roman army. The narrative on Jerusalem during the First Jewish Revolt in B. Gittin 55b-56b contains themes and topics that would be familiar and of interest to students of the ancient world. Choosing this text also introduces students to the Talmud's narrative on the origins of the rabbinic

---

14, 2015, http://www.brandeis.edu/mandel/pdfs/Bridging_working_papers/Rubenstein_5610.pdf.

22 Holzer and Kent, *Philosophy of Havruta*, 97, 208-11; Orit Kent, "A Theory of *Havruta* Learning," in Levisohn and Fendrick, *Turn It and Turn It Again*, 293; Rubenstein, "From History to Literature," 6.

23 Holzer and Kent, *Philosophy of Havruta*, 209; Jeffrey L. Rubenstein, *Talmudic Stories: Narrative Art, Composition, and Culture* (Baltimore: Johns Hopkins University Press, 1999), 9; Rubenstein, "From History to Literature," 4-5.

24 Ibid., 5.

25 Holzer and Kent, *Philosophy of Havruta*, 210.

26 Ibid., 208-11.

movement—with Rabban Yohanan ben Zakkai's famous escape from Jerusalem and request for "Yavneh and its sages."[27] Thus, the students moved from the familiar (a Roman siege) to the strange (rabbinics).

We read the text together in the classroom, where I asked the students to take turns reading passages aloud. I stopped the reader frequently to summarize what he or she just read and to think about how what they were reading fit into the broader narrative.[28] This provided an opportunity to correct erroneous connections that students can make on their own. I also challenge students to make connections with other texts, concepts, and ideas discussed at other points during the course and to articulate opinions that are grounded in the source material. I interject at times to provide additional background and to clarify specific terms or turns of phrase. In doing so, I strive to articulate how each word and each detail is "the tip of an iceberg," a fragment, that with proper and thorough investigation, we can begin to understand and appreciate the size, shape, and contours of the great mass that lies beneath the surface.[29] I also prompt the students to think about structure and reoccurring themes.

In continuously provoking the students to think while we are reading, the approach aligns with Keene and Zimmermann's work on the qualities of proficient readers. Namely, proficient readers activate relevant, prior knowledge (cognitive schema) while they read. When students think about their own reading *while* they read, they think of questions that provoke additional questions. They then make connections (and articulate distinctions) between what they know and what is new information. In short, proficient readers are "metacognitive" in that they think about their own

---

27   On this text, see Rubenstein, *Talmudic Stories*, 139-75; Peter Schäfer, "Die Flucht Johanan b. Zakkais aus Jerusalem und die Gründung des Lehrhauses in Jabne," in *Aufstieg und Niedergang der Römischen Welt II.19.2*, ed. H. Temporini and W. Haase (Berlin: de Gruyter, 1979).
28   I advocate a slow, deliberate reading that resonates with that discussed by Jane Kanarek, "The Pedagogy of Slowing Down: Teaching Talmud in a Summer Kollel," *Teaching Theology and Religion* 13, no. 1 (2010): 15-34; reprinted as Jane Kanarek, "The Pedagogy of Slowing Down: Teaching Talmud in a Summer Kolel," in Levisohn and Fendrick, *Turn It and Turn It Again*, 128-57.
29   Alexander, "Why Study Talmud," 11.

thinking while they read.[30] Intensive intervention by the instructor can also foster active learning and serve as a model for working through a text.[31] The students commented that they appreciated the interjections I made, as these created an atmosphere of openness and connectedness, in which they felt free to interject with their own observations. My overall objective with the students is to transform the classroom into a "living commentary" on the text, whereby the elucidation of the material is a collective enterprise.

This approach proved to be effective, as the students came to understand the straightforward meaning of texts as we worked through them and became attuned to their literary qualities. At the same time, however, a number of other challenges rose to the surface. First, there were difficulties in identifying the referents to particular pronouns—that is, who is the *he* referred to in the text? One student said that she had read the text multiple times to identify the referents to certain pronouns in preparation for class, but with little success. Indeed, this could be classified as a "good problem," as such ambiguities reflect the character of the text in its original languages. Nevertheless, it constitutes yet another obstacle to accessibility and comprehension for neophytes.

A second challenge was the structure of the narrative. Rabbinic texts are famous for going off on tangents, but it was often unclear to the students where tangential discussions began and ended. Other challenges that the students faced included making sense of parables and metaphors, as well as understanding how prooftexts work. It was not always apparent to them how prooftexts related to the issues at hand. Unlike the ancient rabbis for whom these texts were originally written, the students lacked a comprehensive knowledge of the Hebrew Bible or an ingrained sense of how it is used in classical Jewish texts.

While narratives are surely easier to grasp than legal discussions, *aggadot* also pose their own unique challenges. For example, when Yohanan ben Zakkai went to see Vespasian, students wondered whether the "meeting"

---

30 Ellin Oliver Keene and Susan Zimmermann, *Mosaic of Thought: Teaching Comprehension in a Reader's Workshop* (Portsmouth, NH: Heinemann, 1997), 22-23.
31 Satlow, "Teaching Ancient Jewish History," 232. On the importance of teachers as model readers in the classroom, see Stephanie Harvey and Anne Goudvis, *Strategies That Work: Teaching Comprehension to Enhance Understanding* (York, ME: Stenhouse, 2000), 7; Keene and Zimmermann, *Mosaic of Thought*, 22-23.

took place in Jerusalem or Rome. Such questions may suggest the development of reading skills, as proficient readers often create a mental map of the principle characters in order to attain comprehension of the text.[32] Here, the question opens a discussion on the nature of rabbinic *aggadah*—namely, how it can be so concerned with some details of the past, yet unconcerned with others. This presented an opportunity to make the point that such details do not necessarily matter to the rabbis. The interests of rabbinic texts may or may not align with the interests (or even values) of modern readers. Indeed, part of gaining proficiency and objectivity is recognizing what is important and unimportant to the authors of an ancient text.

The layered texture of rabbinic literature is new to these students, as they are struck by the all-knowing rabbis who simply interject themselves into an ongoing conversation. More unique qualities of rabbinic narratives are brought out when we read a brief passage from Josephus on how the inhabitants of a besieged Jerusalem hid in tunnels in an attempt to escape the battle.[33] The historiographic texture of Josephus's writings provides a stark contrast with the Bavli's *aggadah*. The narrative section on Emperor Nero produced the most consternation. In B. Gittin 55b-56b, Nero is (initially) pegged as God's instrument of destruction. But then he becomes learned in Torah and converts, and the Talmud identifies him as an ancestor of Rabbi Meir. Students with a background in classics and ancient history know something about Nero and are disturbed by this free rewriting of history.[34] In some respects, the students' perplexity is a good sign, as they are trying to connect the new and the strange (in this case, the Talmud) with what they already knew.[35] While the students seek to make text-to-text connections between the Bavli's "Nero" and the historical Nero, an inability to do so illuminates the unique texture of rabbinic *aggadah,* which features

---

32 Harvey and Goudvis, *Strategies That Work*, 7.
33 Josephus, *War* 6.392.
34 Similarly, see Rubenstein, "From History to Literature," 1-2, who also notes that classical sources have no knowledge of Nero setting out to fight Judea or converting.
35 Thereby activating their "schema," which Harvey and Goudvis, *Strategies That Work*, 21, define as the sum total of one's background knowledge and experience that one brings to his or her reading. See also Keene and Zimmermann, *Mosaic of Thought*, 22-23.

occasional cameos by historical figures such as kings and emperors.³⁶ I also use this opportunity to discuss modern scholarly ways to handle the text, distinguishing the "historical kernel" approach pursued by some scholars from holistic and literary approaches by others.³⁷ As we continued to read about Yohanan ben Zakkai's encounter with Vespasian, the students giggle, recognizing that this is not meant to be interpreted as a historical account. In this way, they began to appreciate the unique texture, genre, and interests of *aggadah*. In learning how to read talmudic texts, they also gained a better understanding of the Talmud's character.³⁸

Reading these texts also brought up a number of other issues that students face when reading texts in translation. First, while puns and wordplay (Qamza, Kalba Sabua, etc.) are often explained in the translation's footnotes, they predictably lose their intended impact in translation. Second, rabbinic names are foreign to students without background, as they frequently confuse individuals with similar names, such as Yohanan bar Nappaha and Yohanan ben Zakkai. Rabbi Judah (bar Ilai) is confused with Rabbi Judah the Prince. Third is the problem of unusual words, such as *biryoni* and *Sicarii*, for which translators usually provide only minimal explanation. Looking up such words in reference books, moreover, was challenging due to differences in transliteration and spelling.

Identification and Access

There were additional advances in research skills. During the semester, students brought to light a number of technical barriers in identifying and accessing sources. Those students learning to read Talmud for research purposes should be able to identify references to primary sources (as cited in

---

36 Harvey and Goudvis, *Strategies That Work*, 21, define text-to-text connections as "connections that readers make between the text they are reading and another text, including books, poems, scripts, songs, or anything that is written."

37 Compare, for example, the approaches to this text by Gedalyahu Alon, *Jews, Judaism, and the Classical World: Studies in Jewish History in the Times of the Second Temple and Talmud*, trans. Israel Abrahams (Jerusalem: Magnes Press, 1977), 269-313; Rubenstein, *Talmudic Stories*, 139-75.

38 The challenges of teaching *aggadah* to the uninitiated are also discussed by Rubenstein, "From History to Literature," 1-8.

a scholarly work) and locate those sources in an English translation, so that they can read them within their broader literary contexts. Students repeatedly indicated that this task was complicated by the multiplicity of methods of citing rabbinic texts, noting that abbreviations and transliterations of the names of rabbinic compilations and tractates differed from one reference work to another. This made it not only difficult for them to look up primary sources, but also to make meaningful connections between texts.[39] Similarly, when students encounter rabbinics for the first time and are reading scholarship flooded with transliterations, it is understandable how *'Abod. Zar.* (SBL style) could be confused with *Aboth* (Herbert Danby's *Mishnah*) and *Šeb.* with *Šebu.* (both SBL). The citation of compilations can also be problematic. Note, for example, how the Jerusalem Talmud, also known as the *Yerushalmi*, the Palestinian Talmud, and the Talmud of the Land of Israel; all can be abbreviated as *j., p., y.,* JT, TJ, and PT.

Similarly, as discussed earlier, translations and transliterations of key names and terms vary, making it difficult for students to thematic connections between one text and another. For example, it can be difficult to know that *tsedaqah* in one source should be equated with *sedaka* in another. Similarly, when they see "Akiba" mentioned in one reference work, students understandably do not know to look him up as *'Aqiva' Ben Yosef* in another, or that Jacob, Yaakov, and Ya'aqob may all refer to the same person. Students have expressed anxiety, both in researching (as they try to determine if two similar-looking words found in different books or articles refer to the same concept) and in their writing, as they are concerned that a small misspelling of a Hebrew word in transliteration may inadvertently refer to a concept that they had not intended to mention.

---

39 Compare, for example, the abbreviations and transliterated titles in Patrick H. Alexander et al., eds., *The SBL Handbook of Style: For Ancient Near Eastern, Biblical, and Early Christian Studies* (Peabody, MA: Hendrickson, 1999), 79-80 (which lists three different ways to cite each tractate); Adele Berlin, ed. "Common Abbreviations Used in This Work," *The Oxford Dictionary of the Jewish Religion: Second Edition* (New York: Oxford University Press, 2011), xvii-xviii; Fred Skolnik and Michael Berenbaum, eds., *Encyclopaedia Judaica*, 2nd ed. (Detroit: Macmillan Reference USA and Keter Publishing House, 2007), 1:184-96.

Independent Research Projects

In teaching students how to acquire the skills needed to make use of rabbinic literature for their own research, my goals are similar to those of Martin Goodman and Philip Alexander, who dedicated a volume to making rabbinics more accessible to Roman historians.[40] Goodman lays out many of the obstacles for non-rabbinicists, such as the uncertain provenance, dating, and transmission of rabbinic texts. Rabbinic texts are written in genres that are unfamiliar to most audiences, as they are characterized by esoteric modes of expression. Translations, Goodman notes, are not always trustworthy.[41] As I have discussed earlier, even accurate translations are not necessarily written in ways that are accessible to readers without background in rabbinics. In addition to problems inherent in the primary sources, Goodman highlights a dearth of scholarship in rabbinics that attempts to transmit a specialist's findings in ways that are accessible to non-specialists. In short, non-specialists looking to use rabbinic literature in their own research face problems both with primary texts and secondary literature that is based heavily on rabbinic sources.

For my graduate course, independent research projects consisted of student presentations and seminar papers, which were aimed to develop skills in presenting one's ideas orally and in writing.[42] In their papers and presentations, I found that some students demonstrated an ability to access and critically read primary texts on their own. For example, in a discussion of a text on burial practices in tractate Semahot, one student wrote:[43] "Does this discussion lead to the conclusion that sheets were not used in secondary

---

40 Martin Goodman and Philip Alexander, eds., *Rabbinic Texts and the History of Late-Roman Palestine* (Oxford: Oxford University Press for the British Academy, 2010).
41 Goodman, introduction to *Rabbinic Texts*, 1-3.
42 On the importance of writing assignments for teaching classical Jewish texts, see Kanarek and Lehman, "Assigning Integration," 18-32, which seeks to develop seminary students' spiritual connections with the text. My goal is to promote the integration of rabbinics into graduate students' areas of personal research interest—both, I believe, can be categorized as different types of text-to-self connections, as elucidated in Keene and Zimmermann, *Mosaic of Thought*, 21.
43 The title of the external tractate Semahot ("Gladness") is a euphemism for its subject matter, as it addresses laws related to death, burial, and mourning. It has been dated to the third or eighth century CE; see Eyal Ben-Eliyahu, Yehudah Cohn, and Fergus Millar, *Handbook of Jewish Literature from Late Antiquity, 135-700 CE* (Oxford: Oxford University Press for the British Academy, 2012), 56.

burials? No. The fact that there is a discussion about the role of a sheet in ossuaries insinuates: (1) sheets were used—otherwise, there would be no reason to counsel against them; and (2) there is a difference in opinion concerning proper burial, suggesting various methods were probably employed." She continued that when the rabbis enact a prohibition, we should be skeptical of the extent to which it was followed. Such prohibitions may also indicate that the rabbis were responding to real practices that were known to them. This demonstrates knowledge of the prescriptive—rather than descriptive—character of rabbinic literature, as well as the early rabbis' lack of authority and other important current scholarly views of rabbinic literature.[44]

Both the specific challenges of secondary scholarship and the students' success in overcoming them became apparent through their research. This was evident, for example, in a co-presentation by two students on a scholarly dispute over the interpretation of possible ritual baths found in Jerusalem.[45] These articles, like many studies on the archaeology of ancient and late antique Israel, draw heavily on rabbinic sources, integrating their concepts and terminology throughout. The students' first impression was that the authors of the articles presumed that rabbinic literature is *sui generis,* unique, and thus untranslatable to the uninitiated. They noted that many issues were left unexplained in the articles, leaving the students to wonder if the absence of explanation was a product of the authors' own lack of clarity or that the authors felt no explanation was needed, because the point would be well-known to those in the field.

Illustrative were the students' handouts that they themselves prepared for other students to better understand the material. One included a glossary of terms, such as *avodah, terumah, zavim,* etc. Notably, the handout

---

44 On rabbinic authority, see Seth Schwartz, *Imperialism and Jewish Society, 200 B.C.E. to 640 C.E.* (Princeton: Princeton University Press, 2001), 103-28. On the prescriptive character of rabbinic literature, see Michael L. Satlow, *Tasting the Dish: Rabbinic Rhetorics of Sexuality* (Atlanta: Scholars Press, 1995), 8.

45 This project contrasted the following studies: Yonatan Adler, "The Ritual Baths Near the Temple Mount and Extra-Purification before Entering the Temple Courts: A Reply to Eyal Regev," *Israel Exploration Journal* 56, no. 2 (2006): 209-15; Eyal Regev, "The Ritual Baths Near the Temple Mount and Extra-Purification before Entering the Temple Courts," *Israel Exploration Journal* 55, no. 2 (2005): 194-204.

included *miqveh* together with its plural form *miqva'ot* and two alternative spellings—*miqweh, mikweh*—again highlighting the difficulties that differences in transliteration can create for non-specialists. The handouts also included a reconstruction of the layout of the Temple compound, which the scholarly articles had not provided. Here we see the students using visual methods to better understand the texts at hand, both the scholarly literature and the rabbinic material on which it is based. As I noted earlier, creating visual and other sensory images from the text is an important attribute of a proficient reader.[46] In analyzing the aforementioned discussion of ritual baths, the students also demonstrated an understanding of the kinds of assumptions that each author made with regard to the authority of the rabbinic texts.

That students had developed a good grasp of modern scholarly discourse on rabbinics was also evident in their increased awareness of various methodological problems. For example, in comparing ossuaries to a rabbinic discussion of burial practices, one student pointed out the difficulties in "projecting rabbinical values on archaeological material predating the genesis of the rabbinic period (circa 200 CE)" and "interpreting archaeological data with an anachronistic lens." Understanding that it was necessary to address the chronological gap, she cited and discussed scholarship that takes the position that early rabbinic texts can reliably preserve traditions from the late Second Temple era. In this particular case, she juxtaposed and analyzed approaches by Catherine Hezser and Jodi Magness, siding with Magness.[47] Indeed, the student's awareness of this issue and her ability to argue a particular side of it demonstrate a level and type of proficiency I was seeking to develop—namely, the ability to read and understand scholarship that is based heavily on rabbinics.

Similarly, another student's research showed an insightful understanding of the methodological issues involved in using M. Middot for research on the Temple Mount, which had been destroyed long before the tractate was

---

46 Keene and Zimmermann, *Mosaic of Thought*, 22-23.
47 Catherine Hezser, "Correlating Literary, Epigraphical, and Archaeological Sources," in *The Oxford Handbook of Jewish Daily Life in Roman Palestine*, ed. Catherine Hezser (Oxford: Oxford University Press, 2010), 9-27; Jodi Magness, *Stone and Dung, Oil and Spit: Jewish Daily Life in the Time of Jesus* (Grand Rapids, MI: Eerdmans, 2011).

compiled. This project demonstrated a good grasp of studies by Naftali Cohn, Joshua Schwartz, Yehoshua Peleg, and others, as the student had displayed an excellent understanding of the nuances of these scholars' arguments.[48] The student concluded by highlighting the limitations of using M. Middot as a source for the layout of the Temple compound.

In assessing the independent research projects, there is strong evidence that some students sought out, accessed, read, and analyzed the primary sources on their own. For some students, however, whether this was achieved was more ambiguous. In these cases, it was difficult to determine if the students accessed and read the primary texts on their own or limited their search to texts that were discussed in secondary scholarship. In reassessing my goals, it seems unlikely and perhaps counter-productive for all students whose scholarship does not focus on Jewish studies to be reading these texts without the opinions of specialists in hand. To be sure, even understanding the specialists' opinions in scholarly writings presents obstacles that must be overcome.

The students' research projects also brought to the fore an interesting paradox in teaching Talmud to the uninitiated at the university level. On the one hand, neophytes can understandably confuse terms that may look similar, such as Mishnah and Midrash. And yet, they also had read these texts in a highly critical way and within their late-antique historical contexts, both due to the fact that they were unencumbered by the perspectives and presuppositions that often come with learning to read Talmud in a traditional setting.

Narratives and Material Culture

In assessing my teaching and student performance at the end of the course, I find that narratives and material culture provide especially effective frameworks for teaching students to read rabbinic literature. The effectiveness of introducing rabbinic literature through narratives supports the approaches of Holzer, Kent, and Rubenstein that I discussed earlier. Just as they

---

48 Naftali S. Cohn, *The Memory of the Temple and the Making of the Rabbis* (Philadelphia: University of Pennsylvania Press, 2013); Joshua Schwartz and Yehoshua Peleg, "Are the 'Halachic Temple Mount' and the 'Outer Court' of Josephus One and the Same?" in *Studies in Josephus and the Varieties of Ancient Judaism: Louis H. Feldman Jubilee Volume*, ed. Shaye J. D. Cohen and Joshua J. Schwartz (Leiden, Neth.: E. J. Brill, 2007), 207-22.

demonstrated the effectiveness of narratives as an entry into rabbinics for Jewish educators, in adult education and in other popular educational settings, I find that narratives are effective for introducing rabbinic texts to graduate students at a secular university.[49] Moreover, whereas Holzer and Kent promote the use of "miniature narratives" of just a few lines long, I add that longer narratives are equally effective.

The very broad range of material culture, from architecture to religious and domestic items, also provided a useful inroad to teaching students to read and use rabbinic texts.[50] The students who engaged with rabbinic literature the most were those whose research projects focused on material culture. The visuality of material culture presents some advantages for the uninitiated, as visuals can help compensate for a reader's lack of background knowledge.[51] Material culture can strengthen the students' understanding of a text by forging tangible and visual connections with the subject matter.[52]

Those interested in material culture, moreover, have much to gain by learning to read and use rabbinic texts. The rabbis were extensively interested in how laws applied to all aspects of daily life, such as cooking, eating, building, and weaving. This produced discussions that included intricate details on the features and uses of pots and pans, lamps and houses, and clothing and courtyards—all items valuable to cultural historians.[53] For example, the ancient uses of ceramic oil lamps found throughout Near Eastern archaeological sites can be illuminated by the discussion of Sabbath laws in M. Shabbat 2:1-3, which includes details on the kinds of materials used for wicks (e.g., cedar fiber, raw silk, flax) and the oils used as fuel (e.g., sesame oil, nut oil, fish oil, olive oil).[54] Similarly, the potential uses for the baskets found at the Cave of Letters (second

---

49 Holzer and Kent, *Philosophy of Havruta*, 208-11; Rubenstein, "From History to Literature," 5-8.
50 The usefulness of archaeology and material culture for teaching rabbinic literature has also been noted by Levisohn, "What are the Orientations," 62.
51 Harvey and Goudvis, *Strategies That Work*, 7-8.
52 On using different senses to foster meaning and understanding for readers, see ibid., 7, 22; Keene and Zimmermann, *Mosaic of Thought*, 22-23.
53 Leib Moscovitz, *Talmudic Reasoning: From Casuistics to Conceptualization* (Tübingen: Mohr Siebeck, 2002), 47.
54 For an overview of oil lamps and their importance in the study of late-antique Judaism, see Gregg E. Gardner, "City of Lights: The Lamps of Roman and Byzantine Jerusalem," *Near Eastern Archaeology* 77, no. 4 (2014): 284-90.

century CE) are illuminated by rabbinic discussions of the *quppa*, i.e., a wicker basket.[55] Yehoshua Brand's massive collection and analysis of rabbinic discussions of ceramic vessels attests to the importance of objects to the rabbis and, in turn, the Talmud's usefulness for modern-day students of material culture.[56] In short, attention to material culture can provide effective motivation and a useful aid for non-specialist students to learn to read rabbinic literature.[57]

Conclusions

In this chapter, I have explored and reflected upon the application of Jonathan Z. Smith's goal to make the strange familiar in the teaching of Talmud to graduate students at a secular university.[58] Rabbinic texts *are* strange. Written by and for a small circle of Torah scholars who lived long ago, their language, form, modes of reasoning, and presuppositions make them difficult for non-rabbinicists to penetrate, even in an English translation. All of this makes learning to read the Talmud significantly difficult. However, many of these challenges can be overcome. I have explored how students can learn to read rabbinic literature for the purposes of pursuing their own research.[59] I have found that narratives and attention to material

---

55 Gregg E. Gardner, *The Origins of Organized Charity in Rabbinic Judaism* (New York: Cambridge University Press, 2015), 63-83. While most references to *quppa* in rabbinic texts denote a wicker basket, in a handful of instances *quppa* refers to a communal charity fund.
56 Yehoshua Brand, *Ceramics in Talmudic Literature [Hebrew]* (Jerusalem: Mosad ha-Rav Kuk, 1953); likewise, see the classic work of Samuel Krauss, *Talmudische Archäologie*. 3 vols. (Leipzig: G. Fock, 1910-1912). For more recent studies, including methodological assessments for integrating material culture and rabbinic texts, see Yaron Z. Eliav, "Samuel Krauss and the Early Study of the Physical World of the Rabbis in Roman Palestine," *Journal of Jewish Studies* 65, no. 1 (2014): 38-57; Catherine Hezser, ed. *The Oxford Handbook of Jewish Daily Life in Roman Palestine* (Oxford: Oxford University Press, 2010); Joshua J. Schwartz, "The Material Realities of Jewish Life in the Land of Israel, C. 235-638," in *The Cambridge History of Judaism: Volume Four: The Late Roman-Rabbinic Period*, ed. Steven T. Katz (Cambridge: Cambridge University Press, 2006), 431-56.
57 See further Gregg E. Gardner, "Reading Between the Strata: Teaching Rabbinic Literature with Material Culture," *Teaching Theology and Religion*.
58 Smith, "God Save This Honourable Court," 382-83, 389.
59 One student commented in the evaluations that he or she appreciated the focus on practical research methods, "It's more important for us to learn to research, rather than just

culture can provide effective entry points to learn to read and effectively use rabbinic literature for those who specialize in other areas of the ancient world. By the end of the semester, many students who had never seen nor heard of the Talmud previously could skillfully work their way through secondary scholarship, access and interpret the primary sources (to varying extents), and integrate all of this into a graduate-level research project in fields such as early Christianity, ancient history, archaeology, and classics. If not entirely familiar, I believe that the Talmud was made significantly less strange to my students.

---

knowing the material." Similarly, another student wrote, "Perhaps what I found most beneficial from the course was learning how to refine my research skills. ... This class was more than just knowing the material, but knowing how to question and use the material. This is a skill I will be able to take with me throughout my academic career."

CHAPTER 6

■ ■ ■

When Cultural Assumptions about Texts and Reading Fail: Teaching Talmud as Liberal Arts

Elizabeth Shanks Alexander

How do undergraduates with superficial or no previous exposure to Judaic texts learn to read the Talmud in translation within the context of a liberal arts education? This question has actively shaped my teaching of Introduction to Talmud at the University of Virginia since I first offered the course in 2001. Students opt to take this course for all sorts of reasons, which range from a genuine and enduring interest in the topic to purely pragmatic considerations (e.g., it helps them fulfill a requirement and fits their schedule). Typically, 15-25% of students enrolled in the course are Jewish. Most of the other students come from Christian denominations, many with a strong sense of religious identity.

When teaching the course initially, as their instructor, I assumed the most important service I could provide was cultural translation. Having invested considerable energy in identifying, describing, and analyzing the Talmud's repertoire of argumentational and interpretive moves, I felt my greatest asset as a teacher was the ability *to explain* talmudic dialectic in language and concepts familiar to my students. Students from early iterations of the course had helpfully pointed out that they would have liked it if I had done more than explicate the Talmud in plain language. They explained that they were not enthusiastic about investing time and energy in the difficult task of learning *how* to read Talmud, without clarity about *why* they should care to read Talmud in the first place. As I have revised the course over the years, I have experimented with different ways to emphasize the

Talmud's relevance—for Jewish culture writ large, but also for them, whomever they may be, Jewish or not, religious in any tradition or not. I want my students to feel positively invested in the task of reading Talmud, enough so that they stay with it, challenges and setbacks notwithstanding.

This past semester, I experimented with a new way to make Talmud study more compelling in the context of a liberal arts education. I styled the students as partners in the instructional process. I made them responsible for monitoring their own successes and failures and the pace of their development as readers of Talmud. I drew on some of L. Dee Fink's work, which I had read during an intensive summer workshop on course design several years ago. He argues that significant learning experiences have six basic components. They provide opportunities and encourage students to: (1) understand *foundational knowledge*; (2) *apply* that knowledge; (3) *integrate* course materials with other disciplines, perspectives, and subject matter; (4) learn about oneself and others (the *human dimension*); (5) *care* about the subject matter, and (6) *learn how to learn*.

Fink emphasizes that the six components of significant learning experiences are not mutually exclusive. Rather, "each kind of learning is related to the other kinds of learning and ... achieving one kind of learning simultaneously enhances the possibility of achieving the other kinds of learning. ... For example, if a teacher finds a way to help students learn how to use the information to solve certain kinds of problems effectively (application), this makes it easier for them to get excited about the value of the subject (caring)."[1] My course seeks to facilitate all components of significant learning experiences, but this past semester, I was particularly drawn to the sixth component (learning how to learn). This emphasis led me to design assignments asking students to reflect on and take responsibility for parts of the learning process. I hoped that these assignments would focus students' attention on the "how" of their reading practices and give them an opportunity to consider their effectiveness when engaging talmudic texts. This shift in pedagogic emphasis provided an interesting "hook" for the students, motivating them to work with material that was difficult and unfamiliar, even when they were manifestly discouraged, as is inevitable with beginning students of Talmud.

---

1   L. Dee Fink, *Creating Significant Learning Experiences: An Integrated Approach to Designing College Courses* (San Francisco: Jossey-Bass, A Wiley Imprint, 2003), 32; see also ibid, "A Taxonomy of Significant Learning," 27-59.

Assignments Focused on "Learning How to Learn"

In past versions of my course Introduction to Talmud, writing assignments required students to practice the tasks and drill the skills reviewed in class. For example, following a unit that presents strategies for making sense of midrashic passages, students wrote a paper demonstrating their ability to perform this task independently, using passages not discussed in class. Such an assignment emphasizes components 1 and 2 of Fink's taxonomy. Students use concepts and vocabulary presented in class (foundational knowledge) to read a midrashic passage (application). When teaching the course this time, I retained some assignments emphasizing components 1 and 2 from prior years, but I also included newly designed assignments that required students to reflect on aspects of the learning process.

In one new assignment, students were required to write a weekly 200 to 300 word posting for our class blog, to be read by their class peers and me (people outside the class did not have access to the class blogsite). The assignment was designed to alert students to the many steps involved in learning to read something as manifestly difficult and unfamiliar as Talmud. I wrote prompt questions to guide them when they sat down to compose the blog posts. The questions were designed to accomplish two things. First, I wanted to draw students' attention to various aspects of the reading experience so that they could reflect on which strategies they found to be more effective and which were less so when engaging talmudic texts. Second, I wanted to nudge them gently toward strategies that I thought would serve them well when engaging these texts. Students had the freedom to respond to whichever prompt they felt would be most generative in a given week.

Below are the prompts that I gave the students; each is followed by a brief commentary about the pedagogical motivations for these prompts:

1. What was confusing, counterintuitive, or simply opaque to you from the reading? Where and why do you think the breakdown in understanding occurred? What is it about the text that makes it hard for you to understand? Alternatively, what makes you a less-than-ideal recipient of the text's meaning?

The first question in this prompt reflects my view that effective learning occurs when students *focus on* rather than *skim over* difficulties. Students may be tempted to ignore the discomfort of not understanding something in the hope that the feeling will soon pass. At some point in the middle of the semester, I realized that students experience mild shame when they do not understand course materials. This prompt creates a space *within the learning process* for experiencing failure without shame. I want students to recognize that I do not expect them to succeed the first time or all the time and that frustration can be a source of insight. Their "failures" may actually guide them toward future success. The follow-up questions in this prompt encourage students to reflect on the reasons for their difficulty. The last question (What makes you a less-than-ideal recipient?) helps students recognize that their *assumptions* about the goals and process of reading may impede their success with Talmud, a book that comes from a culture very different from their own. I want students to recognize that culturally conditioned assumptions about what reading is and how it is done can impact reading outcomes.

2. Summarize what you take to be the key point of the assigned secondary source. Be generous in your reconstruction of the author's internal logic. How does the article help you make sense of the primary texts? What "tip" or "trick" can you glean from it?

This prompt is designed to communicate the value of secondary sources in the project of learning to read Talmud. The prompt steers students toward the "tips" and "tricks" within the article that will help them make sense of the primary texts. Each in-class lecture introduces students to a feature of talmudic discourse (e.g., Mishnah's tendency to arrange traditions topically and obscure the biblical roots of the legal tradition) and showcases one or more illustrative examples of this feature. This second prompt encourages students to anticipate the lecture and "teach themselves" what to look for and what to regard as significant in the primary source selections.

3. Reflect on your reading process. What was the first thing you did when you encountered the primary text? What did you do next? Which steps were more effective and which were less? Was there a certain point at which the text started to make sense? When and why?

Alternatively, did the text never make sense? Why do you think that happened?

This set of questions expands on a theme from the first prompt, namely, that how one reads is culturally conditioned. The questions help students identify the assumptions that govern their own reading practice by tuning in to what they actually do when they sit down to read. The questions promote heightened awareness of the concrete ways in which students interact with texts. Additionally, the questions prompt an evaluative process in which the students distinguish between more and less successful approaches to reading the text.

4. Tell us about a detail that caught your eye in a primary text. What makes this detail compelling and noteworthy? What does it reveal about the text's commitments, concerns, or resolutions? Why does it resonate with you?

The fourth prompt offers students a specific strategy to employ when interacting with talmudic texts—asking them to focus on a concrete detail. Over the years, I have observed that students naturally gravitate toward some reading strategies over others. It is not uncommon for students to accord greater importance to the general themes of a text than to specific details featured in the text. While gathering-up general themes and trends is important, *reading for generalities* has limited utility when interacting with talmudic texts, which typically are structured around very specific questions and numerous textual details. This prompt encourages students to allow specific textual details, rather than overarching themes, to guide the reading experience.

In addition to the weekly blog post, a second assignment was inspired by the goal of helping students "learn how to learn." In the final paper, I asked students to narrate their development as a reader of Talmud over the course of the semester. I directed them to address the following issues in their narrations:

1. What is the difference between how you approached these texts at the beginning of the semester and how you approach them now? What were you engaging in the texts initially? What do you notice now? What did you expect of yourself then and now? What were key moments of insights for you? Which insights led to other insights?

2. What did you learn about yourself as a reader? Are the skills you gained in the process of learning to read Talmud transferrable? If yes, how are they transferrable? If not, why?
3. Which reading had the most impact on you? Which class discussion? Which blog post felt most like a breakthrough?

Students were instructed to illustrate moments of key insight with reference to specific primary texts. The requirement that students cite and discuss specific primary texts ensured that my focus on the sixth component of Fink's taxonomy (learning how to learn) did not come at the expense of more traditional pedagogical goals, generally understood in terms of the first two components of the taxonomy (foundational knowledge and application). Students would have to demonstrate competence in reading texts in order to narrate the process by which they came to be able to do so.

Two distinct concerns led me to design these assignments. First, as I have already explained, I wanted to provide students with a forum in which the process of learning itself would be a focal point. I hoped that incorporating a "learning how to learn" component into the course would increase students' integration of the course content, as per Fink's suggestion that different kinds of learning mutually reinforce each other. Ideally, having students focus on the process of learning to read would also help them (1) master foundational knowledge central to Talmud study, (2) apply that knowledge to the reading of texts, (3) develop a new passion for Talmud study or strengthen an existing one, (4) reflect on connections between Talmud study and other subjects, and (5) ultimately, learn something about themselves.

My second motivation in developing the new assignments was to provide a source of data (in the form of student testimonials) for *my* reflection on the process whereby my students were learning to read Talmud. In the body of this chapter, I report on two themes that emerged as I reviewed, sifted through, and synthesized the students' blog posts and final papers. One trope that returned in various ways concerns the manner in which students focus their attention when reading. Their natural tendency seems to have been to read with the goal of perceiving an overarching narrative, or a general sense of the whole. Students reported that this approach to reading led to frustration when working with talmudic texts. Over the course of the semester, they realized that they needed to shift their focus from the big picture to textual details in order to read talmudic texts effectively. A second prevalent theme is best understood in terms of students' underlying assumption about what texts are and what they do. Students' natural tendency here seems to have been to regard texts as *things*. When texts are understood in this manner, the goal of reading is to grasp or hold the "thing." That is, students want to know what the text "is"—what it claims or what it means. In order to become successful readers of Talmud, students reported having to learn to regard the texts differently, namely, as providing access to a "thinking process." Students found that the texts made much more sense to them when they read them in order to *experience the thought process* that lies behind them. That is, they succeeded as readers when they understood the act of reading as a means to reproduce and experience anew the thoughts and arguments of the talmudic sages. In this new paradigm, reading prompts an *experience* of thinking and arguing.

It appears that culturally conditioned ideas about texts and reading shaped what they did when they sat down with a text, what they looked for when reading, and what they expected to gain from interacting with a text. Data from this course, then, suggests that one can maximize students' success if one encourages them first to observe their instinctive and culturally conditioned ways of interacting with texts, and subsequently to modify them. When students become aware of their natural patterns of engaging texts, they strengthen their capacity to intervene deliberately and adopt a set of learned practices better suited to Talmud.

My Goal for the Students

I measured my students' success as readers of Talmud by their ability to read, understand, and explain the back and forth of a complex dialectical argument by semester's end. I did not expect my students to be able to achieve understanding independently; rather, I wanted them to be able to follow my explanations of the material to the extent that they could accurately explicate the text in their own words. The choice to emphasize competency in reading halakhic passages, rather than aggadic, reflects my desire to equip students to make sense of the Talmud's *overarching discursive framework*. I do not want my students to experience Talmud as a series of disconnected aphorisms or sage stories, though these genres offer significant insight into the thought world of the talmudic sages. Rather, I want students to be able to make sense of the Talmud as a *genre of literature*. By familiarizing them with dialectical interests, devices, and movements that reappear throughout the Talmud, I am giving students tools to enter the Talmud's meandering conversations on any page, provided they receive guidance in the specific topics treated.

Rava and Abaye's discussion of *yeush shelo midaat* (see my translation of this phrase below) centers on the question of whether the owner of an object needs to be aware of having lost it in order for the object to become "ownerless." A lost object's status as ownerless determines the finder's rights and obligations with respect to the object. If a lost object is ownerless, the finder becomes its legal owner. If the object is not ownerless, the finder must advertise the find so that the owner may claim the object, as it still belongs to him. In order for the lost object to become ownerless, the original owner must despair of having it returned to him. The question that the sugya deals with is whether an object can become ownerless in the interval between when the owner loses the object and he becomes aware of his loss. If such a lost object is considered ownerless, the finder may keep it. If it is not considered ownerless, the finder may not.

Rava and Abaye agree that when the owner is *aware* of his loss he despairs of its return, the lost object becomes ownerless, and the finder may keep it. They disagree in the case of an owner who is *not aware* of his loss. Being unaware of his loss, the owner cannot despair of retrieving it. Abaye says that when the owner is unaware of his loss, the original owner retains ownership rights, and the finder does not become the object's new owner. Rava has a different approach. Confident that the owner will eventually become aware of the loss and despair of its return, Rava invents the concept of *yeush shelo midaat* (despair without [conscious] knowledge). This concept allows Rava to regard the lost object as ownerless *at the moment that the finder discovers it, even though the owner has not yet consciously despaired of retrieving it*. Since the object is ownerless when the finder discovers it, he becomes its rightful owner. Rava uses the concept of *yeush shelo midaat* to grant ownership to the finder in cases where the owner is not aware of his loss when the finder discovers it.

Abaye, on the other hand, disallows the concept of *yeush shelo midaat* and argues that the finder takes legal possession only when the owner actually despairs of retrieving the object.

In this sugya, Rava and Abaye bring authoritative sources (mishnayot, baraitot, and halakhic midrash) to support their respective positions on the concept *yeush shelo midaat*. We read this argument on the last two days of class. In order to follow the argument, students needed to have mastered an extensive body of knowledge and skills. They need to be able to:

1. Identify and distinguish among different textual strata within the sugya (tannaitic, amoraic, and stammaitic)
2. Understand how mishnayot, baraitot, and halakhic midrash are interpreted to support the respective positions of Rava and Abaye
3. Recognize that the tannaitic sources cited in the sugya can be legitimately understood in more than one way
4. Understand some fine points of Jewish law, such as the difference between ownership and being a guardian for the owner
5. Grasp that the *point* of the argument is not to adjudicate between the two positions, but to appreciate how each sage uses the same authoritative sources to support his own position

Reading this sugya serves as a wonderful culminating exercise for the students. In order to do a successful reading of the argument, students need to have mastered and integrated terms and concepts from throughout the course, as the above skill list illustrates. Gratifyingly, the students' final blog posts[2] reflect many feelings of accomplishment at the semester's end. Georgia[3] writes, "First of all, I would just like to state that this is the first time I've read the primary text and turned to the secondary text with an understanding of the former that was RIGHT ON!" Michala subsequently writes, "I have to start by

---

2 I have introduced minor edits into the blog posts for ease of reading and focus. For example, I do not include ellipses where I have skipped over a few words or sentences to get to the main point. I have also corrected spelling mistakes, as the blog posts reflect unedited writing. I have not, however, corrected diction, usage, or capitalization patterns to conform with professional scholarly standards, as I want readers to be able to access the students' voices in as authentic terms as possible.

3 I have changed the names of all students to preserve anonymity and their privacy.

congratulating Georgia. … Her 'ah-ha' moment was very well expressed through her post, and I enjoyed reading about it. It's fun to see that we're all progressing in our journey to understand the world of Talmud study." Their joy is palpable. Caitlin echoes these sentiments in her post, "I would say that, by far, this was my most enjoyable reading. I felt that I somewhat experienced a partial review of everything I have learned. I could see the beit midrash of the Amoraim come to life [in the argument between Rava and Abaye]."

Big Picture versus Textual Details

The accomplishments at semester's end did not come easily to my students. Culturally conditioned habits developed in other classroom settings and when reading other literatures did not necessarily serve them well when reading talmudic texts. They had to become aware of what they were doing instinctively that was not productive for Talmud if they were deliberately to cultivate an alternate set of reading practices. One habit that students grappled with is the tendency to gloss over details in the hope of stabilizing meaning by detecting an overarching narrative. Listen to Georgia as she begins to recognize what she is doing and how this glossing over does not serve her well when reading talmudic materials for this course. Her post was composed one month into the semester. (I have added numbers to her text that clarify the order in which she performed the tasks she set for herself as she worked through the reading. Note that task 5 is mentioned after task 6. The numbers correspond to the order in which she *performed* the tasks, not the order in which she *narrates* them):

> (1) The first thing I did when reading B. Bava Metsia 59b was quickly read through the passage in an attempt to get the "gist" of what it was saying. I was startled by how I wanted to know what the text meant right then and there after breezing through it only once. (2) Then, I read through it much slower. I read each paragraph carefully, restating each sentence's meaning in my head before moving onto the next sentence, and then restating each paragraph's meaning before moving onto the next. If I couldn't get the full meaning of the paragraph or didn't understand a sentence after trying to re-word it to myself, I would look to the

When Cultural Assumptions about Texts and Reading Fail | CHAPTER 6

next paragraph or sentence to see if it could shed light on the part I was confused by. (3) Then, I wrote down any questions I had for that section or new questions for other sections, in light of the information I had just read. (4) Finally, I read the passage in its entirety to see if I got answers to my questions. Halfway through this step—right after re-reading the whole passage and at the start of processing through it—my friend texted me to say he was in my parking lot waiting to pick me up for dinner. So—more so by chance than by choice—(6) I was forced to return to the text a few days later, at which time (5) I read the other primary texts and the secondary source.

The more effective steps in my learning process included the second step (2) of reading really slowly, trying to gain understanding for each piece of information before moving to the next, as well as the last (unintentional) step (6) of returning to the piece at a later time and re-reading it alongside prior notes and questions. I learned that reading a passage quickly to get the gist of it before rereading it slower (step 1) didn't really aid my learning. Though I gained more understanding of the text by re-reading it slower the second time (step 2), I don't think that the text really started to make sense until I re-read it a third time that day (step 4), and a fourth time today (step 6). I think this is because I only could understand the whole of the text by first understanding it in bits and then combining [those] bits together slowly to form a whole. Additionally, I had read the secondary source packet (step 5) the fourth time (step 6) I read it and had also given my brain a break from strongly focusing on the text, both of which gave me a clearer head while reading. This has made me very self-aware as a learner, as I've found myself trying to implement what worked well and avoid what didn't work well in readings for other classes this week.

Georgia's first instinct was to read the text in a superficial manner to "get the gist." She hopes to gain a sense of the whole by reading quickly and glossing over details. She reasons that if she can identify an overarching narrative or structure, she will know what to do with the myriad of details she encounters. While this assumption may serve her well with other literatures, it frustrates her when reading this talmudic passage: "I was startled by how

I wanted to know what the text meant right then and there, after breezing through it only once". Georgia finds that she cannot get a sense of the whole without painstakingly attending to details. She does much better when she "reads each [sentence and] paragraph carefully," making sure not to move to the next sentence or paragraph until she has a grasp of the current one. She finds that she can "only understand the whole of the text by first understanding it in bits and then combining bits together slowly to form a whole." Georgia is aided in her ability to fit the bits into a whole by having read the secondary source. Reading the secondary source eliminates many potential ways to configure the bits and offers a few suggestive patterns. In the end, Georgia achieves a sense of the whole, but she has to work in unfamiliar ways.

The final paper of another student reflects on an initial resistance to reading slowly and paying attention to details. Like Georgia, Anna finds it helpful to review the text several times.

> I had to adapt my reading strategies in order to better understand the [Mishnah]. Taking the time to [look up the biblical sources of a mishnah] was new for me. I also realized that I needed to slow down and read deliberately and with intention. Full comprehension was not attainable if I was reading under a time constraint or if I was distracted. Under those circumstances, I would read on a superficial level, in which simply getting the words into my head was my main goal. Realizing this flaw forced me to create a new strategy that involved multiple readings, each with a different focus. The first reading was the same, in that I read for content alone, but in addition, I would read a second, if not also a third, to focus on questions such as: Why is this information grouped together? What is the significance of word choice and repetition? What has been extrapolated from the biblical text?

Anna finds that she has to "adapt [her] reading strategies" in order to make sense of the Mishnah. Her observation that reading on a "superficial level" is nothing more than "getting the words into my head" echoes Georgia's sense of the futility of quickly skimming through the text. Though one hears hints of mild resistance to the practice of looking up the biblical sources of the Mishnah, Anna's reading is enriched by engaging such details. Like Georgia, Anna also benefits from multiple readings, each one achieving a different degree of integration. Only on the second or third time through the text can she address questions that reveal what is interesting about the passage: "Why is this information grouped together? What is the significance of word choice and repetition? What has been extrapolated from the biblical text?"

Michala also has to fight a natural tendency to skim over details that slow her down. The following post was composed about three-quarters of the way through the course:

> For my reflection, I decided to address a problem that I tend to have with the primary readings in this course as someone who comes from an Episcopalian faith. Plainly put, I don't usually know *what* I'm reading. I might understand what I'm reading *about*, but I often make it through an entire piece without even knowing *what* I'm reading. In the Episcopal Church, we work with the Bible and the Book of Common Prayer. When it comes to studying, the Bible is the only text we focus on. Judaism has much more material, all of which is referred to by different names. I'm still training myself to take the time to figure out *what* I'm reading when I sit down with a primary text from Judaism as opposed to immediately jumping into the content.
>
> When I first sat down with the syllabus, I noted the assigned text, "m. Shevu'ot, chapter 3." I knew that the 'm' signified this piece to be part of the Mishnah. This might seem insignificant, but considering we've been looking at texts that start with familiar names like "Genesis" or "Exodus" [as in Genesis or Exodus Rabbah], as well as unfamiliar things like "b. Baba," a little "m" can really help differentiate texts. I flipped back to my notes from our last class and refreshed my memory on the differences between midrash and mishnah. We have been reading a lot of midrash, especially in preparation for our papers, so I wanted to make sure I was clear on the difference. I recalled from my notes that the Mishnah [had] a topical arrangement [that] brought together all the verses on a particular topic from many different sources. So, in our reading for today, I could expect one main topic as the subject and explanations and clarifications brought together by many sources. I noted from the primary packet that the Shebuoth was part of the Tractate Nezikin. A quick Google search revealed that this was part of the Mishnah's order on civil damages.

In the first paragraph, Michala admits that she often skims over cumbersome information. It "takes time to figure out *what* [she's] reading," and until now, she has not felt that time spent in this manner is a worthwhile investment. Underlying her disinclination to clarify the name of the document from which she reads is her assumption that such details are irrelevant to understanding the text properly. Michala accounts for her inattention to detail by referring to a feature of her religious upbringing. When people engage text in her church, they do not need to pay attention to which book they are reading, as all readings are drawn from the same book ("the Bible is the only text we focus on"). Like Georgia and Anna, Michala resists taking the time to focus on details that initially appear trivial. She finds that she is well served, however, when she slows down and pays attention to the "little m." She returns to her notes from the previous class to recall salient features of the Mishnah—for example, that it had a topical arrangement that beneficially informs her subsequent reading of the primary sources ("I could expect one main topic as the subject").

My last student example, Derek, likewise develops as a reader of Talmud when he shifts his gaze from the "big picture" to smaller units of text:

> I came into this class with the most questions about the process of talmudic argumentation. I had read passages from Talmud in previous classes, and had looked at Mishnah and Baraitas. However, whenever I attempted to approach one of these passages, I was always driven towards a summary or some other abridgement.

Unlike a number of other students in the class, Derek had enough prior exposure to Talmud to have a particular interest in "the process of talmudic argumentation." Derek's previous experiences, however, did not give him reading strategies to make sense of argumentation. One guesses he may have encountered Talmud in an excerpted format, perhaps in the form of pithy wisdom sayings or sage stories. Derek shares with the other students an initial resistance to focusing on details. The fact that he "was always driven towards a summary or some other abridgement" reflects his assumption that a text is most effectively amalgamated when it is stripped of its particularities and reframed in generic terms. Derek does not seem to know what to do with textual details aside from moving quickly past them as distractions to a higher understanding. He grows as a reader, however, when he learns to focus on, rather than gloss over, textual details:

> What was pivotal for me was the Boyarin article. Specifically, Daniel Boyarin states that the semiotic elements of the Torah "function for the rabbis much as words do in ordinary speech." This really illustrated an important reading strategy for the rabbis, atomization. It helped me to think of the Torah, not as a collection of tales from different authors nor as a linear and coherent narrative, but as a series of passages, which Boyarin describes as being like a dictionary. Each phrase from the Torah can operate as an independent lexeme in Midrash and Mishnah.

This passage captures Derek in the process of learning to see biblical verses through the lenses of the rabbis "as a series of passages" that (in Boyarin's words) "function for the rabbis much as words do in ordinary speech."[4] Mastering the rabbinic genre of midrash means learning to see the Torah through the eyes of the rabbis. Derek observes that the rabbis atomize biblical verses and then combine the atomized bits so that each "operate[s] as an independent lexeme in Midrash and Mishnah." The atomized bits become the "words" of rabbinic discourse. For Derek, reading Torah like a rabbi entails engaging textual details in a new way. Textual details are no longer trivial data to be subordinated to a larger narrative framework ("tales" or "a linear and coherent narrative"). In order to experience fragments of biblical verses as the building blocks of rabbinic discourse, Derek must attend to, rather than gloss over or reduce, their particularity.

Each of these students initially resists focusing on textual details. They regard textual detail as something to be transcended, at best, and a minor nuisance to be quickly dispensed with, at worst. Instinctively, they find it easier to read for big ideas and themes. Each finds, however, that making sense of midrash, Mishnah, and Talmud requires giving into, rather than fighting, the details. A usable sense of the whole cannot be achieved unless they engage and address textual detail.

---

4 Daniel Boyarin, *Intertextuality and the Reading of Midrash* (Bloomington: Indiana University Press, 1990), 28.

CHAPTER 6 | Elizabeth Shanks Alexander

The Fallacy of One Right Answer and the Importance of "Process"

A second challenge that my students faced came from the assumption that texts have one correct meaning and from using their instinct to organize reading around the task of finding that one meaning. Reading in this manner did not position students to make sense of the texts easily. In reviewing Michala's mid-semester blog post, one can see her reading of midrash is structured as a quest for the right answer:

> I was confused by Genesis R[abbah] 1.4. This passage is discussing whether the Torah or the Throne of Glory was created first. Many opinions about the correct answer are expressed through quotes. However, I simply don't understand which one is determined to be the right one. Is there a right answer?

Michala expects her reading of the midrash to resolve into a single "correct" view. She effectively identifies the passage's subject matter (the place of the Torah and the Throne of Glory in the order of creation), but is less successful at understanding the purpose of the midrash's discussion. Assuming that the text aims to convey a "correct answer" to readers, she is frustrated that she cannot discern it. Eventually, Michala learns to structure her reading of midrash around the *insight it provides into* rather than *the answer it offers about* biblical verses. In this excerpt from her final paper, she explains how she was able to move beyond the frustration expressed above:

> In lecture, I was introduced to [the idea that] multiple answers do not cloud one's understanding, as I had originally thought, but rather provide readers of Midrash with different ways of making sense of the material. My notes serve as evidence of the moment during class when the light bulb went off—There is <u>no</u> accepted view! But now we know the text in a deeper way. So the goal is to know the text better.

In Michala's new way of thinking, midrash helps the reader "know the [biblical] text in a deeper way." Michala makes peace with the fact that the passage does not make clear whether the Torah or the Throne of Glory was created first, because she realizes midrash offers her something else instead. It familiarizes her with the biblical verses that support each position, which she learns to read in new ways. Though she formerly glossed over certain details as insignificant, she now regards them as the basis for each unique position. Michala no longer reads midrash to learn answers. Her new orientation is to use midrash to "know the [biblical] text better."

Anna's learning trajectory is also shaped by an initial assumption, which she must first recognize and then suspend—that texts have a single meaning readers should acquire in the act of reading. Like Michala, she writes in her final paper that she "had to embrace [the fact] that sometimes there is no right answer to a question and that significance is found in the process of [seeking] explanation." In her new way of thinking, reading stimulates a "process of explanation." As she formulates the matter, the goal of reading is not acquiring a *thing* ("the answer"), but having an *experience* ("a process"). In the final papers, several students (including Anna and Michala) retrospectively realize and adopt a new found focus on "process" as central to their eventual success, as opposed to what they variously call "answers," "content," and "literal meaning." Michala, whose frustration is evident in the mid-semester blog post we read above, also resolves her problem by shifting the focus of her reading from finding "answers" to experiencing "process." In the final paper excerpted above, she distances herself from her former orientation and explains that "the goal is not always to get a clear answer. When it comes to Talmud study, the point is to interact with the Torah in a special way, to see the beauty in many different perspectives, and to understand the thought processes involved in arriving at those perspectives." Michala's new perspective is that one reads to "understand the thought processes" of the sages whose "conversations" are recorded in the Talmud. Reading is now about recreating and experiencing anew a conversation implied by the Talmud's words. The words do not carry meaning in and of themselves. Instead, they are clues from which she recreates what she, later in the paper (and not quoted in this chapter), calls the "original 'thrust and parry' that took place in the study houses."

Excerpts from Caitlin's final paper eloquently and passionately identify the same shift in perspective—from a focus on "content" to one on "process"—as

CHAPTER 6 | Elizabeth Shanks Alexander

central to her success as a reader of Talmud. The paper's introduction sets out basic ideas that she explores in the body of the paper:

> Coming into the course, I failed to realize that the course objective was to understand the Talmud's study process just as much as the Talmud's content. I focused on the historical and intellectual framework surrounding the primary texts we were examining. My failure to grasp the full objective skewed my encounter with all the materials up until when midrash was introduced. When midrash was presented as an intellectual disposition from which the rabbis read the Torah, as well as a literary record of that activity, my eyes for the Talmud were opened and I finally saw it for what it was: a beautiful literary record of the live arguments that went on in the Amoraic beit midrash, arguments that went on in order to keep Written Torah alive through a continual creation of Oral Torah.

Here, Caitlin distinguishes between two approaches to reading: one that seeks to understand the text's "study process" and the other approach, only its "content." Since the course is called Introduction to Talmud, she, as a student, expects it to familiarize her with the Talmud's content, and, initially, she orients her study toward that goal. By focusing on the "historical and intellectual framework surrounding the primary texts," she engages Talmud through the familiar paradigm of its content. By semester's end, however, she approaches the Talmud with a different end in mind. Seeing it now as a "literary record of live arguments," she seeks to replicate the rabbis' experience as thinkers, readers, and arguers in their own right. Adopting the "disposition from which the rabbis read the Torah" enables her to think the thoughts that they thought. Her new approach focuses on the "Talmud's study process" (i.e., the study process that lies behind the text) over and against its content. In the body of the paper, Caitlin returns to this key moment of insight:

> Then, on the day, in the class, in the very moment that Professor Alexander explained midrash as a "literary record of the intellectual activity of reading in a midrashic way," the Talmud and the activity of Talmud study

was forevermore transformed in my heart and mind; in that one moment, it all came alive, and I saw all the puzzle pieces fall together (Cox, notes). For the first time in the course, I was freed to fully to see what we were doing with our class: we were studying a record of a form of study. Unlike my other academic classes, we did not have to take sides and pick a perspective from within a debate and argue why one [view] was right over another.

The unstated question that Caitlin grapples with here is, "What is a text and to what does it point?" In other classes, texts inform her about issues that can be debated. She learns in those classes more about the issues by "picking a perspective and arguing why it is right." There, the goal is to understand "the thing," that is, the issues, to which the text points. When texts point to things, they are ontologically singular. That is why Caitlin is instructed to pick only one perspective to argue. The instruction to argue a single perspective resonates with Michala and Anna's preoccupation with the task of identifying the correct answer. They too expect texts to point to a single thing, "the answer." My course offers Caitlin a different way to think about texts. According to the new paradigm, texts point to an "intellectual activity." The delight in her voice is palpable as she realizes, "we were studying a record of a form of study." The implication here is that in class we were not studying a subject, informational content, or a perspective that could be held, acquired, or disputed. Rather, we were engaging in an experience that consisted of reliving the rabbis' study process.

Conclusion

The students whose voices appear in this chapter embraced and succeeded at the assignments that emphasized "learning how to learn." They used the blog posts and their final papers to cultivate awareness of both habits and assumptions that shape them as readers. For these students, the sixth component of Fink's taxonomy of significant learning experiences worked in conjunction with his other components in a mutually reinforcing manner. Students came to care about the subject matter. Recall Michala's enthusiasm for Georgia's success with her "Ah-ha! moment" and the success of the entire class at the end of the semester, as they followed each other "on-blog." Students also connected what they were doing in this course to work from other courses, as we saw in an early blog post from Georgia, who said, "I've found myself trying to implement what worked well and avoid what didn't work well in readings for other classes this week." And students mastered foundational knowledge and learned to apply it. Students also learned about themselves, as becomes apparent in a last excerpt of Anna's final paper at the conclusion of this essay.

Collectively, the student reflections cited in this chapter offer a relatively coherent account of some of the cultural assumptions about texts and reading that cause difficulties for liberal art students who are learning to read Talmud for the first time. My students at the University of Virginia learned about what they intuitively focus on "seeing" when they read a text (an overarching narrative) and what they assiduously ignore (textual details). They also learned about what they expected a text to provide them (answers or content, as opposed to access to a study process). Armed with increased alertness, curiosity, and a newly found respect for *how* to read, these students were able to self-intervene and adopt assumptions about texts and reading that are better suited to interact productively with Talmud. They came to understand that when reading Talmud they were not aiming to achieve the same things as when reading other literatures.

As is inevitable, of course, not all students in the course were as strong as the ones featured in this chapter, and not all students were enamored with this approach to teaching Talmud. One disgruntled student wrote in the anonymous online evaluations that "the central conceit of self-evaluation and changing the way we thought seemed grandiose and overblown, and the results were completely underwhelming. I would have learned way more about Talmud from a traditional lecture." These reservations notwithstanding, on the whole, students found the course worthwhile. When asked by the online course evaluation system to reflect on the statement "I learned a great deal in this course," 85% of students indicated that they "strongly agree," while the remaining 15% indicated that they "agree." In comparable courses,[5] only 53% state that they "strongly agree." By all measures, then, the course succeeded in effectively conveying course content to the students.

It is important to recognize that most of the students who took this course are not likely to find themselves reading Talmud again soon. For them, the course's value should not be measured in Talmud-specific terms, but in what they take forward. The final paragraph of Anna's final paper offers a nice summary of how an Introduction to Talmud course at a large public university can contribute to the broad goals of a liberal arts education:

> I learned a lot this semester about how I personally read and relate to [all] texts. I began to develop a more patient understanding [of how to interact with texts; my new method is] characterized by multiple readings, synthesis, and dedication. I found that understanding does not come without effort, and that, sometimes, even effort cannot clear obscurities. I became more comfortable asking questions and admitting confusion, a skill I have never had to cultivate until this course. The most important skill I have acquired is the ability to see where my presuppositions are at odds with the methods I need to employ to analyze this material. Looking at a first-century or a seventh-century document through a twenty-first century lens prevented me from appreciating the perspective of authors of the [ancient texts]. It was hard to admit when my learning methods failed me, but it was with that failure that I reinvented my approach to the texts.

Anna's summary of what she learned from this course is firmly connected to the goals of the course. She developed habits of engaging texts that are particularly well suited to Talmud. For example, she formed an approach that includes "multiple readings, synthesis, and dedication" and she came to recognize where her "presuppositions are at odds ... [with] the perspective of the [ancient authors]." And yet, Anna frames her insights in a manner that

---

5 Evaluation data on all 3000-level courses taught during the semester in question at the University of Virginia's Department of Religious Studie was provided in conjunction with the results of my own course for comparative purposes.

makes clear that these new habits have relevance moving forward. She has a new willingness to ask questions, admit confusion, and live with uncertainty, as when she admits that "sometimes even effort cannot clear obscurities." She displays a new disposition to learning that will inform how she engages difficult tasks in the future. Even though continued Talmud study may not be in the future of this environmental science major, the course has contributed to her intellectual formation.

CHAPTER 7

Talmud in the Mouth: Oral Recitation and Repetition through the Ages and in Today's Classroom

Jonathan S. Milgram

To the memory of a master pedagogue, our colleague and teacher

Professor Dov Zlotnick z"l, *'the Tanna of Riverdale'*

Talmud scholars have recognized the fundamental role of oral recitation and repetition in the production, publication, and dissemination of rabbinic literature from the rabbinic to the geonic period. The part played by oral recitation and repetition in educational settings in centuries past, however, has been of lesser academic concern. Certainly, the simulation of ancient and medieval models of recitation and repetition in the context of the contemporary classroom has been, for the most part, ignored.[1] The goal of this article is to chart and discuss the presumed functions of oral recitation and repetition in tannaitic, amoraic, and geonic educational contexts and entertain the possible benefits reaped from the integration of age-old study models into my contemporary college classroom. That is, to answer the question, "Can the imitation of these methods benefit modern pedagogy and contemporary students?"—and, if so, "How may these methods help my students learn how to read Talmud?"

---

1 The primary exception is the recent strategy of Pinchas Hayman employed for the study of Mishnah. See the summary of these methods, "Conference on Teaching Rabbinic Literature," http://www.brandeis.edu/mandel/teachingrabbinics/abstracts.html#Anchor-The-7200. I thank Jon Levisohn for bringing this approach to my attention.

CHAPTER 7 | Jonathan S. Milgram

In my undergraduate class, Sugyot about Sukkot, taught at the Albert A. List College of Jewish Studies, the secular Jewish Studies college of the Jewish Theological Seminary,[2] I used a method of group oral recitation and repetition similar to what is known in contemporary education as "choral reading."[3] First, I read the talmudic discussion, or sugya, out loud, section-by-section, and the entire class repeated each section in unison after me (for a detailed description, see below, "The Course and Its Goals"). The regular incorporation of this class exercise was meant, in part, to simulate the oration of texts assumed by scholars to have taken place during the tannaitic, amoraic, and geonic periods (first century CE-eleventh century CE).

Admittedly, there is an inherent anachronism in my imitation of ancient and medieval exercises in the context of the contemporary classroom under the guise of approximating what the talmudic sages and their textual inheritors, the geonim, practiced. Unquestionably, we cannot reproduce—in any real sense—whatever took place in the classrooms of the academies of yore, since we know so little about the activities of those educational settings, and our contemporary pedagogic framework is so dramatically different.[4] Unfortunately, the historical truths will be concealed from us forever. We can, however, experiment with the imitation of these presumed practices—especially when we observe the benefits of these methods to our students' education, as simulation can result in stimulation.

Below, I first explore some aspects of oral recitation and repetition in the educational contexts of the tannaim and amoraim and, the later geonim. Following, I introduce my college course and the goals I set out

---

2   3080 Broadway, New York, NY.
3   I wish to thank Ms. Lisa Schlaff, Director of Judaic Studies, SAR High School, Riverdale, NY, for first introducing this term to me when I once described to her how I intuited conducting my Talmud class. In searching for bibliography on choral reading, the following article by Joyce K. McCauley and Daniel S. McCauley, "Using Choral Reading to Promote Language Learning for ESL Students," *The Reading Teacher* 45 (March 1992): 526-33, served my needs exceptionally well and meaningfully informed the discussion herein.
4   One obvious distinction is that the tannaim, amoraim, and geonim recited and repeated oral texts. They had no written or printed exemplars in front of them. In my classroom, of course, we used printed editions. Regarding the situation among the rishonim, see the Addendum.

for my students. Finally, I explain the actual process of recitation and repetition that took place during each class session and discuss why I think that the incorporation of these methods enhanced my students' educational experience, enabled the accomplishment of the academic goal to read and comprehend Talmud better, and even solidified the students' appreciation of talmudic literature. As evidence, I draw from the students' course evaluations.

Oral Recitation and Repetition through the Ages

In his seminal study, "The Publication of the Mishnah,"[5] Saul Lieberman argued that the Mishnah was never published in writing,[6] only orally,[7] and suggested how the Mishnah was published and disseminated *viva voce* in antiquity. In one notable instance, he entertained the role[8] of orality in the educational context of the tannaim, saying that when the master taught his disciples:

> [h]e taught the new Mishnah to the first Tanna; afterwards he taught it to the second Tanna ... then to the third etc. ... After the ... Tannaim knew it thoroughly by heart, they repeated it in the college in the presence of the master who supervised its recitation, corrected it ... and gave it its final form.[9]

---

5   Saul Lieberman, "The Publication of the Mishnah," in *Hellenism in Jewish Palestine* (New York: Jewish Theological Seminary, 1950), 83-99.
6   This did not mean, argued Lieberman, that some writing of traditions did not exist; see Lieberman, "Publication," 87, where he discussed the private notes of students. However, in a more recent consideration of the data, Yaakov Sussmann argued that, in fact, tannaitic and amoraic rabbinic culture were qualitatively different from other contemporaneous societies that employed both oral and written media. According to Sussman, writing was not at all used by the rabbis in the creation or transmission of halakhic traditions. See Yaakov Sussmann, " '*Torah shebeal peh,*' *peshutah kemashmaah: koḥo shel kotzo shel yod,*" in *Meḥqerei Talmud III, Part I: Talmudic Studies Dedicated to the Memory of Professor Ephraim E. Urbach,* ed. Yaakov Sussmann and David Rosenthal (Jerusalem: Magnes Press), 328.
7   For a challenge to this view, see Elizabeth Shanks Alexander, *Transmitting Mishnah: The Shaping Influence of Oral Tradition* (Cambridge: Cambridge University Press, 2006), 19-21.
8   He carefully begins his paragraph by stating, "[t]hen the procedure adopted by the master was *probably something like the following* ..." (Lieberman, "Publication," 93) [emphasis, JSM].
9   Ibid.

Lieberman hypothesized that the educational function of oral recitation and repetition in antiquity was to internalize the text by committing it to memory[10] and, later, to correct it, leading to the official and authoritative version.[11]

Yaakov Elman's recent claim for a "pervasive orality"[12] in talmudic Babylonia (fourth century CE-fifth century CE) presented a compelling corollary to Lieberman's conception regarding the earlier tannaitic period.[13] Elman asserted that the legal material found in the Babylonian Talmud was orally transmitted, and that the latest layer, made-up of dialectical and redactional elements, known as *stam hatalmud*,[14] was also orally composed.[15] As Elman correctly noted, a shift took place between the time of the production of the Babylonian Talmud's latest layers and the age of the geonim (roughly 589 CE-1038 CE), "[I]n the geonic period ... oral transmission of the Babylonian Talmud was a conscious choice, given the prevalence of book culture in Islamic Iraq."[16] Indeed, in this period, an age during which oral recitation and repetition of talmudic literature remained predominant and privileged, technologies for publishing (hand-written) books were prevalent.[17] And, despite the existence of written book publishing, the new methods seemingly did not

---

10 *Cf.* Jacob Neusner, *Oral Tradition in Judaism: The Case of the Mishnah* (New York: Garland Publishing, 1987), 102. See also Dov Zlotnick, "Memory and the Integrity of the Oral Tradition," *JANES* 16-17 (1984-85): 229-41 [=Zlotnick, *Iron Pillar Mishnah* (Jerusalem: Bialik, 1988), 51-71; see also *ibid.*, "Some Aspects of Mishnaic Repetition," 72-106].

11 Lieberman, "Publication," 87.

12 Yaakov Elman, "Orality and the Redaction of the Babylonian Talmud," *Oral Tradition* 14, no. 1 (1999): 52-99.

13 For suggestions on the possible differences between oral transmission in Palestine and Babylonia, see Martin Jaffee, *Torah in the Mouth: Writing and Oral Tradition in Palestinian Judaism 200 BCE-400 CE* (Oxford: Oxford University Press, 2001).

14 The bibliography on the nature and scope of this redactional layer is vast. For a summary of the issues, see both "Eliezer Diamond, "Rabbinics in the *New Encyclopaedia Judaica*," *Judaica Librarianship* 16, no. 17 (2011): 181-84 and Jonathan S. Milgram, "Then and Now: A Summary of Developments in the Field of Talmudic Literature through Contributions to the First and Second Editions of the *Encyclopaedia Judaica*," *Currents in Biblical Research* 11, no. 1 (October 2012): 131-33.

15 Elman, "Orality," 52.

16 Ibid., 57.

17 Ibid. See also the discussion in the magnificent study by Neil Danzig, "*Mitalmud al peh letalmud bikhtav: al derekh mesirat hatalmud habavli velimudo biyemei habeinaim,*" Bar Ilan 30-31 (2006) [=*Meir Simcha Feldblum Memorial Volume*], 49-112.

impact the oral study of Talmud among the geonim. This we are to understand from the tenth-century eye-witness account of Rabbi Nathan the Babylonian, who chronicled his visit to the geonic academies,[18] describing the educational setting in which the orally transmitted text of the Babylonian Talmud was studied. He wrote:[19]

> And when the head of the academy wants to examine them concerning their study texts (*girsa*), they gather around him in the four Sabbaths (i.e., weeks) of the month of Adar, and he sits and the first row recites before him, and the other rows sit silently ... Then he reads[20] and they are silent.

The description here is of a repetition exercise, during which the students recited to the master the text they learned, and the master subsequently recited his version of the text back to them.[21]

The central role of oral recitation and repetition in the tannaitic, amoraic, and geonic periods is clear. What remains to be examined are the possible benefits, if any, of the imitation and integration of said methods into the contemporary college classroom. The potential pedagogic gains provided by oral repetition and recitation will, in the end, define the new role of oral recitation in the next stage of its historical implementation. It is my hope that my undergraduate course, Sugyot about Sukkot, marks the humble beginnings of that next phase.

---

18 On Nathan the Babylonian and the history of his narrative, see: M. Ben-Sasson, "The Structure, Goals and Content of the Story of Nathan HaBavli," *Culture and Society in Medieval Jewry: Studies Dedicated to the Memory of Haim Hill Ben-Sasson*, ed. M. Ben-Sasson, et. al. (Jerusalem: Zalman Shazar, 1989) [Hebrew], 137-96; and the literature cited in Rober Brody, *The Geonim of Babylonia and the Shaping of Medieval Jewish Culture* (New Haven: Yale University Press, 1997), 26-30.
19 This translation is from Brody, *Geonim*, 46. For the Hebrew translation of the original Judeo-Arabic, see A. Neubauer, *Mediaeval Jewish Chronicles and Chronological Notes* (Oxford: Clarendon Press, 1895), vol. 2, 87-88.
20 Although "reading" is usually done from a written text, here the verb is used to indicate oral recitation from memory. On the use of the verb "to read" as a description of oral recitation of Talmud, see Danzig "*Mitalmud al peh*," 77. And on the possibility that here the author of the text is influenced by the use of the verb "to read" in Arabic, which can designate oral recitation, see the literature cited in Danzig, "*Mitalmud al peh*," 77, note 99.
21 On this, see Danzig, "*Mitalmud al peh*," 77-78.

CHAPTER 7 | Jonathan S. Milgram

The Course and Its Goals

The class I taught, Sugyot about Sukkot, was an undergraduate course designed for intermediate level students; that is, students with some previous exposure to Talmud study in the original. The material covered consisted of select discussions (sugyot) from the Babylonian Talmud's tractate Sukkah, relating to the fall holiday of Sukkot (known in English as the Feast of Tabernacles). The topics covered in these sugyot included the physical dimensions of the sukkah (temporary dwelling constructed for use on the holiday) (B. Sukkah 2a-2b); how many meals one is obligated to eat in the sukkah during the week-long festival (B. Sukkah 27a-27b); the required attributes of the lulav and etrog (respectively, the palm frond and citron fruit, shaken daily for the duration of the seven-day holiday) (B. Sukkah 31a-31b); the conditional gifting of the lulav to another for ritual use in expectation of its eventual return (B. Sukkah 41a); and the legality of using a stolen lulav on the first day of the holiday (B. Sukkah 29b-30a and 31a).

During the semester, the class met twice weekly for one hour and fifteen minutes. Of the nine students in the class, eight were graduates of Jewish high schools and had varying degrees of previous exposure to rabbinic texts in the original. The one student who was not a graduate of a Jewish high school took a course at the Jewish Theological Seminary in Talmud text the semester before taking my course. Certainly, none of the students had previously been taught through any method of group oral recitation and repetition. At most, some had been called on individually to read aloud from texts during high school Talmud classes.

The primary course goal was that students would be able to decode the text of the Babylonian Talmud in the original (Hebrew and Aramaic) by the end of the semester. Decoding, as I saw it in the context of this course (and other courses I teach), entailed the students mastering several skills the authors of other chapters in this volume emphasize as well:[22] (1) knowing the meaning of every individual word, in context, in the talmudic

---

22 See, for example, chapters 3 and 4 by Jane Kanarek and Marjorie Lehman, respectively, in this volume.

discussion; (2) reading the words and phrases in the original language(s) fluently; (3) pronouncing the words accurately; (4) understanding the function of technical terminology; and (5) following the flow of the logical argument presented in the text.

Recitation and Repetition in the Context of the Contemporary College Classroom

During the course of the semester, at each class session, I recited the text of the sugya, line-by-line, and the entire class repeated it *verbatim* in unison. My recitation included enunciation and inflection, emphasis on the proper pronunciation of each word in the text, and a stress on the technical role of each term and statement in the sugya. Below is a table, in which I describe the recitation and repetition exercises that took place by citing a selection of the sugya at B. Sukkah 2a in three columns (from right to left, as in Hebrew, columns I-III), with boxes representing rows (A-G). Each box in the column that is farthest right, column I, includes a discrete unit of the original text in Hebrew and Aramaic; the middle column II provides the translation[23] and, in brackets, brief explanatory remarks made by me to the students; the column that is farthest left, column III, indicates the function (question, answer, etc.) of the text in column I for that row (A, B, C, D, E, F, or G). Before presenting the text and describing the oral recitation and repetition exercise, a summary of the Talmud's discussion is in order.

The first mishnah in tractate Sukkah invalidates a sukkah whose height is more than twenty *amot* (sing., *amah*; a talmudic measurement equivalent to the length from the tip of the middle finger to the elbow, also translated as "cubit"). The subject under discussion in the talmudic sugya is: Why is a sukkah built higher than 20 *amot* not acceptable? Three amoraic opinions are cited by Rabbah, Rabbi Zeira, and Rava; and, interspersed, are two challenges by the amora Abaye. The text follows in Figure 1:

---

23 The translation is based on Isidore Epstein, ed. *The Babylonian Talmud* (London: Soncino Press, 1935-1948), with changes as I felt appropriate.

III	II	I	
Question	How do we know this? [i.e., that the maximum height of the sukkah should be 20 cubits?]	מנא הני מילי?	A
First answer	Rabbah said: for Scripture states, "That your generations may know that I made the children of Israel dwell in booths" (Lev 23:43). Until [the height of] 20 cubits, a person knows that s/he dwells in a sukkah; higher than 20 cubits, s/he does not know that s/he dwells in a sukkah, since his/her eye will not catch sight of it [i.e., the *schach*, the covering on top of the booth].	אמר רבה: דאמר קרא "למען ידעו דרתיכם כי בסכות הושבתי את בני ישראל." עד עשרים אמה - אדם יודע שהוא דר בסוכה, למעלה מעשרים אמה - אין אדם יודע שדר בסוכה, משום דלא שלטא בה עינא.	B
Second answer	Rabbi Zeira said: From here [i.e., from the following verse, it is derived], "And there shall be a sukkah for a shadow in the daytime from the heat" (Isaiah 4:6). [In a sukkah] up to 20 cubits [high] a person sits in the shade of the sukkah, [but] higher than 20 cubits, the person does not sit in the shade of the sukkah, rather in the shade of the walls.	רבי זירא אמר: מהכא "וסכה תהיה לצל יומם מחרב," עד עשרים אמה - אדם יושב בצל סוכה, למעלה מעשרים אמה - אין אדם יושב בצל סוכה, אלא בצל דפנות.	C
Challenge	Abaye said to him: Rather, from here, if a person makes his/her sukkah in *Ashtarot Karnayim* [a valley between two mountains where the sun does not shine]. [Would it] also not be a [valid] sukkah?	אמר ליה אביי: אלא מעתה, העושה סוכתו בעשתרות קרנים, הכי נמי דלא הוי סוכה? -	D
Response to challenge	He [R. Zeira] said to him [Abaye], there [i.e., in the second case], remove the *Ashtarot karnayim* and there will [still] be shade from the sukkah. Here [i.e., the first case], remove the walls of the sukkah and there is not shade from the sukkah [just shade from the walls].	אמר ליה: התם, דל עשתרות קרנים - איכא צל סוכה, הכא דל דפנות - ליכא צל סוכה.	E

Third answer	And Rava said: from here [i.e., from this verse, it is derived], "You shall dwell in sukkot seven days" (Lev. 23:42). The Torah declared, for the whole seven days leave your permanent abode and dwell in a temporary abode. [With a sukkah] up to 20 cubits [high] one makes his/her abode a temporary one; [in one] higher than 20 cubits, one does not make his/her abode temporary, rather, a permanent abode.	ורבא אמר: מהכא "בסכת תשבו שבעת ימים." אמרה תורה: כל שבעת הימים צא מדירת קבע ושב בדירת עראי. עד עשרים אמה - אדם עושה דירתו דירת עראי, למעלה מעשרים אמה - אין אדם עושה דירתו דירת עראי, אלא דירת קבע.	F
Challenge	Said Abaye to him [i.e., to Rava], rather, from here, if he made walls of iron and placed the [proper] covering over them, would [it] also not be a [valid] sukkah?	אמר ליה אביי: אלא מעתה, עשה מחיצות של ברזל וסיכך על גבן - הכי נמי דלא הוי סוכה? ...	G

Figure 1 B. Sukkah 2a.

During the oral exercises, I first read a section of text in the original; for example, IA, out loud. Then I translated the text and gave minor explanatory notes, for instance, as per IIA, and indicated whether the text being recited and repeated was a question or an answer, such as, per IIIA. Following my recitation, translation, and explanation of an entire row, i.e., IA-IIIA, the students recited only the original text, IA, out loud in unison. Then the same procedure took place for IB, IIB, and IIIB; and then for IC, IIC, and IIC, and so on, until we completed the entire sugya in this fashion. After completing the sugya, we recited and repeated only column I (e.g., IA, IB, IC, and so on)—that is, without the translation and explanation in columns II and III—multiple times, until it was clear to me that the group was able to accurately express the contents of the sugya orally in unison. By hearing the group emphasize, enunciate, and inflect, I was able to gauge the group's mastery of the text (to read more on this, see below). For the most part, because of the repetition and recitation exercises, students would immediately realize whether the statement read was a question or an answer, whether a sage was simply stating something or aggressively defending a position and whether a proof was rebutted or upheld. After the oral exercise was completed, students asked content questions about the material and, together, we consulted the commentary by Rashi printed on the side of the page in standard printed editions.[24]

In the contemporary classroom, my students and I simulated—to a certain degree—the drills described by Lieberman for tannaitic educational methods and similar exercises likely carried out in talmudic Babylonia in the context of the "pervasive orality" of the day and noted in the eyewitness account of Nathan the Babylonian. When engaging the text through oral recitation and repetition, the students affirmed that they internalized elements of the material and "owned" the texts in a qualitatively different way than if they had just read the texts out loud as individuals, with me guiding their reading and its rhetorical qualities (see student evaluations below for their testimony). I suggest that group repetition helped students to be confident in their expressive reading of the dialectics of the sugya, without any individual being "put on the spot" to perform out loud the reading of the text in front of classmates. The group performance and repetition after my recitation provided a different and comfortable experience with a positive outcome: students learned to read Talmud better. Indeed, the other side of Walter Ong's observation that "[w]riting separates the knower from the known and thus sets up conditions for 'objectivity,' in the sense of personal disengagement or distancing ..."[25] is that oral performance provides for the opposite: a cognitive closeness and unparalleled internalization of the text recited, as affirmed by student G, "[o]ne of the things I love most about Talmud is the sound, or the *niggun*, which the learning brings, the moving sound that comes out of reading the text. Hearing or imagining the tone of

---

24 Rashi's commentary was also read out loud by me or read by a student when called on. However, students were not required to repeat the text of Rashi after me. In truth, I attempted at the beginning of the semester to have the students recite Rashi's commentary after me as well. However, Rashi's syntax—while concise and precise, is still, at times, longer and less predictable than the language of the Talmud—and proved to be too clumsy and difficult for the recitation and repetition exercises. Therefore, I abandoned the idea of students repeating this text.
25 Walter Ong, *Orality and Literacy: the Technologizing of the Word* (London and New York: Methuen, 1982), 45-46.

voice that the rabbis used and repeating it out loud multiple times helps me to understand the argument of the text. Given my processing, this kind of learning helped me to better internalize the texts."

For some, the experience of oral recitation and repetition helped with, what we might term, fluency and grammatical accuracy when reading. It also provided a sense of appreciation of the Talmud's literary and intellectual program and, as a result, a connection with a broader ideal of Talmud study. As student A observed, "For me, my mistakes in punctuating the Talmud text prevent me from fully grasping the dynamics of the dialogue. Reading aloud in class helped me with punctuation and therefore also intonation. But even more than this practical matter, I think that reading the text aloud … highlights the very nature of the Talmud and, by extension, Talmud study." Indeed, this student's comments relate well to the findings of some educators regarding the benefits of oral recitation and repetition of poetry and short stories in the classroom, including matters more mechanical, such as better diction[26] and fluency.[27] The student's evaluation also expresses an increased general appreciation for the literature studied, a benefit of oral repetition and recitation documented by some reading specialists.[28] Student C emphasized a different enhancement to the ability to read Talmud, one that was provided by the oral exercises, "I think that I also had a better comprehension of what the sugya meant, because I could understand how individual words were emphasized within their sentences. So, when we spoke with certain emphasis on one word or the other, I could follow and comprehend the sentence itself better." Improved comprehension is another skill that reading teachers note students acquire through the practice of oral recitation and repetition.[29]

---

26 Donna R. Hall, "Oral Interpretation: An Approach to Teaching Secondary English," (paper presented at the joint meeting of the Central States Speech Association and the Southern Speech Communication Association, St. Louis, Missouri, 1987); cited in McCauley and McCauley, "Choral Reading," 527.
27 John M. Bradley and Mary R. Thalgott, "Reducing Reading Anxiety," *Academic Therapy* 22, no. 4 (1987) 349-58; cited in McCauley and McCauley, "Choral Reading," 527.
28 John W. Stewig, "Choral Speaking. Who has the Time?" *Childhood Education* 58, no. 1 (1981): 25-29; cited in McCauley and McCauley, "Choral Reading," 527.
29 See the bibliography noted for improved understanding and vocabulary; ibid., 527.

The effects of the pedagogic paradigm of oral recitation and repetition on retention of material by students of English as a second language are discussed by Joyce K. and Daniel S. McCauley in their study, "Using Choral Reading to Promote Language Learning for ESL Students."[30] I draw here, specifically, from the study by McCauley and McCauley on students of English as a second language, because the challenges confronted by this population are, at times, similar to those encountered by my students of Talmud, for whom Hebrew and Aramaic are certainly second languages.[31] The study by McCauley and McCauley focused on the application of the pedagogic practice known as "choral reading," described by the authors in accordance with M. H. Arbuthnot's[32] definition as, "the oral reading of poetry that makes use of various voice combinations and contrasts to create meaning or highlight the tonal qualities of the passage."[33] It goes without saying that a dialectical literature such as the Talmud, composed and transmitted orally over generations, is expressed best when read out loud. But choral reading is more than just oral recitation. It is also about repetition, and it is this significant act that promotes the progress charted by reading teachers. As documented in McCauley and McCauley's article, reading specialists have discussed the benefits of oral recitation and repetition for over one-hundred years, starting with the now classic study by Edmund Burke Huey, *The Psychology and Pedagogy of Reading*.[34] More recently, Peter A. Schreiber emphasized that repeated reading enhances the student's ability to "recognize what kind of syntactic phrasing is necessary to make sense of the passage."[35] Other reading specialists stressed improved self-confidence and a sense of empowerment as a result of choral reading strategies.[36] Student

---

30 See footnote 3.
31 In truth, even for the occasional native Hebrew speaker who may attend my class, talmudic language, with its integration of both Hebrew and Aramaic, is foreign. Only a select few will be comfortable with textual constructions because of backgrounds in intense Talmud study.
32 May Hill Arbuthnot, *The Arbuthnot Anthology of Children's Literature* (Glenview, IL: Scott Foresman and Co.), 1961.
33 McCauley and McCauley, "Choral Reading," 527.
34 (Boston: MIT Press), 1908.
35 Peter A. Schreiber, "On the Acquisition of Reading Fluency," *Journal of Reading Behavior* 12, no. 3 (1980): 182; cited in McCauley and McCauley, "Choral Reading," 528.
36 McCauley and McCauley, "Choral Reading," 527.

C in my class echoed that this was also a byproduct of my course, "[o]verall, reciting the text orally was empowering, because it allowed me to understand the language used by the sugya."

More than just summarizing the research on choral reading, McCauley and McCauley argue for the benefits specific to students of English as a second language. In that setting, according to the authors, choral reading is successful, in part, because it is a "low anxiety activity":

> All children can (and do) participate; there is no failure, no tension. The children are safe. Their individual mispronunciations are absorbed by the overriding voices of the group; even children with the least facility in English can experience fluent reading.[37]

For McCauley and McCauley, fluency is achieved in the group setting because of the creation of a "safe space." My students affirmed the safe and enjoyable context of oral recitation and repetition in my classroom, plainly stating, "This is a cool thing to experience"[38] and "it was actually pretty fun to read together."[39]

Conclusions

The implementation of oral recitation and repetition—age-old methods for the study of rabbinic texts—yielded positive results in my college Talmud classes. As evidenced by students' comments, the methods enabled the accomplishment of the course goals I set out for my students. Furthermore, the oral recitation and repetition was enjoyable and solidified the students' appreciation of talmudic literature.

The classroom recitation and repetition provided a template for the oral final exam, which was individual recitation of the texts in my office.[40] During the exams, the students applied what they learned and were pushed to reproduce what had been done in class as part of the group, but this time as individuals (and without me reciting before them). Certainly, for some

---

37 ibid., 528.
38 Student A.
39 Student C.
40 There were two exams: a midterm and a final.

students, the exam experience was not stress free. For some, the inability to rely on the group for support made the exercise extra challenging. Student C commented on this issue specifically, "I think that it would have been useful to do individual recitations [i.e., during class time], so that we could each practice the sugya with our own voice. Though, I still think that reading the text orally together did help me with the oral exam." All in all, the students performed exceptionally well. Student G even attributed success during the exam to the group recitation and repetition experience, "Because our exams were oral, which I most prefer and find that I learn the most from, it was especially helpful to read out loud as a class and repeat multiple times the texts in front of us that we were later to be tested on."

The educational outcomes of oral recitation and repetition in my class, Sugyot about Sukkot, matched the results researched by advocates of choral reading in meaningful ways. The implementation of the strategies I describe here provided a positive educational experience for my students and significantly improved their Talmud text reading skills and comprehension. It is my hope that others, too, will benefit from the integration of oral recitation and repetition in their Talmud text classes when they teach their students *how to read Talmud*.

Addendum

A Note on the Oral and the Written in the Period of the Rishonim and the Potential for Its Imitation in the College Classroom

Talmudic texts were transmitted orally for centuries and only were officially committed to writing during the early Middle Ages.[41] The Talmud being written down only affected educational settings by the time of the rishonim (1038-1565) and resulted in the eventual secondary role of oral recitation and repetition and a new primary position for written technology in Talmud study. Among the rishonim, in fact, the Talmud came to be studied exclusively in written form.[42] The mode of instruction in the great medieval academies of Franco-Germany remained oral lectures however, as evidenced

---

41 See Danzig, "*Mitalmud al peh*."
42 Ibid., 49-50.

Talmud in the Mouth | CHAPTER 7

in the time of the tosafists (11th century-13th century), when oral communication in the form of lectures still played a central role in educational settings, even while writing and the use of written Talmud texts had become the norm.

In a formal exercise of medieval instruction known as *reportatio*, the master dictated the text of his lesson to a disciple. Beryl Smalley described the program of the medieval *reportatio* from a student perspective:

> The *reportatio* ... is a product of the classroom, arising directly from the needs of the student ... The 'reporter' is not a professional stenographer but a pupil, who, instead of merely taking notes, tries to get down a full, consecutive account of the lecture.[43]

As Haym Soloveitchik added, the process among the tosafists included the dictation of the lessons and interpretations by the teacher to the student, followed by the master's review of the student's report which, if necessary, he corrected and then certified as accurate. The text was then titled as *tosafot* (additions) or *perush* (commentary) of the master, as transcribed by the student.[44] Hence, works such as *Perush HaRashbam shenikhtav lifnei Rashi* (*The Commentary of Rashbam written before Rashi*) were born.[45] The authenticating mark of the *reportatio* was the addition at the end of the work of מר, *mipi rabi*, certifying that the work was "from the mouth of my teacher," a formula preserved in better medieval manuscripts (but absent from others and printed editions). Some copyists, not understanding the significance of the formulation, removed the certifying "signature" from the end of the transcripts. Moreover, the names of the works themselves were shortened. The above title, for example, became just *Perush HaRashbam* (*The Commentary of Rashbam*),[46] as it is known even today.

An imitation of the *reportatio* could be integrated into the contemporary college classroom and, I believe, could be positively productive. Students, after

---

43 *The Study of the Bible in the Middle Ages* (Oxford: Blackwell, 1952), 201.
44 Haym Soloveitchik, *Wine in Ashkenaz in the Middle Ages* (Jerusalem: Zalman Shazar 2008), 118.
45 Soloveitchik, *Wine*, 118.
46 Ibid.

taking notes[47] based on the class lecture and discussion, could submit their notes as a record of what was said to the instructor for "certification" that the contents are accurate. Indeed, the relationship of students' notes to the information and analysis provided by instructors is of significant concern to contemporary educational researchers, since the students' knowledge acquisition and methodological training depends not only on the professor's presentation, but also on the students' capable summarization for later consultation. As recently noted by Jaques van der Meer, professors should not assume that contemporary students come to the college classroom knowing how to take notes properly, and new methods for assisting student note-taking should be explored and implemented. Van der Meer emphasized that the inherent issues are not resolved by learning support structures implemented in institutions of higher education, since, often, note-taking is field specific.[48] Developing appropriate note-taking for Talmud classes, therefore, is essential.

Partnering with our students on their note-taking—while arguably for some a seeming reinvention of how university instructors would approach teaching—can become an opportunity to better guide our students in developing skills necessary to master comprehension of rabbinic texts. Teachers requiring and then checking students' outlines and summaries of sugyot[49] is, certainly, an advance in this regard. The challenge remains, however, to find a way to incorporate a running abbreviated commentary to the Talmud text in the outlines as well.[50] Perhaps this problem could be resolved with the use of educational technology that would allow for an outline in electronic form, with links to windows that would then briefly explain the contents of a statement in the Talmud, a matter worthy of further consideration.

---

47 Whether electronically or in writing.
48 Jaques van der Meer, "Students' Note-taking Challenges in the Twenty-first Century: Considerations for Teachers and Academic Staff developers," *Teaching in Higher Education* 17, no. 1 (February 2012): 13-23 (and, for our discussion, especially 13-16).
49 See, for example, the discussion of outlines in Marjorie Lehman's "And No One Gave the Torah to the Priests: Reading the Mishnah's References to the Priests and the Temple" chapter 4 of this volume.
50 To be sure, some instructors require students to indicate in their outlines when the sugya records a tannaitic vs. an amoraic statement or where in the text a question vs. answer is provided. This does not constitute commentary in the classical sense of the word; as well, it does not, usually, include an explanation of the contents of the statements by the sages or questions and answers given.

CHAPTER 8

Talmud that Works Your Heart: New Approaches to Reading

Sarra Lev

The Philosophy: Reading for What?

Michaelson asks: "Of what value are sorrow and tears? How can one put them to use for purposes of a life politics?" Let me try to answer what is perhaps intended to be nothing more than a rhetorical question, a question for which no answer is really desired. ... Call it sentimental, call it Victorian and nineteenth century, but I say that anthropology that doesn't break your heart just isn't worth doing any more.[1]

Some years ago, a rabbinical student who was several weeks into his first semester of Talmud study approached a colleague of mine and said, "When you teach me Talmud, you are assuming this is the *first* time that I am studying it." My colleague was stunned, and as the student paused for effect, he thought, "I *have* been thinking this is the first time that my students are learning these texts. Have I been underestimating them? Should I be shooting higher?" The student then continued, "This is not the *first* time I am studying Gemara ... this is the *last* time. I will never open this book again. So, you'd better teach me what you want me to know." Setting aside, for the moment, the tone with which the student expressed himself, there is something important to be learned here. At best, this student feels that the Talmud

---

1 Ruth Behar, *The Vulnerable Observer: Anthropology That Breaks Your Heart* (Boston: Beacon Press, 1996), 176-77. Behar cites Scott Michaelsen, from David E. Johnson, Scott Michaelsen, *Anthropology's Wake: Attending to the End of Culture* (New York: Fordham University Press) 2008.

| 175

cannot be harmonized with his values and, at worst, that it is downright immoral. This student is not alone. Every semester, there is at least one student who enters my class already hating the Talmud.

These students echo feelings that I myself have had on reading certain passages, and yet, I am compelled by the Talmud—by its depth and by the *way* in which it is traditionally studied. So, I ask myself, "Can we read Talmud to create a kinder, more compassionate, empathetic, and self-reflective society?" English professor Ihab Hassan once asked his student teachers, "Is it possible to teach English so that people stop killing each other?"[2] That is the question that this reading system addresses. *Can* we read *Talmud* so that people stop killing each other?

Usually, a student will leave my beginners' Talmud class able to identify the parts of an argument; understand how those parts relate to one another; know what the keywords are that produce the argument; recognize how the argument fits into the greater context; and know the named rabbis, as well as some information about the text's historical relevance. But over recent years, I have been asking, "Is this enough?"

"Reading to work the heart" is far less clear-cut than other reading methods. I could say to the students, "I want you to be able to translate all the words" or, "I want you to be able to tell the earlier layers from the later ones"—but this would only address a small part of my ultimate goal. Rather, I am asking them to read Talmud by addressing its moral (and immoral) issues. I want to teach them how to read *all* of the stories, including those in which the rabbis reject saving a non-Jew's life if it would mean transgressing Shabbat;[3] those in which they debate the mechanics of sex with a three year old girl;[4] and those in which they (on more than one occasion) even commit murder.[5] I want to provide students the opportunity to use their encounters with rabbinic texts to deepen themselves in multiple ways: as individuals, in their relationships with others, and in their relationship with the material itself. And so, I premiered the course Talmud Through a Moral Lens to investigate a mode of reading Talmud that

---

2 Mary Rose O'Reilley, *The Peaceable Classroom* (Portsmouth, NH: Boynton/Cook Publishers, 1993), 9.
3 M. Yoma 8:7.
4 B. Niddah 45a.
5 See, for example, B. Yoma 22a-23b and B. Bava Kamma 117a.

both excites and scares me. I wanted to know: "Is there a way to read Talmud that will help us grow, even when the Talmud *itself* does not reflect our values? What qualities can we cultivate in ourselves through encounters not only with the Talmud's "friendly" sides but even (or perhaps, particularly) with its "unfriendly" ones? In short, I wanted to know if there is a way to read Talmud that not only "works the brain," but also "works the heart."

The way I determined to set about this was to treat the Talmud as a new genre[6]—which I will call "summons."[7] By that, I mean to treat the texts of the Talmud as if they exist to help us achieve holiness, not by telling us what is or what should be, but by impelling us to interact with the text. It is a text that pushes our buttons and by which we can be pushed to become ever more reflective, understanding, empathetic, discerning, and expansive.

Methodological Background

The idea of reading to "work the heart" draws largely from Hans Georg Gadamer's philosophical hermeneutics, in which the interaction with a text is an I-Thou encounter. From this perspective, the text itself is an "Other" with whom the reader is in conversation. The primary purpose of that encounter is for the reader to develop self-understanding. The text is historically situated, but so too is the reader, who is "prejudiced" by the lens of her own historical moment.[8] Although "understanding" is never achievable, the encounter itself has ethical "significance":

> [T]he understanding of the Other possesses a fundamental significance. ... In the end, I thought the very strengthening of the Other against myself would, for the first time, allow me to open up the real possibility

---

[6] For more on the question of rabbinics and genre, see Julia Watts Belser, "Between the Human and the Holy: The Construction of Talmudic Theology in Massekhet Ta'anit" (PhD diss., University of California, Berkely, 2008), 36-43; Barry S. Wimpfheimer, *Narrating the Law: A Poetics of Talmudic Legal Stories*, 1st ed., Divinations, Rereading Late Ancient Religion (Philadelphia: University of Pennsylvania Press, 2011); David Charles Kraemer, *Reading the Rabbis: The Talmud as Literature* (New York: Oxford University Press, 1996), 3-9, 142-50.

[7] I did not have this word at the time I was teaching the course but feel that it best describes the work I was doing.

[8] Prejudice is not a derogatory term for Gadamer, but simply a given condition of all understanding.

of understanding. To allow the Other to be valid against Oneself—and from there to let all my hermeneutic works slowly develop—is not only to recognize in principle the limitation of one's own framework, but is also to allow one to go beyond one's own possibilities, precisely in a dialogical, communicative, hermeneutic process.[9]

Gadamer is insistent that the meeting of Oneself with the Other must take place through truly seeing the Other in that "Other's" fullness and not as a mirror reflection of ourselves. Filled with unfamiliar characters making choices we ourselves would not make, plus a foreign language and a foreign culture, the Talmud here plays the role of paradigmatic "Other."

If the Gemara becomes the Other that must be "valid against Oneself," then the self has the opportunity to grow through the encounter with the Gemara, whether or not one likes (or even "accepts") what the Gemara seems to be saying. The encounter with the Gemara as summons excites self-reflection, making us more ethical human beings—not through being told or shown, but through offering us an encounter with the wholly "Other."[10]

In addition to the heavy influence that Gadamer's philosophy has had on my work, while teaching and writing I stumbled across the theory of transformative learning (TL):

> Transformative education involves experiencing a deep structural shift in the basic premises of our thoughts, feelings and action. It is a shift of consciousness that dramatically and permanently alters our way of being in the world. Such a shift involves an understanding of ourselves and our self-locations, our relations with other humans and with the natural world ... our visions of alternative approaches to living; and our sense of possibilities for social justice and peace and personal joy.[11]

TL does not stop at increasing knowledge or developing skills. It also changes the learners' understanding of themselves, of other people, and of the world

---

9 Hans-Georg Gadamer, "Subjectivity and Intersubjectivity, Subject and Person," *Continental Philosophy Review* 33, no. 3 (2000): 284.
10 See also Martha Craven Nussbaum, *Poetic Justice: The Literary Imagination and Public Life* (Boston: Beacon Press, 1995). Nussbaum advocates teaching literature in order to "cultivate humanity."
11 Edmund O'Sullivan, Amish Morrell, and Mary Ann O'Connor, *Expanding the Boundaries of Transformative Learning: Essays on Theory and Praxis*, 1st ed. (New York: Palgrave, 2002), 18.

and opens the mind and heart wider. At the same time, TL does not do away with the need for mastery of content. On the contrary—that mastery is essential; but so too is the possibility for transformation that emerges from the encounter with the material. The result is a learning experience that directly employs the theories of Gadamer.

The philosophies of Gadamer and TL are truly inspiring, but they offered only theory and provided little practical advice on how to apply that theory. To begin with, particularly with Gadamer, material on *how* teachers implemented these philosophies in the classroom was hard to come by. In addition, I found no TL material to address the teaching of religious texts, particularly those with complicated value systems. I was suggesting an entirely new enterprise that required reading the Talmud, not as we have traditionally, but as a new genre, as it were—a genre whose intent was to awaken us and to summon us to become our best selves.

Course Background

I taught Talmud Through a Moral Lens at the Conservative Yeshiva in Jerusalem, once a week for fourteen weeks. I could give the students no mandatory homework by the rules of the Yeshivah. The participants were ten college-educated students in their later twenties to thirties. Most considered themselves progressive Jews. They had a wide range of experience with Talmud, from those who knew almost no Hebrew or Aramaic, to those who had spent three years in rabbinical school and had significant exposure and some proficiency with understanding the texts. With these different levels of experience, I decided to present each text in both the original and in translation.

On one hand, the students were unique in their disposition for this work. All of them had taken a year of their lives to move to Jerusalem and to study at the Conservative Yeshiva, an institution tailored to teach only religious subjects. Simply by virtue of this, they were already invested and responsive to a reflective experience. Some articulated that they were searching for the meaning in their own tradition that they had found in the religious traditions and texts of other cultures and religions. On the other hand, while halakhic Jews study the Talmud as a religious practice and seek to understand it in the context of their daily lives, this would not necessarily be the case for progressive, non-halakhic Jews. For them, the texts have no intrinsic legal-practical value, and they have no pre-defined or natural connection to these texts. Could non-halakhic liberal Jews read texts that differed vastly from their own value systems and ways of thinking with the goal of becoming better human beings? With this question, I entered the semester.

Personal Challenges

There are two challenges in teaching how to read "Talmud as summons" that I realize are particular to my personality, but I believe they are worth mentioning as they do inform my pedagogy. To begin with, I had to over-come my discomfort with the hubris of saying, "I use these texts to be self-reflective, and I'm going to show you how to do that." It was difficult for me to find words to explain what it was that I wanted them to do without (inadvertently) suggesting to a class of wonderful students, many of whom I had not met before, that they are not yet "kind enough," "empathetic enough," or "self-reflective enough," and that I wanted them to learn or improve those skills through our reading.

The second challenge was that, while teaching this class I learned much about my own fear of venturing into the world of emotional reactions and "the work of the heart" in the context of a classroom. While I knew the only way to read the Talmud as summons was to enter the sphere of the personal, I feared invading my students' privacy in general and, specifically, of pushing them too hard, demanding vulnerability from them without knowing them well, asking them to do something beyond "ordinary Talmud study" in a Talmud class, and as well, displaying my own vulnerability in order to model the behavior I sought from them. I feared asking any number of questions that pushed *too far*, or having a conversation drift *too far* into the emotional—I was afraid of losing them in the process of helping them to find themselves. My journal as I prepared for the sixth class shows my concern for these issues:

> I am afraid of asking the difficult questions. I am afraid I don't know what those questions are. I keep giving-up on the writing exercises and just doing the text. Last week, I told the story [of the Mittler Rebbe][12] ... I should have asked my students, "Have any of you ever done that? Ever

---

12   See below 191 for story of the Mittler Rebbe.

tried to find that place inside when someone says something you can't believe they are saying?" But I didn't do that. I was not brave in the moment. So we did other things in class. Good things. But not *that*.

Where this discomfort most often played out was in transitions from the very intense textual analysis that served as the base for the personal work and the personal work itself. My journal after the first class read, "What I most wonder about is how I am going to transition in class from our intensive work on the Talmud text to the question of what this means about us as human beings. I want to do that organically, but I do not know how."

Methods and Techniques

This process defied linearity, at every step requiring skills *a fortiori* that we were to learn as we went through the process itself.[13] Included in these competencies were the performance of complex analyses; the ability to stand in the "Other's" shoes; the awareness that the Other is *not* the same as me; proficiency in thinking outside of the box; facility in considering options rather than jumping to immediate conclusions; and heavy doses of empathy, compassion, and kind-

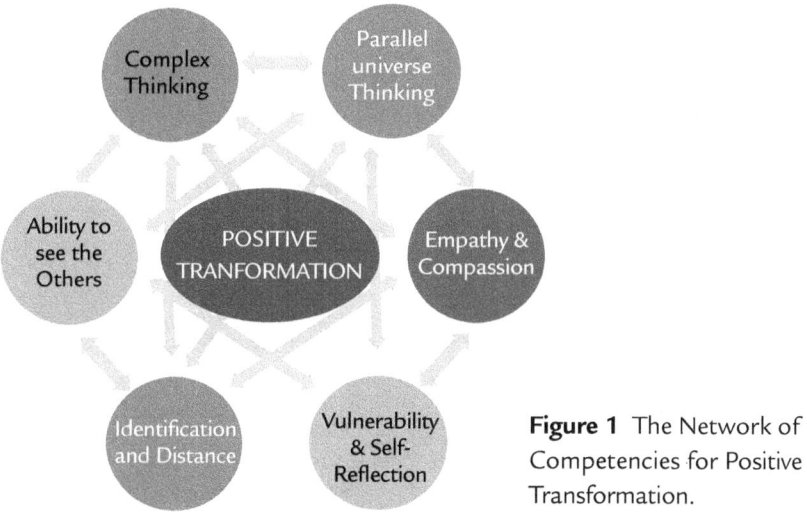

Figure 1 The Network of Competencies for Positive Transformation.

---
13 My thanks to Rabbi Toba Spitzer for her assistance in articulating this aspect of skill acquisition.

ness.[14] The process is, in Gadamer's words, "dialogical." One cannot place one of these goals before the other (see Fig. 1). For example, in order to acquire empathy, we need to learn to engage in "parallel universe thinking,"[15] which requires complex thinking and the ability to see the Other. The ability to see the Other, in turn, requires empathy. Gadamer's recognition that reading in this way "is to allow one to go beyond one's own possibilities" is true, both in terms of process and outcome. That is, in order for me to engage, I must allow myself to go beyond my current possibilities as I perceive them. And this opens me further to even more possibilities. In other words, there is no "first step." The only way to acquire these skills, habits, and character traits, is to jump right in.

Stage 1 of my methodology was to do a close reading of the text in order to foster complexity and build some of the aforementioned skills. This would lay the groundwork for Stage 2, which involved reading the text as "summons" and would reinforce certain of the skills, as well as engage some of the others. The techniques I used in this first stage to cultivate uncertainty and foster complex readings were as follows:

1. Choosing material that would allow the students to be critical but could also push them to understand and empathize with the Other
2. Leaving ambiguity or multivalence in my translations
3. Putting the text "on stage"
4. Providing information about unfamiliar concepts and making available aids to understanding our text, when necessary
5. Providing historical context and employing *"historical thinking,"*[16] in order to dislodge assumptions or preconceived notions
6. Examining the text in literary context

---

14   The fields of TL and social justice divide into three basic foci of transformation; my interest primarily is in the outcomes of the third: "a theory of existence, which views people as subjects, not objects, who are constantly reflecting and acting on the transformation of their world so it can become a more equitable place for all to live." See Heather L. Stuckey, Edward W. Taylor, and Patricia Cranton, "Developing a Survey of Transformative Learning Outcomes and Processes Based on Theoretical Principles," *Journal of Transformative Education* 11, no. 4 (2013).
15   The practice of exploring multiple explanations to explain a person's behavior.
16   Samuel S. Wineburg, *Historical Thinking and Other Unnatural Acts: Charting the Future of Teaching the Past*, Critical Perspectives on the Past (Philadelphia: Temple University Press, 2001).

By the time we reached Stage 2, most of the "real" work had already been accomplished. We had repeatedly challenged ideas about right and wrong, judgments about what was happening in the text and ideas about what the text intended to convey, as well as calling into question the students' own personal relationships to the text. Stage 2 carried through some of the techniques of stage 1 (primarily cultivating uncertainty), but the goal of stage 2 was to read the text as summons (although, at the time, I was not framing it that way). In order to do so, the added techniques I used in class were:

1. Framing my approach to understanding the self through poetry and story
2. Remaining complex: techniques to avoid reductionism
    a. Staying close to the text
    b. Asking questions about the text that bridge between it and ourselves
    c. Asking questions about ourselves that reflect back on the text
3. Encouraging and exhibiting vulnerability and self-reflection

Stage 1: Fostering Complexity—Balancing Intimacy and Alienation

When I have taught Talmud in the past, I have noticed two opposite ways that students experience the text—for some, it feels remote and alien, while for others, it feels intimate, sacred, and infallible.[17] The first student will reject the texts. The second will run circles around the texts to make them conform to what he/she believes the text should say or wants it to say,[18] ultimately opening the text to presentism, ethnocentrism, and egocentrism. Neither group's response allows for complex analysis.

Both my choice of texts and my teaching require a careful balance between making the strange familiar and making sure that the familiar is not *too* familiar. Although the idea of cultivating uncertainty in a classroom may

---

17 An equal but opposite manifestation of intimacy occurs when a student feels so identified with the text that she must utterly reject it, so as not to be implicated by its problematic aspects.
18 This phenomenon creates what Paulo Freire refers to as "circles of certainty." Paulo Freire, *Pedagogy of the Oppressed*, 30th anniversary ed. (New York: Continuum, 2000), 38-39. For the relationship between uncertainty and social justice education, see Doris Santoro, "Teaching to Save the World: Avoiding Circles of Certainty in Social Justice Education," *Philosophy of Education Yearbook* (2009).

seem incongruous, it is essential to my teaching. In my methodology, "disequilibrium," Piaget's theory of resolving new information into current schemas, which he believed was vital to the development of logical thought, is a prerequisite to seeing the "Other" in our relationships.[19] If a reader is convinced that her way of understanding is the only way, it is likely that this will translate to her life as well. The uncertainty of the skillful reader with a refined approach is what helps her to continually reassess as new information is introduced or greater understanding is achieved.

"Working the heart" is meant to cause a disruption in what Paulo Freire calls "circles of certainty,"[20] by identifying (and dispelling) responses to a text that are entirely based on what we *think* we know. But, while trying to dispel the predisposition to "know and judge," I also want to keep my students close enough so that reading Talmud *matters*. How can they truly meet the Other, if they do not feel at all attached to the text? Reading the Talmud as "summons" demands the ability to hold both enough distance to quell our assumptions and enough familiarity to feel something, to create meaning. I want the students to grow through *getting to know* a text that is laden with religious meaning, is entirely foreign, and yet, they can claim as their own. As I see it, this has to take place on several levels, some that support familiarity, some that support healthy distance, and some that maintain a balance of both simultaneously.

Where Do We Begin? Framing. Both what I do in the classroom and how I prepare for the classroom is directly affected by these considerations. In my preparation, this is reflected in what materials I choose to teach, and in how I translate that material. To preserve the balance between familiarity and healthy distance, I feel texts that might disrupt the students' equilibrium would likely facilitate deep discussion and engagement. Thus, for this class, I chose texts in which the message (and many times the plot itself) was unclear, and they could legitimately be read in a number of ways and on multiple levels. In part, classroom discussion involved sifting out possible readings of the Talmud text from unlikely ones, still allowing for multiplicity. I wanted to provide for indeterminacy, while not slipping into moral or literary relativism,

---

19 See, Jean Piaget, *The Equilibration of Cognitive Structures: The Central Problem of Intellectual Development*, trans. Terrance Brown and Kishore Julian Thampy (Chicago: University of Chicago Press, 1985), 10.
20 Freire, *Pedagogy of the Oppressed*.

Talmud that Works Your Heart: New Approaches to Reading | CHAPTER 8

or sentimentalism. At the same time, for today's liberal reader, the Talmud does little to promote identification with the characters and more often evokes estrangement (and sometimes derision). Hence, I chose texts that could bridge between this altogether different reality, the Other, and the students' own cultural reality, and offer access to the familiar as well as the strange. Additionally, if a text had elements with which the students might disagree, that friction itself could stimulate conversation. I did not want to alienate them entirely with "terrible texts" merely to provoke discussion and regress into sensationalism, and yet, I wanted to deal head-on with highly problematic material. Ultimately, my basic organizing principle for choosing my texts was to present texts that were as complex as the Talmud itself.

My final criterion for choosing texts was that they had to be engaging and interesting. In what follows in this chapter, I will use B. Yoma 23a, a story about a priestly murder that we studied during the semester. The story had intricacies that could lead to in-depth conversations, and was both familiar (murder) and strange (Temple practice) at the same time:

> Our Rabbis taught: It once happened that two priests were tied as they ran and ascended the ramp. One of them ran ahead into his colleague's "four cubits of the altar," He took a knife and thrust it into his heart. R. Tsadok stood on the steps of the Hall and said: "Our Brothers of the House of Israel, listen! Behold it says [in Torah], 'If a corpse is found in the land then your elders and judges shall go out ...' (Deut 21:1) For whom shall we bring the heifer whose neck is to be broken? On [behalf of] the city or on [behalf of] the Temple Courts?" All the people burst out weeping. The father of the boy came and found him while he was still in convulsions. He said, "May he be your atonement. My son is still in convulsions and the knife has not become impure." [His remark] comes to teach that the purity of their vessels was graver for them than the shedding of blood.[21]

Translating the texts. It was not only the materials I chose, however, that went into my preparation. On the most basic level, if my readers were to have any investment in these materials, they needed, first, to be able to simply

---

21 For an extended analysis of this passage, see Marjorie Lehman, "Imagining the Priesthood in Tractate *Yoma*: Mishnah *Yoma* 2:1-2 and BT Yoma 23a," *Nashim: A Journal of Jewish Women's Studies and Gender Issues* 28 (Spring 2015): 88-105.

| 185

decipher the text. Since few of them had a mastery of Hebrew and Aramaic, a translation was necessary.[22] However, given that exploring multiple meanings is a key element in a complex reading, I could not use a translation that "answers" a question before the readers ever realized there *was* a question. Thus, in order to challenge students to interrogate their own judgments through an encounter with the "wholly Other," I created and distributed translations that preserved the multivocality and ambiguity of that Other—the talmudic text.[23] This meant maintaining the terse and ambiguous style of the original text, sometimes leaving an ambiguous word or phrase untranslated (substituting a transliteration), and sometimes dealing with translation issues in the classroom, as we did with the above Yoma text.

Choosing an appropriate text would set the stage for this method of reading, but it was during the classroom discussion of that text that the primary work took place. There, I needed to create the relationship that Gadamer advocates: a balance between the distance that ensures careful critique and the intimacy that allows for a full knowing of the Other, (in this case, the talmudic text). This challenge was heightened by the short amount of time we had to cultivate a relationship with the texts as a whole.

The primary way to disrupt understanding, while allowing students access to the texts, was through translations *in class*. In texts where I left words transliterated, I located other contexts in which the word or phrase appeared and reviewed those in class, giving students multiple meanings with which to work. We then used these to determine possibilities for how *our text* might be contextualizing that word or phrase. In the Yoma text, however, the ambiguity that I wished to highlight lay in the father's response (*harei hu kaparatkhem ve-adayin beni mefarper ve-lo nitmeah sakin*) and was difficult to transmit in a written handout. Thus, after reading the above translation in class, I listed on the board other options for the meaning of the father's statement:

1. The first half of the statement:
    a. May he be your atonement
    b. May this be your atonement

---

22 I always included the original text alongside the translation for those who wanted to refer back to it.
23 I translated with an eye toward staying close to the language of the original Hebrew and Aramaic.

c. Behold, he is your atonement
d. Behold, this is your atonement
2. The second half of the statement:
a. My son is still in convulsions and the knife has not become impure
b. *And* my son is still in convulsions and the knife has not become impure
c. *That* my son is still in convulsions and the knife has not become impure

I then had the students read various combinations of the father's statement in a variety of tones of voice, asking them to experiment with different emotions behind the tones expressed. Some students read the father's words (1a, 1b) somberly, as a wish or a hope for the priestly clan that either his son, the (still pure) knife, or some other "this" should atone for the murder. Others read them (1c, 1d) as didactic. Some students suggested that however one reads the statement, the father is likening his dying son, stabbed with a knife normally used for sacrifice, to a sacrificial animal used for atonement.

A student raised the question, "What does the extra '*and* my son' (2b) contribute to the meaning?" Was the father linking "may he be (or this is) your atonement" to the fact that his son was still in convulsions? Another student read "*that* my son" (2c) to mean, "It is your atonement that my son is still in convulsions and [thus] the knife has not become impure." In this case, the student pointed out that the father offers the purity of the knife *as the atonement* for the murder, rather than offering his son as the equivalent of a sacrifice. One student suggested that the father was like Aharon at the death of his sons, not truly responding emotionally. Another suggested that he was responding like a proud father who extols his son for hanging on to life until the sacred knife is removed from his body, so as not to defile the knife. At the end of the discussion, I introduced another possibility: "How would he be saying these words if he was angry?" This elicited a discussion of whether the father might ultimately be speaking sarcastically, critiquing, rather than cleaving to the cult of purity.

Did the father care more about the purity of the knife than his son's death? Were his words ironic or sincere? Was his voice breaking or was he indifferent and unmoved by his son's death? Was he included in those who cared more for their vessels or was he reprimanding them? Without veering from the text in any way, multiple interpretations emerged from this exercise. The more that new options for reading were introduced, the less certain students became of their original readings, responses, and judgments; and the less likely they were to extract simplistic moral lessons from the text.

Situating the Text in Historical and Literary Context. Cultivating uncertainty or balancing between familiarity and distance also came into play when thinking about our story relative to its context, and not only when working with multiple translation options. This meant learning more about how the text was situated historically and textually, clarifying entirely foreign concepts, but also investigating what assumptions we brought to the texts, both about the texts themselves and about our own values. Sam Wineburg tells us:

> The narcissist sees the world—both past and present—in his own image. Mature historical knowing teaches us to do the opposite: to go beyond our own image, to go beyond our brief life, and to go beyond the fleeting moment in human history into which we have been born.[24]

Even with translation, unfamiliar concepts can make the text impenetrable. I began each unit, therefore, by explaining these blatantly foreign concepts in advance, using a "things you must know to understand this text" introduction. For example, Rabbi Tzadok's direct challenge to the priests, asking them, "For whom shall we bring the heifer whose neck is to be broken?" is unintelligible to anyone unfamiliar with the ceremony of the *eglah arufah* (heifer whose neck is to be broken), which takes place upon finding a murdered corpse in an open field (Deut 22). The ritual is performed when the murderer remains unknown and is carried out by the elders of the nearest town. Only upon understanding the ritual, did students realize that Rabbi Tzadok's question was not what it appeared, given that the case concerned a *known* murderer and took place on the grounds of the Temple. Once the students understood this, a discussion ensued about what Rabbi Tzadok was *really* asking about, if not the logistics of the ritual. Likewise, I brought in a picture of the ramp and the altar for the students, which allowed

---

24 Sam Wineburg, *Historical Thinking and Other Unnatural Acts: Charting the Future of Teaching the Past*, 24. Wineburg also relies on "the tension between the familiar and the strange" and, likewise, depends on this tension as a method of "humanization." See, in particular, ibid., introduction and chapter 5.

them to visually imagine a stage for the story. Later, when I asked questions such as, "How would this look on a stage?" or "What would you do to direct this production?" the visual background to the story was essential.

A more insidious, ensnaring problem than the blatantly unfamiliar, however, is that which *appears familiar*, or known. The students' familiarity with rabbis of today or with the orthodox Jews of today, for example, was far too easily projected onto the rabbis of the Talmud. Students assumed that the rabbis would be unwilling to critique their own religious system and that rabbis and priests worked in harmony. B. Yoma 23a, however, must be understood in the context of the historically *tense* relationship between the rabbinic and priestly communities. This rabbinic text reports on a priestly murder and critiques the institution of priesthood. So too, Rabbi Tzadok's dual roles as both priest and rabbi, spanning two communities with complicated relationships, heightens the complexity of the scene. Likewise, at the outset of our discussion, for example, one student commented that the priests racing up the ramp was a debasement of the Temple, missing entirely the fact that this was a practice established *by* the priests. The student applied current perceptions of decorum to the Temple cult. The realization that they could not simply map their own reality onto the text gave them pause and opened space for more questions about historical context.

Interpreting both the unfamiliar and the seemingly familiar as products of historical development offered a deeper "knowing" of the text, and, at the same time, an "un-knowing." The latter curtailed the impulse to hang onto their assumptions about the motivations or choices of the characters and restrained presentism (applying their own historical position to the text).

Not only the historical context of the text but also the literary context, in which the later sages use this story, is relevant to our own understanding. Thus, after discussing the story on its own terms, we returned to the mishnah that preceded it. Unlike the tannaitic[25] story that we told above, which appears in the Gemara, the mishnah that parallels this story ends by addressing the issue of competition. Coupling the two texts opened up the question of what these texts are *about* and what critique is being offered. Are the parallel stories about competition? Purity? Or, perhaps, it is something else entirely that binds them together?

---

25 Belonging to the same historical period as the Mishnah.

Stage 2: Translating Our Reading into a Summons

Achieving a balance of differentiating between ourselves and the Other, while still understanding and empathizing with the Other, would not emerge from solely intellectually analyzing the text. We needed a process to shape the nature and extent of that encounter. The more we pulled at the material, in order to know the texture of every thread, the more we exercised that skill, and the more we were able to translate it into our understanding of *many different* "Others." But pulling at the threads is only one essential aspect of this process. *How* we pulled was equally essential. While the reader must come to know and understand the text on its own terms, she must also cultivate an ability to see herself in those who appear within the pages of the Talmud and in their circumstances. Once we had accomplished the complex analysis of the text, we needed to take the reading to the next stage—understanding how the text summons us to become our best selves.

Where Do We Begin? Framing. Some of the outside tools that I introduced to frame this very complex and unfamiliar reading process in the classroom included two poems and an old Hassidic story. Each of these demonstrated skills for understanding the Other (whether person or text) in all his/her/its complexity and viewing her/him/it with compassion.

Thich Nhat Hanh's poem "Call Me by My True Names"[26] focuses on the philosophy that we each embody all possibilities for right action, for wrongdoing, for both victim and perpetrator. Creating changes in out thinking requires identifying these places in ourselves and having compassion and a will to change:

> I am the twelve-year-old girl,
> refugee on a small boat,
> who throws herself into the ocean
> after being raped by a sea pirate.
> And I am the pirate,
> my heart not yet capable
> of seeing and loving...
>
> Please call me by my true names,
> so I can hear all my cries and laughter at once,

---

26 Nhất Hạnh Thich, *Peace Is Every Step: The Path of Mindfulness in Everyday Life* (New York: Bantam Books, 1991).

so I can see that my joy and pain are one.

Please call me by my true names,
so I can wake up
and so the door of my heart
could be left open,
the door of compassion.

For Thich Nhat Hanh, a renowned Buddhist monk and spiritual guide, only when we acknowledge *all* of who he is are we "calling him by his true names." I wanted the students to understand and apply this teaching: that we all have within us that which we tend to condemn in others.

Yehudah Amichai's poem, "From the Place Where We Are Right," echoes Gadamer's call to recognize the failings of our own framework and to radically open ourselves to the Other. Amichai calls on us to let go of "the place where we are right" and to question our convictions and behavior in order to make room for a place where "flowers will grow."[27]

Finally, the story of the Mittler Rebbe, Dov Ber Schneuri, ends as the Rebbe explains to one of his chassidim that he is only able to advise his parishioners to repent for their wrongdoings by first seeking the place inside of *himself* that would commit that particular wrongdoing. I explained that this story had changed me profoundly as a young adult and that it embodies the process that I seek when we are reading the Talmud: to take on the words or actions of a particular rabbi or of the "narrator" (if only for a brief time), whether or not we like them, in order to seek the way in which we may do *teshuvah* (repentance) for that wounded place inside of ourselves.

These particular ways of seeing the world are not self-evident nor are they normally understood as prerequisites for studying Talmud. Thus, it was important to introduce them explicitly early on in the course so that they would be front and center during the second stage of the process.

Avoiding Reductionism. Reductionism is one of the main pitfalls of a project designed to take complicated material and have students apply it to their lives. In planning for my fourth class, I wrote the following in my journal:

---

27 Amichai, Yehudah, *The Selected Poetry of Yehuda Amichai*, trans. Chana Bloch and Stephen Mitchell (Berkeley: University of California Press, 2013), 34.

The most difficult thing has been to figure out a way to get them to use the text to self-reflect, while still keeping to the text itself, rather than just say to them "OK, now you're Moses. How do you feel?"[28] Identifying the elements that make this a more complex process than that—*that* is the challenge.

I did not want the text to become a jumping off point from which to just talk about ourselves or to flatten the text's depth by glibly applying our own experiences to it. Avoiding reductionism and cultivating the above skills and characteristics, first and foremost, required keeping the discussion close to the text, even while self-reflecting. In order to maintain depth and complexity, we did this while reading the text and through class discussions.[29] Maintaining the variety of perspectives we had accumulated in stage 1 allowed the students more entry points into the material *and* offered them much richer material for analyzing their own behaviors. Hand in hand with this range of perspectives, I sought to apply "parallel universe thinking" to the text, "challenging oneself to identify the many alternatives to the interpretations to which we may be tempted to leap, on insufficient information."[30] I wanted my students to understand that while perhaps they *could* judge the text the way they originally had (whether positive or negative), they must not *necessarily* do so. Indeed, in each text, we took time to question particular judgments based on elements in the text and to introduce alternative and equally plausible readings.

In addition to staying close to the text, I tried to ask searching questions. The types of questions that would elicit discussions leading us down the path of self-reflection varied greatly from text to text. I asked the students,

---

28 My thanks to Rabbi Susan Silverman for this phrasing.
29 See, for example, Nel Noddings, *Educating Moral People: A Caring Alternative to Character Education* (New York: Teachers College Press, 2002), 70-72; Jacques Derrida, "The 'World' of the Enlightenment to Come (Exception, Calculation, Sovereignty)," *Research in Phenomenology* 33, no. 1 (2003); Steven I. Meisel and David S. Fearon, " 'Choose the Future Wisely': Supporting Better Ethics through Critical Thinking," *Journal of Management Education* 30, no. 1 (2006); Tara Fenwick, "Responsibility, Complexity Science and Education: Dilemmas and Uncertain Responses," *Studies in Philosophy & Education* 28, no. 2 (2009).
30 See Jean Koh Peters and Susan J. Bryant, "Five Habits for Cross-Cultural Lawyering," in *Race, Culture, Psychology, & Law*, ed. Kimberly Barrett and William George (Thousand Oaks, CA: Sage Publications, 2005). The authors used this method to challenge their students' negative responses to clients of different cultures.

for example, what it might have been like to have lunch with the priest who did the stabbing on the day before the incident. What did they imagine about his character? Would they necessarily have noticed anything about him that was "different"? My goal here was to draw attention to the fact that the text presented no indication that the perpetrator was in any way different than his compatriots; rather, it attributed the disaster to a systemic issue—that of the priesthood's emphasis on competition. Imagining possibilities for who he was and what brought the murderer to stab a fellow priest challenged the perpetrator/victim reading, and opened a conversation about institutional pressures and instances in which we ourselves have failed individuals by conforming to values or practices of an institution. Even as we engaged in this self-reflection, we remained closely anchored to the text as our base, moving back and forth from personal experience to text, rather than allowing for a stream of consciousness conversation that left the text behind.

My purpose throughout was to cultivate an encounter that views the text as summons, a call to look within, not only by leading with bridging questions (such as that above), but by *explaining* the types of questions that this approach requires as we apply the text to our own lives: "What is it that I am not understanding about these opinions or behaviors?" "What information do I need to collect to understand more?" "How can I read this differently if I approach it with compassion?" "What will I learn about myself if I meet this text without beginning at a place where I am right?" All of these questions serve to bridge between the text and the reader, not by *leaving* the text and *moving* to the reader, but by applying parallel methods to understanding ourselves as readers and to understanding the text itself.

Taking the Path of Most Resistance: Inventing Vulnerability and Self-Reflection.

N. Elias reminds us that summoning ourselves is no easy task:

> It is hard for human beings to get away from preconceived ideas about themselves and the world and when philosophers suggest "Know thyself" most people are likely to respond "no thanks, we don't want to know that much."[31]

---

31 Quote from N. Elias, *Le Sociedad De Los Individuos* (Barcelona: Peninsula, 1990), 96. Translated to English in Martha Traverso-Yepez, "Examining Tranformative Learning Amidst the Challenges of Self Reflection," in *Narrating Transformative Learning in Education*, ed. Morgan Gardner and Ursula Anne Margaret Kelly (New York: Palgrave Macmillan, 2008), 157.

CHAPTER 8 | Sarra Lev

Reading the text as summons requires us to see the struggles, decisions, opinions, and behaviors of those in the texts as connecting with and relevant to our own lives, even when those behaviors or opinions do *not* seem to reflect our own. The skills that are required to truly come to know (that is, to understand and to feel for) the characters of the text necessitate a certain level of vulnerability. It is certainly not a given that adult students taking a class in Talmud, usually a highly intellectual exercise, will be willing to make themselves vulnerable enough in front of classmates and teachers to self-reflect. It was my hope, however, that I could find ways to make that happen aloud in class. I did this both by asking particular questions that required them to be vulnerable and by pushing myself to be vulnerable with them.

Creating a classroom atmosphere of kindness and compassion (which I hoped would allow them a place to be vulnerable) was easy with this particular group. Nevertheless, I myself struggle with both my own and my students' vulnerability in the classroom. I felt this discomfort acutely when managing transitions from textual analysis (Stage 1) to the discussion of how it impacted our lives (Stage 2). I overcame that discomfort by asking my students outright to engage in this experiment with me, making it a joint effort. I also felt it was important to let them know that whatever they were thinking about, they were not alone in their concerns or fears. In class, after studying the story in Yoma, I told them that when I first read this text I had recorded the following thoughts:

> "I cannot believe that this is our religious text." I went into it with an incredible amount of judgment about this being the "thing" that we're supposed to be looking at in order to figure out how to be Jews. ... And for me what happens is when I take it apart like this, it helps me go from "How could that possibly be the story?" to "Wow, that's really the story. It's the story all over the place. It's the story that I'm in. It's the story that everybody else is in." And then the question is—how do we deal with that story?—as opposed to—*how could they ever have done that*?! I asked myself—"[referring to a story a student told]. ... What are the moments when I am so completely submerged in the life of something "bigger," like the institution, or whatever it is, that I cannot see past that?" And that is a story that we are all in. So, it just helps me to feel like this story is actually telling me something; this is actually pulling me somewhere, and I have to look at this.

But, while I could *say* that the story was universal, *showing* it is ultimately more powerful. To do this, I tried modeling what I wanted them to do by exposing outright my own encounters with the text. I myself did each exercise that I assigned to the students and then posted my writings for them. While this did allow me to *model* the process, I also hoped that my own vulnerability would invite them to follow suit.[32] This approach also eased my reticence to ask them to share their own vulnerability and my concerns about the hubris of the enterprise. If during class I was able to demonstrate areas where I myself needed to grow, I was somewhat more comfortable asking them to do so. I wanted my own participation to open a space for them to be able to do the same.

One very straightforward way in which I asked for their vulnerability was through personal questions. Of course, they could choose not to answer, but the questions made room for the personal to be a part of the class. Toward the end of the unit on Yoma, I asked them to consider the underlying transgressions in the story. A selection of those the students suggested included: caring more about ritual and religion than about people (the murderer and the father); putting the institution above the individual (the father and the priests); and competing for "holiness" (the priests, the murderer, the murdered priest). I had them consider whether they themselves had ever been guilty of such transgressions. Could they understand the obsession with ritual that allowed other human beings to become secondary? Had they ever felt ritually competitive? Albeit, in the Yoma text, these impulses resulted in murder and, perhaps (depending on how we read the father's response), an indifference to the death of a loved one. By reading the text "to work the heart," I was looking for students to identify with the character's impulse itself and not necessarily with its outcome in the story. After we had brainstormed the transgressions, I asked, "If you choose one of these—if one of these people or groups of people came to you and said, 'I did this,' and you were the Mittler Rebbe, how would you suggest that they do *teshuvah* (repent)? And then the question is, how did you get there?"

I also ended some units with an in-class writing exercise, in which I asked a question prompting students to examine their lives in light of our discussion about the text. The first unit's writing exercise simply asked, "Is there anything in this text that spoke to your life, made you think differently

---

32 I also encouraged them to post to our blog board, though none did.

about yourself, made you question something, or helped you learn something about yourself?" Answering these questions produced a bridge from the material to their very personal experience.

Evaluating: The Past and the Future

My primary method of assessing this reading process was to ask the students two types of questions: those that would evoke the types of readings that I wanted them to get to (below) and direct and transparent questions about whether the process I described was working for them. An example of the latter occurred toward the end of the course, when I asked whether they thought they had changed as a result of any of what we did (see series of responses below). Whether (and how) we were able to achieve complex thinking and to grow to see the "Other" was reflected in the responses to these questions. After studying Yoma, one student spoke of how this reflective process opened his eyes to the complexity of the text and his own biases:

> I think the one thing that might be a little different for me is just reading the text ... It's hard not to read it with your own kind of presupposition of what you think the text is going to be saying about what is good and bad, as opposed to then pulling it apart in this way to see the twelve different permutations of what the father says and how that can really influence what the moral judgment is about what it is in the text.

The exercise in which we interpreted the father's exclamation about his murdered son, introduced into our discussion both the nuance and the uncertainty that reading the Talmud as summons demands. No longer could the student remain with his pre-judgments.

All of these methods—supplying more than one translation, complicating the reading using historical context, and rarely giving an unequivocal answer to a "factual question"—fostered a feeling that the totality of our "knowing" must be examined and re-examined. At the same time as students were accruing more "data" to stand on, they were feeling that accretion of information shifting uncertainly beneath their feet. This made it difficult to map their own assumptions and preconceptions onto the text, and opened multitudes of possibilities. Paradoxically, these processes served to bring students closer to the text, as one aptly demonstrates:

> I think that, like a lot of rabbinic texts, coming into it and looking at the social picture that it's painting ... initially coming into the text, it looks very alien and kind of blocky (inaudible), and it's like a thing that was happening out there separate from me. And it's really hard to really understand what human stuff is going on underneath all the alien pageantry. But this conversation helped me really ... If I'm going back and reading the story again, I'll be seeing the characters as much more human, acting in ways that I can intellectually understand where they are coming from and less as dolls strutting across the rabbinic puppet stage.

My journal entry from February 25th records a student's comment to me that was made outside of class:

> G told me that he has never considered poetry in the context of Talmud before, and that the two exercises ... were great for him ... That they made him think more deeply about the complexity.

A third student said that it was the modeling I had done that helped him "to see ... this as relevant and meaningful in our day-to-day lives. Things we can actually relate to."

> It was your email that talked about your retreat and this conversation[33] that really helped me see the relevance of this text to modern life. And I'm still trying to figure it out. What I'm taking away is something along the lines of the theme we discussed in class, like don't be too righteous. But this specifically deals with institutions, and as L was saying—understanding the individual and detaching yourself from institutional values—so, I'm playing with that. Seeing this as relevant and meaningful in our day-to-day lives. Things we can actually relate to as opposed to a guy stabbing another guy on the altar.

In each of these responses, one specific technique can be identified (the conversation, the exercises, or my personal post) as having served to trigger a

---

33 Referring to my post that week. See pp. 194-195.

change in the student. For the first and third students, the utterly alien text is no longer "separate from" the student—it is "much more human" or "relevant and meaningful in our day-to-day lives." In the second example, the student changed his way of reading the particular text so that his response was no longer as simple as it had seemed to him at first. In all of these writings, however, I believe that the change could not have taken place without all of those elements being present. I am still pondering how to ask *self-reflection questions* that are multi-dimensional and mirror the complexity of the text, as well as how to produce exercises that might evoke these types of changes. For example, the question, "How would you feel if you were in that position?" is not as compelling if the complexity of the position itself is not explored. I asked myself, "How do I begin to ask the kinds of questions that can change a person's life?"

The students' varied responses taught me that the work takes place differently for different people and that reading in this way may require many techniques simultaneously. Of course, this is the case with all reading but here that was heightened by the fact that the students were required to take the extra unfamiliar step of "reading as summons."

Regarding the ability of students to be vulnerable and to self-reflect, while classes for the first two-thirds of the semester contained *moments* of self-reflection, they primarily consisted of more impersonal intellectual conversations about the text. It was quite a while into the semester before students showed vulnerability. Because of my own discomfort moving between the intellectual and the personal, I worked up to being quite transparent about the transition from examining the material's content to reading the material as "meaning maker." I told them directly that I was interested in their reflecting on their own culpability for transgressions they had related to in the text. I was moved when a student took on the challenge directly and began to tell a story about himself in relation to the text. That student opened up the space for others to talk about situations that they had been in where they themselves had made these types of choices.

A few examples of what students spoke about demonstrate the range of ways in which they related to the story in Yoma. One student spoke about a close relative dying just after she had converted and being haunted still by her choice to follow a halakhic opinion not to say kaddish over that non-Jewish relative—making a choice to adhere to the authority of the institutional and ritual establishment, at the expense of her own intuition. Another spoke about a decision to follow the institutional rules and to fail a student for a late paper without querying the circumstances that had led to the delay. A third student spoke about watching to see if others performed all the motions during prayer correctly, sometimes to check himself against others and sometimes to check if they "knew what they were doing." A fourth student spoke of being shamed precisely for an attempt to pray every word, when one time it had taken him longer to finish than the rest of the group. Overlaid onto these stories was a conversation about repentance and how we would counsel the transgressor (or ourselves) to repent. But what was more significant was the active interweaving into our personal stories of references back to the text itself. In one case, a new interpretation of the father's response to his son's death emerged from our reflections about ourselves in response to the text. In another, a student offered a suggestion for the type of *teshuvah* that the priests might take upon themselves.

If a part of my goal was to effect a change in their view of the text, the students' comments above reflect that objective was met. Did the text effect a transition of the heart? I do not know. At the same time, I think back on times in my life when an event, a statement, or something I learned has profoundly changed me. Did I realize it then or later? Did I claim it or merely ponder it internally?

There are some lessons that I have learned during this first attempt, this experiment of teaching "Talmud to work the heart," and I consider them here briefly. I believe these lessons will significantly improve my methods and approach for the next time I teach this course.

Methods of Evaluation. We did discuss the initial comprehension of texts in class, but it would have been useful to have taken the time to really register initial *reactions* and to *write them down,* in order to have better noticed our own transitions. At the time, I believed this was a poor use of precious time, but it would have allowed us to compare these responses to post-discussion responses. I realized this late in the course, and so, although we sometimes asked these questions informally, I regret not having been more methodical. This would have allowed the class to have a shared sense of whether the process itself was merely adjusting our intellectual readings of the text, or it was also changing our emotional reactions at the beginning of the process, cultivating empathy with positions we had not originally held.

Time. It is difficult to tell why it was not until more than halfway through the semester when I felt we had succeeded in "reading the text as summons." Do I need to explain more clearly? Was it my discomfort with the possible hubris of the project or with the vulnerability it required?[34] Or is it realistically a matter of "personal growth takes time?"

What is certain is that the amount of time allotted to the course was insufficient for the task. My teaching journal reads, "I wish I had more time with them. If I had this to do again, I would insist on more time in the week."[35] I believe that thoroughly familiarizing the students with the material, allowing for a complex reading, and reading the text as summons is a weighty task for a single semester if one wishes to engage with more than one or two texts.

Familiarizing the Strange.[36] In these texts, the rabbis, the father, the murderer, Rabbi Tzadok, the priests, the community, and the *Talmud text itself*—all of these—are our "Other." I know in the next round of this "adventure of the heart," I would spend more time on the redactoral layer. After analyzing the story of Yoma, I asked the students, "Do you feel like [the text] is trying to grapple with the question of how this [incident] could have happened?" One student answered with a strong critique of the text:

> This is, for me at least, the thing that makes it difficult to read the Talmud, more than any other aspect of the Talmud. I think it's pretty clear that the rabbis have a lot emotionally invested in what they are doing. But the method by which they go about discussing it seems to be calculated to hide all of those emotional, personal, moral issues behind this sort of façade of technicality. This sort of polite fiction of what we're actually engaged in is a technical discussion, and we are kind of magisterially viewing this system and making sure that we've got all the details right. There's very rarely points in the Talmud where the rabbis really seem to be like … where you can really detect their jaws dropping open and them saying "something really significant just happened here—we need to do

---

34 See also pp. 194-195.
35 Teaching Journal, Jan. 21, 2014.
36 Jonathan Z. Smith, introduction to *Imagining Religion: From Babylon to Jonestown* (Chicago: University of Chicago Press, 1982), xiii; Jonathan Z. Smith, "God Save This Honourable Court: Religion and Civic Discourse," *Relating Religion: Essays in the Study of Religion* (Chicago: University of Chicago Press, 2004), 383, 389.

something about it." Which I think for me at least is the most morally problematic part of the Talmud, because the rabbis seem to be constantly denying their own personal, emotional involvement in what they're talking about, even though it's constantly breaking through.

This student expresses difficulty with the Talmud's cold, technical reasoning in the face of the tragic or appalling. In this class, we did not enter into the realm of the calculated reasoning (which does follow the story). I feel it would have been beneficial to interrogate this phenomenon as "summons" as well. What does it mean to ignore or miss the importance of the "burning issue" (whatever it is in that particular text) in favor of those technical conversations? Without allowing the *text itself* (rather than just the *characters* in the text) to have a place as "Other," the process of familiarizing the strange cannot be entirely successful. If one successfully reads Talmud as summons, the way the redactors of the text respond to issues should also call to us to become our better selves.

Framing. The type of personal self-reflection that I am looking for requires getting used to and is not taught by the Talmud itself. For this reason, I brought in poems and a story at the beginning of the course in order to frame the process. While these were an asset, reading the poems without discussing them was a mistake. Traditionally, reading Talmud is a process that calls intensely on logic—and rarely on emotion. As I was teaching using the poem texts, I slipped back into "reading" in all of the ways I had previously taught reading.[37] There was so little time to spend on the texts that I did not want to divert our attention to the poems. Reading Talmud as summons, however, *demands* of us to draw upon reading skills and materials from other disciplines and to develop those particular skills in addition to the traditional skills specific to the field of rabbinics. Just as "reading Talmud to work the heart" is not intuitive, neither are the messages of these poems. We can read the poems and even agree with them, but that is different from internalizing them. This was a process that needed to be taught as well. In addition, what I lost by choosing not to discuss the poems was the ability to then connect the content of the poems back to our process of reading of the Talmud texts. The question, "Why do you think I brought in these two poems?" would have been helpful, both to a conversation about the goals of reading and

---

37 See my introductory remarks.

to the actual analysis. I could have then used that discussion throughout the semester to think about how these poems might inform our readings of the texts.

In addition, the mechanism I used to find and ask relevant questions was based largely on the story that I had told them of the Mittler Rebbe. Because I felt that his interior journey was an excellent example of self-reflection, I used the terms of that story to ask them about the talmudic texts, using concepts such as "the transgressions that you find in the text" and "the *teshuvah* that you would advise." At the time that I was teaching the course, I was not yet using the terms "summons" or "awakening" to describe the reading process. I think the framing for the next time I teach this course will include less discussion on a model of transgression (theirs and mine) and more on a model of using the text as a summons to become our best selves.

Assumptions. Along with interrogating the *students'* assumptions, I learned a good deal about *my own* assumptions. Dori Levine, a long-time educator and teacher trainer (and also, my mother) taught me that one responsibility of a good educator is to anticipate. In this class, I failed to anticipate that the differences in values would appear not only between the students and the text, but between my students and *me*, or between one group of students and another. At times, I had to think on my feet, having expected an entirely different response to the text. This reminded me that a critical reading of the text requires me to do a critical reading of *all* possible responses and not only those I expect will be the popular response.

My journal entry after the first class read, "How do we ask questions that will ensure passion and insight?" Ensuring passion and insight requires us to leave open the possibility that there is "something even better" ahead, and to strive for that something in all that we learn. It is when we read Talmud not as legal discourse, as history, or as a source of decisive resolutions, but as summons to self-reflect that we have the potential for a holy process of growth—for that "something better" that we seek. To recast Ruth Behar, with whom I opened my paper—Talmud that doesn't break your heart just isn't worth doing any more. *Through* its problematic, complex, and sometimes painful content, the Talmud can break our hearts. It is *precisely this* that holds the potential to open to us the door of self-reflection. What remains is to invite one another to go through that door.

Postscript

What We Have Learned about Learning to Read Talmud

Jon A. Levisohn

What does it mean to "learn to read"? Typically, we think about learning to read simple texts in one's native language at an early age, in those societies and cultures that support universal literacy across all of their social classes. "Learning to read Talmud" is more than a special case of this general phenomenon; it is an enterprise that is dramatically different in significant ways. Even for native Hebrew speakers, the language of the Talmud is—or more precisely, the languages are—foreign. The syntax is challenging, the issues sometimes obscure, the logic often torturous. In the general case of "learning to read," it typically happens for most people (although of course not all) in literate societies with gentle interventions by parents and educators. In the specific case of learning to read Talmud, it happens only through the most strenuous efforts.

To be sure, there are still many people who learn to read Talmud at an early age. It would be fascinating to examine that process. How does it happen? What challenges do those children face? What are they actually able to do and at what point? But the studies in this book focus on a different demographic, the "emerging adult" (or sometimes slightly older student). How does that population learn to read Talmud in colleges and seminaries? Some of the students whom we meet in these chapters have had significant experience with Talmud, such as Berkowitz's students at Barnard and Tucker's students at Mechon Hadar. Some have had less extensive experience, such as Kanarek's students at Hebrew College, Milgram's and Lehman's students at Jewish Theological Seminary and Lev's students at the Conservative Yeshiva. Others have had little or no experience, such as Gardner's students at the University of British Columbia and Alexander's students at the University of Virginia. All, however, are engaged in the process of "learning to read

POSTSCRIPT | Jon A. Levisohn

Talmud." Even more importantly, their instructors—the authors of the cases above—are uncommonly creative, reflective, and inquisitive about the process.

This concluding chapter will look across the eight cases of learning to read Talmud to see what we might learn about some of the central questions. What do we mean by reading Talmud? What is encompassed by the term, and why? What are the hallmarks or models of "learning" in this particular domain? But before those questions, we will consider an even more primary question: What is Talmud?

What is Talmud?

The question is not merely conceptual or historiographical but rather very concrete. What, in these cases, is this thing we call Talmud, which is the object of study? When we think about learning to read this text, what is the text that we have in mind? The answer might seem obvious: typically, "the Talmud" refers to the Babylonian Talmud, a set of 37 tractates of Jewish law, stories, interpretation, and wisdom, edited from around the third to seventh centuries in Iraq. Actually, however, the answer is anything but obvious. For example, none of the contributors to this volume recommend starting at the beginning of the Talmud and then simply proceeding through the text sequentially. That may be an appropriate practice for the semi-ritual mode of study known as *daf yomi*, but it is not a good way to learn to read. In fact, it is not even clear what "the beginning of the Talmud" even means.[1]

In educational terms, we might frame the issue in this way: the term "Talmud" refers to a text, to be sure, but it also refers to an educational subject or a field of study, as well as to a process. Learning to read Talmud is surely about learning to read a text, but it is also, at the same time, learning to engage in a particular "discipline."[2] In this sense, learning to read Talmud

---

1   See the discussion in Charlotte Elisheva Fonrobert, "The Beginnings of Rabbinic Textuality: Women's Bodies and Paternal Knowledge," in Aryeh Cohen and Shaul Magid, eds., *Beginning/Again: Toward a Hermeneutics of Jewish Texts* (New York: Seven Bridges Press, 2002).
2   The scare quotes around "discipline" are meant to signal that there is, of course, no single methodology for the study of Talmud, nothing that we could readily identify as the "discipline" of Talmud.

might be compared with, for example, learning to read poetry of the Romantic period. There is surely a text or a set of texts that one has in mind when one thinks of "Romantic poetry"—the poems of Wordsworth and Shelley and Keats. But learning to read these works is not a matter of beginning at the beginning and working one's way through the corpus. In fact, notably, "learning to read Romantic poetry" might be said to include the development of one's own understanding of what is within the corpus and what is not, as well as encountering a variety of representatives of that corpus.

When we think about defining fields or domains, we often focus on the boundaries. We look for a marginal case and try to decide if it is in the specified category or not. When we talk about reading Talmud, in some particular context, do we mean the Yerushalmi (the Jerusalem Talmud) as well as the Bavli (the Babylonian Talmud)? Do we mean commentaries as well as the text itself? Do we also implicitly include non-talmudic rabbinic works, such as Tosefta or midrashic collections? But the authors of the cases in this book tended not to pursue these questions. They took a different approach, one that is familiar from curriculum design: they focused on what texts are central and paradigmatic of the Talmud (or, as appropriate, the Mishnah). They defined Talmud for themselves and their students, implicitly, by presenting paradigms.

How? In several chapters, the paradigm is legal argumentation. Alexander, for example, writes about her "desire to equip students to make sense of the Talmud's *overarching discursive framework*," (p. 143) which she equates with the ability to "explain the back and forth of a complex dialectical argument" (p. 143). That is the paradigm for Talmud in this context, and the claim about paradigmatic status is made explicit. "By familiarizing them with dialectical interests, devices and movements that reappear throughout the Talmud, I am giving students tools to enter the Talmud's meandering conversations on any page" (p. 144). "Learning to read Talmud" means learning to make sense of those texts that include those dialectical moves and arguments. It is no surprise that her culminating exercise focuses on *yeush shelo midaat*, unconscious abandonment of an object; the talmudic discussion of this topic is a classic example of complex dialectical legal argumentation.

However, Gardner has a different view. In the specific setting in which he is teaching, focusing on teaching Talmud to graduate students in other academic fields such as classics or ancient history, he argues that it is more important to help these students learn to read rabbinic aggadah, not halakhah or midrash (pp. 122-124).[3] The material is hard enough as it is without also introducing the technicalities of the legal or exegetical material. Narrative or non-legal material is better suited to give students an introduction that might enable their own subsequent, independent access to material that is relevant to their own research projects. "Learning to read Talmud," therefore, is learning to read talmudic narratives. In contrast to Alexander, then, Gardner would never turn to *yeush shelo midaat* as a paradigmatic text.

Nor is this issue limited to the subgenres of rabbinic literature, i.e., halakhah versus aggadah. Lev, in focusing on the teaching of a text as a "summons," offers a different paradigm that cuts across the halakhah/aggadah divide. Both halakhic and aggadic texts can be troublesome texts in the way that Lev describes. And since she is trying to get her students to read Talmud for self-reflection and personal growth, these texts are her paradigms. Lev would not deny that the Talmud also includes many non-controversial, non-problematic texts, of course, any more than Gardner would deny that the Talmud includes an awful lot of legal argumentation. But the question is not subject to quantification. In each of their particular contexts, the identification of paradigms—an implicit definition of what the Talmud is—is inseparable from the goals they have constructed for their students.

Lehman's case is particularly interesting in this regard. She begins from the observation that students enter her classroom with a particular conception of the relationship between the rabbis of the Mishnah and the priests of the Temple—a prior "understanding" that she wants to disrupt. This disruption becomes a focal point of her teaching. Now, this focal point is not the only criterion of selection for the mishnaic material that she chooses to teach in her

---

3   This is particularly notable since the setting—University of British Columbia, a large public university—would seem, initially, to be similar to Alexander's setting at the University of Virginia. But they develop radically divergent approaches to their teaching, due to the differences in their specific student enrollments (graduate students versus undergraduates) and their conceptions of the goals of those students (professional versus liberal education), as well as because of the differences in their own understanding of Talmud. Reading the two cases alongside each other makes this divergence abundantly clear. Yet, without these two cases, one might be forgiven for assuming that teaching Talmud at a large public university to students without prior experience would be a fairly homogeneous endeavor.

class; she does not exclusively teach mishnayot that deal with the Temple. But surely those Temple-focused mishnayot—both aggadic and halakhic—are paradigmatic in this pedagogic setting. If we ask, "What is the Mishnah in this context?" the answer is something like this: the Mishnah is a text that, paradigmatically if not universally, constructs and presents a relationship between its authors and the Temple rites. If, as a thought experiment, you have the opportunity to teach only one mishnah in this setting, the choice is clear: it ought to be a mishnah that displays this relationship in all its complexity.

Thus, regardless of the straightforward syntax of the phrase "learning to read Talmud," the Talmud is not a stable object that is just sitting and waiting for our attention. A book is not a curriculum, nor a subject or discipline. Once we undertake the effort to "curricularize" the Talmud, we operate from within a set of implicit or explicit commitments about our pedagogic purposes (or else we operate from within a set of unconscious or hidden assumptions about purposes). Those purposes then serve as criteria of selection, not just for appropriate teaching practices but for the material itself, the supposedly stable object of study.

Reading Talmud: The Floor

In reading across these cases, it is apparent that almost all of the authors emphasize accuracy and precision as the minimum requirements for competent reading of Talmud—the "floor" as opposed to the "ceiling." They want students to punctuate sentences accurately, to translate verbs precisely, to identify biblical verses correctly, to distinguish layers of argumentation astutely, to explain rabbinic concepts exactly, and to describe the function of technical terminology carefully. Berkowitz, for example, creates elaborate study guides to structure her students' careful translation and explanation of grammatical forms and technical terms. Kanarek refers to her expectations that students learn to "punctuate and divide a sugya into its chronological layers ... translate and explicate a sugya's argument, and define [its] technical terms" (p. 59).[4] And Milgram advances an argu-

---

4   Her case in this volume does not focus primarily on these aspects of reading Talmud, but rather focuses on the work that she does with students around secondary literature. However, in an earlier study of her teaching (in a different setting)—a study to which several of the authors have referred—she focuses on the central task of getting students to

POSTSCRIPT | Jon A. Levisohn

ment for oral recitation that is predicated on the value of accuracy and precision—including, he adds, correct and fluent pronunciation—as paramount educational goals (pp. 164-165).[5]

From a certain perspective, it is not particularly surprising that these authors care about accuracy and precision. After all, they are each academically trained scholars of Talmud themselves. As scholars, they are focused on the kind of reading that they themselves have been trained to do, which is now what they want their students to learn to do. But even if this is not surprising because of that biographical consideration, we might still consider the fact that, in the literature on literacy in general education, accuracy and precision are known to be both important and problematic. In more progressive circles, teachers refrain from imposing norms on either receptive or expressive language too severely; they are eager to encourage students' efforts at sense-making and expression, even if the details get mangled and the spelling gets creative. It is not that progressive educators believe that normative interpretation and normative expression are unimportant. Rather, they are confident that normative interpretation and normative expression will come, as students continue the work of learning to read and write. So why, we might wonder, is Talmud different?[6]

---

slow down in order to increase their accuracy and precision. See Jane Kanarek, "The Pedagogy of Slowing Down: Teaching Talmud in a Summer Kollel," *Teaching Theology and Religion* 13, no. 1 (January 2010): 15-34; reprinted as "The Pedagogy of Slowing Down: Teaching Talmud in a Summer Kolel," in *Turn It and Turn It Again: Studies in the Teaching and Learning of Classical Jewish Texts*, ed. Jon A. Levisohn and Susan P. Fendrick (Boston: Academic Studies Press, 2013).

5   Gardner is a partial exception to the generalization about accuracy and precision; given his focus on narratives, he does not emphasize these aspects, at least in the case as he presents it. A more interesting example, however, is Lev. On the one hand, she does explicitly mention her concern for accuracy and precision (p. 176), even as she also describes her moral-educational goals that go far beyond that (about which more below). But on the other hand, she also emphasizes the ambiguities of the text that are not easily overcome through precision and accuracy, and sometimes turns the question of translation into an opportunity for exploratory interpretive discussion—without necessarily aiming to resolve the ambiguity.

6   Douglas (Dov) Lerea, in his 2012 dissertation, "What Do I Do Next? Teaching an Ancient Text by Listening to What Students Say: A Case Study of Pedagogic Dilemmas," is an excellent example within the field of Talmud pedagogy of a very different view, that emphasizes attention on students' sense-making, even when—or especially when—they are getting it wrong by conventional standards.

To ground this question, consider Berkowitz's discussion of her use of study guides to help her students at Barnard learn to read Talmud. She notes that, when she arrived at Barnard, she discovered students who had strong backgrounds in Talmud from their experience in Jewish day schools and Israeli yeshivot and seminaries. But this was not necessarily a good thing. She writes:

> All this familiarity, however, was precisely the problem. They had enough information to try to fill in the gaps in their understanding, so much so that they stopped being aware of those gaps (p. 5).

These students then had a great deal of trouble with the kind of patient decoding that she expected of them. In order to help them learn to read, she had to slow them down, to disrupt the hasty sense-making that they were accustomed to. So, the answer to the question of why one should focus on accuracy and precision is clear: students are getting things wrong. They are misreading.

But still, we might wonder what's wrong with misreading. After all, cannot we say that the rabbis themselves were masterful misreaders of prior texts? Are not midrashic exegeses replete with creative misreadings of biblical texts? Do not the editors of the Talmud misread earlier rabbinic statements in their work of stitching together a coherent discussion of whatever topic is at hand? Does not later Jewish tradition, likewise, demonstrate brilliant misreadings of prior sources in pursuit of spiritual or existential meaning? Can we ever really be clear about the dividing line between reading and misreading?

One response here is to suggest that the rabbis, when they adopted alternative interpretive strategies, were aware that they were doing something other than identifying the *peshat* (plain-sense interpretation). They were in the business of *derash*.[7] What the authors of the cases in this book are concerned about,

---

7   As Kanarek notes (J. Kanarek, pers. comm.), Michael Fishbane describes *derash* as follows: "Here the ancient sages ... pondered the meaning of Scripture and discovered there theological, historical, and ethical matters reflective of their religious values and worldview. Here too was the closest reading of the words and phrases of the Bible, discovering new and striking meaning by comparing the words in one passage with those in another. For students of *derash*, the context of meaning is Scripture as a whole" (Michael Fishbane, "Introduction to Commentary," *The JPS Bible Commentary: Song of Songs,* JPS,

on the other hand, is not intentional misreading but rather unintentional misreading—not the addition of creative interpretation, but the substitution of an incorrect meaning for an accurate one. This is not the place to enter into a discussion of what the rabbis knew and when they knew it, nor a place to debate to what extent their creativity was a product of conscious efforts at interpretive innovation or was a product of a system of reading that simply operated by different norms—all questions on which there is significant scholarly debate. What we can say, however, is that for these instructors, in these cases, consciousness is clearly an important goal.

Furthermore, it may be helpful to notice a particular feature of what we might call the phenomenology of misreading, which is that there is a kind of directionality to our reading processes: once we learn the accurate translation of a term or the precise parsing of a verb, we cannot go back. We have lost our innocence, as it were. The point is not that we never forget our grammar, which of course is untrue. Rather, the point is that, in the standard case, what was once a reading now becomes a misreading, or perhaps, what was once an unconscious misreading now becomes a conscious misreading. In this way, the norms of accuracy and precision are unlike other, context-specific interpretational norms. We can read a text as structuralists on Monday and then come back on Tuesday and read the same text afresh as feminist critics, without constraint. We can read for halakhic implications on Monday and then come back on Tuesday and read the same text for its mystical connotations. But when someone points out that we have incorrectly parsed a verb on Monday, our option on Tuesday is restricted by that knowledge: we can only consciously misread, rather than doing so unconsciously.

Returning to Berkowitz, we might now notice that she has already emphasized this consciousness as central to the interpretive process:

> When the students face the question ... of whether to insert brackets or parentheses into their translations, when they consider whether a passive participle is an adjective or a verb, when they decide exactly how to label a line of Gemara—they are making interpretive choices akin to choices made within the Talmud when its authors encountered their inherited traditions,

---

2015, p. xxxvi). Kanarek argues, further, that the correct term for the rabbis' efforts is not "misreading" but rather "rereading."

and like all the Talmud commentators who faced the same questions that the students and I face in our classrooms today. (p. 26).

Accuracy and precision is the locus for interpretive choice-making. Emphasizing accuracy and precision is a way of bringing the interpretive process to consciousness, adopting a metacognitive stance toward one's learning (we will return to this point later on).

Before moving on from this discussion of accuracy and precision, however, we should note that, for Berkowitz at least, the emphasis on accuracy and precision generates a pedagogic problem. She explains that her effort to slow down the students succeeds too well: "The students stop making sense so enthusiastically ... that they forget the ultimate goal, which is to make sense of the passage as a whole" (p. 14). The students in her class embrace the work of precision and accuracy, and, as a result, they begin to think about texts as technical problems to be solved. In a pattern familiar from other educational arenas, attention to "the basics" backfires, with the outcome that the students are in danger of never getting beyond the basics.

The challenge, then, is this: How can the conscientious instructor emphasize accuracy and precision, while also making space for the bigger and bolder project of sense-making? How can one help to establish the floor for reading Talmud, while also constructing the aspirational ceiling? This is not the kind of question that is susceptible to an easy answer. In fact, it is not susceptible to an answer at all—it is a tension to be managed, not a problem to be solved.

Reading Talmud: The Ceiling

Each of the authors in this volume struggles with this pedagogic tension—between establishing the floor and encouraging students to reach for a more aspirational version of reading Talmud—in her or his own way. We should therefore clarify a potential misunderstanding of the metaphor of "floor" and "ceiling," according to which the former is necessary and fundamental, while the latter is optional and aspirational. In fact, none of the authors believes this. Even Milgram, who presents us with a case of oral recitation as a pedagogy to support the development of accuracy and precision in reading Talmud, argues that oral recitation in Talmud, like in other domains of

POSTSCRIPT | Jon A. Levisohn

reading, "increase[s] general appreciation for the literature studied" (p. 169).[8] So we need an aspirational ceiling, as part of the work of learning to read Talmud, as well as a floor. But what exactly is that ceiling? How can we conceptualize the broad range of skills or stances encompassed by reading Talmud?

Alexander, in her case, explains that some of her students come to understand that reading Talmud is not like reading a textbook. The words of one student demonstrate this broader view:

> When it comes to Talmud study, the point is to interact with the Torah in a special way, to see the beauty in many different perspectives, and to understand the thought processes involved in arriving at those perspectives (p. 153).

What this student is proposing, and the stance toward the text that Alexander is trying to cultivate, is that reading Talmud is a matter of context-sensitive encounters (with biblical texts and with the rabbinic interpretations of those texts) more than the acquisition of knowledge. That is why standard reading strategies—skimming, summarizing—are so unhelpful. Precision and accuracy are necessary, to be sure, but so is openness to the encounter and a willingness to explore multiple interpretive possibilities.

Others think about the ceiling differently; indeed, while there are points of contact, each case has a ceiling distinct from every other. For Lehman, students should develop a certain kind of hermeneutics of suspicion about the "polemical impulses at work on the part of the authors of the texts that they were reading" (p. 94); "reading the Mishnah was intimately connected to being suspicious of [the students'] prior views" (p. 106), rather than taking the claims of the Mishnah at face value. Lev, for her part, explicitly declares that her efforts to "work the heart" emerge from her sense that teaching for precision and accuracy is not enough (p. 176). This means, first, that students should learn to recognize multiple possible readings of the same talmudic phrase, and second, that students should learn to engage in moral exploration and develop increased self-understanding—while they struggle with the meaning of the text.

---

8   He quotes a student who reports that "reading the text aloud … highlights the very nature of the Talmud and, by extension, Talmud study" (p. 169).

For Tucker, on the other hand, reading Talmud encompasses the ability to discern not the morally problematic aspects of a sugya, but rather, the textually problematic aspects. For Kanarek, reading Talmud includes reading secondary material on Talmud, to be able to engage with scholarship on Talmud productively—not just for the sake of scholarly competence but in order to gain an awareness of ambiguity and subtext, "connecting a sugya to a wider world of ideas" (p. 57), and more. For Berkowitz, students should be able to "consider ... the Talmud as an intellectual, cultural and religious project" (p. 22). For Gardner, reading Talmud means, especially, accessing the talmudic material that is particularly relevant to whatever a student's scholarly interests happen to be, to be able to access Talmud as an intellectual resource.

When considering this diverse, robust set of reading practices, we may find ourselves mystified. How can it be that "learning to read Talmud" encompasses all this? And if it does, then how does anyone ever succeed in this enterprise? But, on reflection, all these practices are consonant with practices in other domains as well. Learning to read historical texts means, among other things, learning how to critique the moral stances within the texts, while also recognizing the differences in the moral standards of other (historical) cultures. Learning to read scientific literature also means, among other things, learning how to draw on those studies to support or challenge one's own scholarly project. Reading is never simply a decoding of sounds. It is never simply an exercise in translation. To read is to make meaning, and the meaning that one seeks is always a function not just of the text but also of the situation in which one finds oneself and the reasons that one has opened up the text to begin with.

Metacognition

If we were to ask about the hallmarks of learning in this domain, the evidence of these eight cases suggests, first, the importance of what educational researchers and psychologists call metacognition—higher-order reflection on one's own mental processes, or "thinking about thinking." The authors of these cases, in developing their own pedagogies, have independently arrived at the conviction that their students will learn to read better if they can help them to reflect on their reading, to think about what they're doing as they're doing it (or soon after they've done it). Berkowitz writes about "sensitiz[ing] the students to their own process of sense-making ... and encourag[ing] them to reflect on the project of translation and how making sense works differently in different languages" (p. 17). Tucker encourages students to articulate systematically all the problems that they experience in the text. Alexander assigns a set of reflections that provide a scaffolding for metacognition, "to draw students' attention to various aspects of the reading experience so that they could reflect on which strategies they found to be more effective and which less so" (p. 139). A student reports that Gardner "continuously provok[es] the students to think while we are reading," a strategy that Gardner connects to research on schema-activation among proficient readers in general education (p. 125).

The conviction about the importance of metacognition as an aid to learning is not derived from a careful review of the scholarly literature on the subject, even though there is much scholarly literature that supports precisely that conviction.[9] Instead, we might speculate that this conviction derives from the nature of the subject matter, which has been explicitly structured as a *learning-how* task rather than a *learning-that* task, so that reflection seems like an appropriate cognitive complement to the "practical" side. In addition, this conviction about metacognition may derive from the nature of these specific contexts, involving learners who are adults, so that reflection seems like something that they ought to be able to do, but who are also relative novices, so reflection seems like something that they need to do. These instructors, in other words, may not be as committed to metacognition in other kinds of teaching they do (a Jewish history survey course, for example). And other instructors, who teach Talmud to younger students, might not be as committed to metacognition as these instructors in higher education classrooms, because they might not intuit that younger students are as open to or as capable of metacognition as adults. Moreover, the literature on metacognition confirms that not all metacognition is a good thing: if you are trying to learn how to ride a bike or to speak a language, it is not clear that spending a lot of time reflecting on the process is really all that helpful.

---

9   See, for example, discussions in John D. Bransford, Ann L. Brown, and Rodney R. Cocking, eds., *How People Learn: Brain, Mind, Experience and School* (Washington, D.C.: National Academy Press, 2000).

Nevertheless, the consistent presence of metacognition across these cases is surely significant. In fact, the cases demonstrate more than just a shared conviction among the instructors about its importance. They also demonstrate a variety of pedagogic practices—specific techniques—that these instructors have developed to promote what is sometimes called a "culture of metacognition" in their classrooms. On the evidence of these cases, learning to read Talmud in these settings proceeds, at least in part, through the involvement of reflection on what is happening in the text, on what the textual or other difficulties are, and on what one does as one struggles to make meaning.

Competing Models of Learning

How do we conceptualize the development of knowledge in this domain? The eight cases suggest a tension between two competing models. On the one hand, in several, the scholars write about building up understanding bit by bit, slowly accumulating the individual pieces until the students arrive at the point of understanding the whole sugya. We might call this the "building-block" model, and notice that it seems to cohere with the emphasis on precision and accuracy mentioned earlier. On the other hand, there's another model, a version of the hermeneutic circle: in this model, the students move back and forth between some understanding of the whole that informs their understanding of the individual parts and an understanding of the individual parts that informs their revised understanding of the whole.

As an example of the building-block model, consider Alexander's description of the way in which her students begin with "the tendency to gloss over details in the hope of stabilizing meaning by detecting an overarching narrative" (p. 146). They try to skim the text, looking for the big picture. But that strategy, which works well in other kinds of academic reading, is disastrous when it comes to Talmud. Instead, her students have to learn a new approach, a much more patient approach, one that understands words and phrases and sentences, step-by-step through reading and re-reading, cautiously moving forward only when their understanding of the prior sentence has been solidified.

POSTSCRIPT | Jon A. Levisohn

Gardner represents a different instance of the building-block model. For him, the building blocks are not the words and phrases of the rabbinic sugya. Rather, he conceptualizes the building blocks as the background knowledge that must first be in place in order to make sense of the text. "Before teaching Talmud," he writes, "it is first necessary to teach *about* Talmud" (p. 121), to explain to students why the text is important and to provide an overview of the genre in which the students can situate the texts they encounter.[10]

However, other contributors lean toward the hermeneutic-circle model. Tucker, for example, argues that the "first phase of interpretation is nothing less than taking responsibility for the logical coherence of the sugya [as a whole]" (p. 38). This is a striking formulation. Tucker is concerned that the students should practice an ethic of responsibility in their learning, recognizing and enacting this responsibility from their earliest encounter with the sugya. He does so in order to avoid the situation that Berkowitz describes in her classroom, namely, the situation in which students focus so intently on getting the building blocks right that they lose sight of the goal of making sense of the sugya. Notably, Tucker claims that the enactment of this responsibility "throws them into addressing any gaps in their knowledge by precisely defining words, identifying key legal terms, and sharpening the logic of the passage" (p. 38). That is, for Tucker, the big-picture understanding operates in tandem with the technical details—from the very first moments of encounter with the sugya.[11]

Kanarek's focus on integrating secondary material may also be seen as a kind of hermeneutic-circle model. Where some might argue that learning to read scholarship on Talmud should wait until students learn to read Talmud itself, Kanarek adopts a different, more integrated view: what students learn from the scholarship extends or deepens their ability to read the text. To take just one example from several in her case, the scholarly literature helps her student James "to read the range of interpretive possibilities latent in the sugya"

---

10 Notably, Alexander describes her own movement away from this stance. Whereas her prior approach focused on first teaching about the Talmud's relevance to motivate the students' learning, she now seeks to generate motivation by a greater emphasis on meta-cognition (pp. 137-139).

11 In his chapter in this volume, Tucker chooses not to document or explore how this actually happens; his focus is elsewhere. So we must take his claim as an intriguing hypothesis that deserves further investigation. How and in what ways do students (of any age) move from part to whole on a moment-by-moment basis as they encounter a rabbinic text? Such a study would make an enormous contribution to the field of rabbinics education.

(p. 84).[12] Thus, there is, at least in some instances, a back-and-forth dynamic between the secondary material and the primary encounter with the sugya.

Of course, this issue is not entirely unique to reading Talmud. If sense-making in general follows the hermeneutic circle—if we always approach a text or the world with what Heidegger called "fore-structures," provisional understandings of the whole that get refined as we encounter the parts—then reading Talmud should follow the same general pattern. Yet, we could make a reasonable argument that Talmud is a special case, of sorts, because of the difficulty and complexity of the texts that comprise it. So even if it is true that, at some abstract level, the work of reading Talmud can be described in the same hermeneutic terms—even if it is true that we approach a sugya with some anticipations regarding its meaning and its structure—it may also be true that the experience of reading Talmud feels a lot more like the cautious and painstaking assembling of brick upon brick. As a matter of pedagogy, learning to read Talmud may include the development of a certain disposition of patience, the ability to control one's frustration when the whole does not yet make sense while one attends to the meaning of individual terms—even as one also, as Tucker argues, accepts "responsibility for the logical coherence of the sugya [as a whole]."

Conclusion: What We Need to Learn Now

The eight cases in this volume represent an unprecedented set of windows into university and seminary classrooms where Talmud is taught and learned. The authors have shared their pedagogic practice with courage and insight, and with an impressive commitment to ground their analyses in empirical data, drawn from teaching journals, student work, classroom discourse, student evaluations, and other materials.[13] Moreover, the clarity of their shared focus on "learning to read Talmud" allows for generative comparisons, and illumi-

---

12 In Lehman's case, while the encounter with secondary material is not as central a focus as it is for Kanarek, she too writes that she "want[s] the students to learn to move from primary to secondary sources and back to primary sources" (p. 110).
13 This is not the place for a discussion of the methodologies at work in these cases. Readers of the individual chapters will note that some are more systematic and some more exploratory. What is important, however, is that the claims that they make are appropriate to the evidence that they have gathered.

nates the deep diversity encompassed by that deceptively simple phrase. It is also particularly praiseworthy that the authors share with us examples not just of what it looks like when students read well, but sometimes what it looks like when they do not (see, for example, Berkowitz's student, who does a poor job on the study guide, or Lehman's example of a student who seems to revert to her prior assumptions under the pressure of the final exam).

In looking across these cases and seeing what we are able to learn from them, we can also envision the next stage of research on Talmud pedagogy. The cases are like snapshots. Could the next stage of research resemble movies? We might investigate what learning to read Talmud looks like in the specific sense of a developmental process, in which a student, a reader, moves from non-understanding to understanding, or more globally, from illiteracy to literacy over time.

Imagine if we were able isolate specific component elements of learning to read Talmud and then observe how students become better at those particular skills or those particular dispositions—not just over the course of one semester, but over the course of several years. Imagine if we were able to develop, out of that data, an understanding of the typical or common challenges in reading Talmud and how they are overcome over time. Learning to read Talmud may never be susceptible to the kind of systematic analysis that has been accomplished in second-language acquisition, where scholars are able to define specific stages of learning in great detail, as well as to describe the standard trajectories of learning from one stage of proficiency to the next. But at the moment, we lack even the basic categories to describe the differences between novice and expert readers.

This observation, however, is merely an acknowledgement of what we still do not know and of the kind of research that we ought to develop. In the meantime, these authors have provided us with a rich, nuanced, interconnected set of windows into the practice of teaching Talmud, identifying many of the most important pedagogic tensions and challenges in this work. For that, we are in their debt.

Contributors

Elizabeth Shanks Alexander (BA, Haverford College; MA, PhD, Yale University) is Professor of Religious Studies at the University of Virginia, where she has been since 2000 after teaching at Haverford and Smith Colleges. She is the author of *Transmitting Mishnah: The Shaping Influence of Oral Tradition* (Cambridge University Press, 2006) and *Gender and Timebound Commandments in Judaism* (Cambridge University Press, 2013), which was a 2013 National Jewish Book Award Finalist. She and Beth A. Berkowitz are co-editing a volume of collected essays entitled *Religious Studies and Rabbinics*, which explores how the field of religious studies can contribute to and learn from the study of rabbinic literature. Her current research focuses on gender, theology, and body in the Talmud.

Beth A. Berkowitz (BA and PhD, Columbia University; MA, University of Chicago) is the Ingeborg Rennert Professor of Jewish Studies in the Department of Religion at Barnard College. She is the author of *Execution and Invention: Death Penalty Discourse in Early Rabbinic and Christian Cultures* (Oxford University Press, 2006, winner of the Salo Baron Prize for Outstanding First Book in Jewish Studies) and *Defining Jewish Difference: From Antiquity to the Present* (Cambridge University Press, 2012). She is currently working on a book integrating animal studies with rabbinics, called *The Clever Ox, The Escaping Elephant, and Other Rabbinic Animalities: Critical Animal Studies in the Babylonian Talmud*. She is also co-editing a volume with Elizabeth Shanks Alexander, called *Religious Studies and Rabbinics*, which explores how the field of religious studies can contribute to and learn from the study of rabbinic literature.

Gregg E. Gardner is Associate Professor and the Diamond Chair in Jewish Law and Ethics in the Department of Classical, Near Eastern, and

Religious Studies at the University of British Columbia. He holds a PhD in Religion from Princeton University and was a Newcombe Foundation Fellow, a Starr Fellow in Judaica at Harvard University, and a Mellon/American Council of Learned Societies Fellow at Brown University. He is the author of *The Origins of Organized Charity in Rabbinic Judaism* (Cambridge University Press, 2015) and co-editor of *Antiquity in Antiquity: Jewish and Christian Pasts in the Greco-Roman World* (Mohr Siebeck, 2008). He has published articles on classical rabbinic literature and late antique Judaism in *The Jewish Quarterly Review, Journal for the Study of Judaism, Journal of Biblical Literature*, and *Teaching Theology and Religion*.

Jane L. Kanarek is Associate Professor of Rabbinics and Associate Dean of Academic Development and Advising at Hebrew College. She is the author of *Biblical Narrative and the Formation of Rabbinic Law* (Cambridge University Press, 2014). She is currently working on a feminist commentary to tractate Arakhin (Mohr Siebeck). Along with Marjorie Lehman and Simon J. Bronner, she is editing the fifth volume of a series focused on Jewish Cultural Studies, *Mothers in the Jewish Cultural Imagination* (Littman Library of Jewish Civilization). She has published articles in *AJS Review, Journal of Jewish Education, Nashim,* and *Teaching Theology and Religion*. An alumna of the Wexner Graduate Fellowship, she holds rabbinic ordination from the Jewish Theological Seminary and a PhD from the University of Chicago.

Marjorie Lehman (BA, Wellesley College; PhD, Columbia University) is Associate Professor of Talmud and Rabbinics at the Jewish Theological Seminary. She is the author of *The En Yaaqov: Jacob ibn Habib's Search for Faith in the Talmudic Corpus* (Wayne State University Press, 2012), a finalist for the National Jewish Book Award–Nahum M. Sarna Memorial Award in the category of Scholarship. Lehman is working on a feminist commentary to tractate Yoma (Mohr Siebeck) and a book, "Foolish Priests, Revisionist Rabbis: The Transformation of Yom Kippur in Tractate Yoma." Along with Jane L. Kanarek and Simon J. Bronner, she is editing the fifth volume of a series focused on Jewish Cultural Studies, *Mothers in the Jewish Cultural Imagination*, that will be published by the Littman Library of Jewish Civilization. She has published articles in *Jewish Quarterly Review, Jewish Studies Quarterly, Journal of Jewish Education, Nashim,* and *Teaching Theology and Religion*.

Contributors

Sarra Lev has dedicated her professional life to teaching Talmud and Midrash in adult education settings, and trying to do her bit to make the world a kinder place to live in. Before studying rabbinics, she walked in the Great Peace March of 1986 for global nuclear disarmament and lived in the Women's Encampment for a Future of Peace and Justice. Since then, she has engaged in activism toward a just peace between Palestinians and Israeli Jews. She is currently Associate Professor of Rabbinic Texts (Talmud and Midrash) at the Reconstructionist Rabbinical College, Philadelphia, Pennsylvania, and is working on a book project about intersexuality in rabbinic texts. She holds a PhD from New York University.

Jon A. Levisohn is the Jack, Joseph and Morton Mandel Chair in Jewish Educational Thought at Brandeis University, where he directs the Jack, Joseph and Morton Mandel Center for Studies in Jewish Education. He is the co-editor of *Turn It and Turn It Again: Studies in the Teaching and Learning of Classical Jewish Texts* (Academic Studies Press, 2013), the author of *The Interpretive Virtues: A Philosophical Enquiry into the Teaching and Learning of Historical Narratives* (Wiley-Blackwell, forthcoming), and the co-editor of *Advancing the Learning Agenda in Jewish Education* (Academic Studies Press, forthcoming) and *Beyond Jewish Identity: Rethinking Concepts and Imagining Alternatives* (Academic Studies Press, forthcoming). He is an alumnus of the Wexner Graduate Fellowship Program and holds a PhD from Stanford University.

Jonathan S. Milgram is Associate Professor of Talmud and Rabbinics at the Jewish Theological Seminary (New York, NY). He received his PhD in Talmud from Bar Ilan University, Israel, and was a fellow at the London School of Jewish Studies and professor at The University of London's School of Oriental and African Studies (UK). He was Coordinator of the Saul Lieberman Institute for Talmudic Research and Assistant Editor for the *Encyclopaedia Judaica*, second edition, and has published articles and reviews in such periodicals as the *Journal of Jewish Studies, Catholic Biblical Quarterly, Jewish Law Association Studies,* and the *Journal of the American Oriental Society*. He is the author of the book, *From Mesopotamia to the Mishnah: Tannaitic Inheritance Law in Its Legal and Social Contexts* (Mohr Siebeck, 2016).

Ethan M. Tucker is co-founder and rosh yeshiva at Mechon Hadar, where he teaches Talmud and Jewish Law. He currently directs Mechon

Contributors

Hadar's Center for Jewish Law and Values. A recipient of the inaugural Grinspoon Foundation Social Entrepreneur Fellowship and an alumnus of the Wexner Graduate Fellowship, he holds ordination from the Chief Rabbinate of Israel and a PhD in Talmud and Rabbinics from the Jewish Theological Seminary.

Index

A

Abaye, 20–21, 30–33, 74, 76, 144–146, 166–167
Abrahams, Israel, 128n37
Accuracy, 10, 21, 169; Precision, 207, 207n4, 208n5, 209–212, 215
Adler, Yonatan, 131n45
Aggadah, Aggadot, 120, 124, 126–128, 128n38, 206
Aharonim, 40–41
Akiva, Rabbi, 104–105
Alexander, Elizabeth Shanks, xiii, xxiii, xxv, 118n5, 120n9, 121, 121n11, 121n13, 125n29, 137, 161n7, 203, 205, 206n3, 212, 215, 216n10
Alexander, Patrick H., 129n39
Alexander, Philip, 130, 130n40
Alienation, 36, 41, 183–189
Alon, Gedalyahu, 128n37
Ambiguity/Ambiguities, 13, 21, 24, 26, 57, 77–78, 83–84, 96, 107, 116, 126, 182, 186, 208n5, 213
Amichai, Yehudah, 191, 191n27
Amora, Amoraim, 6, 19–20, 48, 55, 146, 160, 160n4
Aramaic, 26, 44, 145, 154, 159–160, 161n6, 163, 165, 174n50
Arbuthnot, May Hill, 170, 170n32
Archeology, 107
Artscroll (Talmud), 39
Assignments, xiii, xxv, 2–4, 8, 27n18, 59–60, 62n7, 66, 73n18, 77–78, 110, 138–143, 155; writing assignments, 59–60, 62–63, 67, 73, 84, 130n42
Assumption, xix, xxvii, 7, 13, 18, 25, 35, 36n1, 38–39, 41, 55, 72, 86n2, 89, 91, 105–106, 113, 123, 132, 141, 143, 147, 150, 152–153, 155, 184, 188–189, 196, 202, 207, 218

B

Babylonian Talmud (Bavli): Avodah Zarah, xvin24, 131; Bava Kamma, 59, 59n2, 65–66, 68, 71n15, 72n16, 73–74, 75n20–21, 77, 83, 176n5; Bava Metsia, 146; Gittin, 92n9, 124, 127; Makkot, 41–50; Niddah, 105n23, 176n4; Sukkah, 3, 6–7, 7n7, 17, 21–22, 25, 28–30, 32–34, 164–167; Yoma, 92–97, 102n21, 105, 176n3, 176n5, 185, 185n21, 186, 189, 194–196, 198, 200
Bain, Robert B., 86n2
Balberg, Mira, 67–68, 67n12, 88n4, 91n8
Barnard College, xxi, 1
Barrett, Kimberly, 192n30
Behar, Ruth, 175n1, 202
Beit Midrash (study hall), 47, 59, 62n7, 146, 154
Belser, Julia Watts, 177n6
Ben-Eliyahu, Eyal, 130n43
Ben-Sasson, M., 163n18
Berenbaum, Michael, 97n16, 129n39
Berkowitz, Beth, xxi–xxii, xxv, 1, 3, 28, 203, 207, 209–211, 213, 216, 218
Berlin, Adele, 129n39
Bernstein, Daniel J., xivn15
Bikkurim, 108–113
Blogpost, Blogposts, 139, 141–142, 145, 145n2, 152–153, 155–156
Boyarin, Daniel, 151n4
Bradley, John M., 169n27
Brand, Yehoshua, 135, 135n56,
Brandeis University, xv
Bransford, John D., 214n9
Brody, Rober, 163n18
Brown, Ann L., 214n9
Brown, Carey A., 117n1
Brown, Richard H., 86n2

| 223

Index

Bryant, Susan J., 192n30
Building-block model, 215–216

C

Caitlin, 146, 153–155
Camp, 86
Chernick, Michael, xn6, 118n5, 122, 122n16, 123n19
Child, xvii–xviii, 2, 23, 77–79, 81, 171, 203; Infant, 77n29, 77–79
Choral Reading, 160, 170–172
Christianity, Christian, xxiv, 119, 122, 136–137
Citation Methods, 120; Problems with Citation Methods, 120
Classics, xxiv, 119–120, 122, 127, 136, 205
Close Reading, 40–41, 49–50, 52, 72, 80, 92, 97, 182
Cochran-Smith, Marilyn, ixn4
Cocking, Rodney R., 214n9
Cohen, Aryeh, 204n1
Cohen, Shaye J. D., 88n4, 133n48
Cohen, Stuart A., 107n27
Cohn, Naftali S., 95n14, 106n25, 133, 133n48
Cohn, Naftali, 95n14, 106n25, 133
Cohn, Yehudah, 130n43
Commentary, commentaries, 40–41, 49–50, 49n4, 54, 57–60, 69, 77–78, 79n32, 87, 122, 126, 139, 168, 168n24, 173–174, 174n50, 205
Commentator, commentators, xvii, 2, 21, 21n14, 26, 40–41, 49, 51, 53, 59–60, 72, 87, 211
Complexity, xiv, xixn32, 37, 54, 56, 58, 65–66, 75–76, 81, 182, 189–190, 192, 193, 196–198, 207, 217
Connections, xviii, xxiv, 69, 74–75, 98n17, 125, 127, 128n36, 129, 130n42, 134, 142
Conservative Yeshiva in Jerusalem, 179, 203
Content, xxvi, 8, 36–38, 42, 74, 79, 101, 119, 142, 148–149, 153–157, 167–168, 174, 179, 198, 201–202
Coppola, Brian P., xn6
Cover, Robert M., 61n6
Cranton, Patricia, 182n14
Creativity, 22, 26, 210
Critical/Critically, xiv, xviin26, xxiii–xxiv, 22, 36–37, 39, 48, 85–86, 86n1, 89, 91, 98, 106n25, 110, 113, 118, 130, 133, 182, 202

Cross, K. Patricia, ixn4, xi, xin7
Crotty, Kevin M., 64–66, 64n10, 75n22, 76, 81
Cult, 89, 92–96, 98, 102–106, 114, 187, 189
Cultural Assumption, xxv, 140, 156

D

Daf Yomi, 37–39, 42–47, 122, 204
Decode, Decoding, xxii, 49, 54, 83, 164
Derrida, Jacques, 192n29
Detail, Details, xxiv, 4, 6, 19–20, 22, 48–49, 59–60, 62, 68, 71, 78, 92, 101, 104, 108, 123, 125, 127, 134, 141, 153, 200, 208, 215–216, 218; Textual Details, xxv, 141, 143, 146–151, 156
Dialectic, 19, 137, 143–144, 162, 168, 170, 205; Dialectical Argument, 143, 205
Difficulty, difficulties, xvii, xxi–xxii, xxv–xxvi, 15, 35–37, 39–41, 44–45, 47, 49–50, 53–56, 66, 75, 77, 88, 91n8, 101, 109, 115, 123, 126, 129, 132–133, 135, 137–140, 156, 158, 168n24, 180, 186, 192, 196, 200–201, 215, 217; difficulty-seeking, 36
Discussion, xiii–xiv, xviin26, 14, 19, 25, 27n18, 41, 43, 46–47, 52, 55, 60, 62, 69, 71–74, 84, 89, 99–100, 103, 105n23, 108, 112–114, 118, 126–127, 130–132, 134–135, 144, 152, 160, 164–165, 174, 184–189, 192, 194–196, 199–200, 202, 205, 208n5, 209–211, 217n13
Disequilibrium, 184
Donoghue, Dennis, xviin26

E

Educational Subject, 204; Discipline, xn6, xi, xin9, xii, xivn16, xxiv, xxviii, 39, 138, 201, 204, 204n2, 207; Field of Study, 204
Egalitarian Yeshiva, xxi
Elias, N., 193, 193n31
Eliav, Yaron Z., 135n56
Elman, Yaakov, 162, 162n12
Empathy, xxvi, 181–182, 199
Estrangement, 185

F

Failure, xxv, 138, 140, 154, 157, 171
Familiarity, xvi, 5, 184, 188–189, 209
Father, 78, 81–83, 99–101, 186–187, 195–196, 199–200

Index

Fearon, David S., 192n29
Fendrick, Susan P., viiin2, ixn3, xn5, 6n6, 111n30, 118n5, 119n7, 123n17, 207n4
Fenwick, Tara, 192n29
Fink, L. Dee, xxv, 138–139, 138n1, 142, 155
Fink, L. Dee, xxv, 138–139, 142, 155
First-grade, xvii
Fishbane, Michael, 209n7
Fonrobert, Charlotte Elisheva, 92n9, 204n1
Fraenkel, Jonah, 2n2
Frank, Yitzhak, 5n4
Freire, Paulo, 183n18, 184, 184n20
Frey, R. G., 61n6

G

Gadamer, Hans Georg, xxvi, 177–179, 178n9, 182, 186
Gap, gaps, xvii, xxi, 5, 22, 35, 38, 51, 132, 209, 216
Gardner, Gregg E., xxiii–xxiv, 90n6, 117, 134n54, 135n55
Gardner, Morgan, 193n31, 203, 205–206, 207n5, 213–214, 216
Genre, 36n1, 37, 78n30, 91, 119, 122, 128, 130, 144, 151, 177, 179, 206, 216
Gentile, 45–47, 52
Geonim, 160, 160n4, 162–163
George, William, 192n30
Ger Toshav (resident alien), 42–48, 51–53
Goodin, Robert, 61n6, 80n34, 82
Goodman, Martin, 123n19, 130, 130n40
Gottlieb, Eli, 86n1
Goudvis, Anne, xvi, xviin, 126n31, 127n32, 127n35, 128n36, 134n51
Grading, 22–23
Graduate students, xvi, xxiii–xxv, 119–120, 124, 130n42, 134–135, 205, 206n3
Grammar, xxi, 3, 5, 7, 10–15, 18–20, 22, 44, 62n8, 210
Grant, Lisa, ixn3
Great Assembly, 89
Greenberg, Moshe, 61n6, 63–64, 64n9
Grey, Matthew, 107n27

H

Haase, W., 125n27
Halakhah, 65, 206; Halakhic concepts, 3, 4n3, 5, 33–34, 143, 145, 179, 198, 206–207, 210
Hall, Donna R., 169
Hallel, 103–104
Hanh, Thich Nhat, 190–191, 190n26
Haran, Menahem, 61n6
Harvey, Stephanie, xvi, xviin27, 126n31, 127n32, 127n35, 128n36, 134n51
Harvey, Stephanie, xvi, xvin23, xviin27, 127n32, 127n35, 128n36, 134n51
Hatch, Thomas, ixn4
Havruta, xvi, xixn32, 23, 46–47, 59–60, 124
Hayes, Christine E., 7n7, 88n4
Hayman, Pinchas, 159n1
Hebrew College, xxii, 58–59, 203
Hebrew, xiii–xiv, xx, xxvi, 1–5, 9–13, 17, 24, 29, 33, 72, 85, 87–88, 115, 117, 120, 123, 129, 164–165, 170, 170n31, 179, 186, 203
Heidegger, Martin, 217
Hermeneutic-circle model, 216
Hezser, Catherine, 61n6, 68n13, 74, 79,83n38, 107n27, 132, 132n47, 135n56
High School, xviin26, xxi, 5, 85, 164
Historical Context, 119, 133, 182, 189, 196
Holtz, Barry, xin9, 76n26
Holzer, Elie, xiin12, xixn32, 23, 123n17, 124, 124n22–23, 124n25, 126n30, 134, 134n49
Horowitz, Shira, xvii, xviin28, xviii, xviiin29, xviiin31
Huber, Mary Taylor, xn6, xin8, xiin13, xiiin14, xivn15
Huey, Edmund Burke, 170

I

Integrity, intellectual, 39
Integrity, textual, 40
Interpretation, xxi–xxii, 19, 26–27, 38, 47, 52–55, 78, 173, 188, 192, 199, 204, 208–210, 212, 216; Interpretive Possibilities, 131
Jack, Joseph and Morton Mandel Center for Studies in Jewish Education, xv
Jastrow (Aramaic-Hebrew-English Dictionary), 5, 11, 11n9, 14–15
Jastrow, Marcus, 5, 5n4, 11, 14–15, 77n29
Jerusalem Talmud, Palestinian Talmud (Yerushalmi), 129, 205
Jerusalem, viiin2, xxiii, xxiv, 86, 97n16, 112, 124–125, 127, 129, 131, 179
Jewish Theological Seminary, xiii, xxiii, xxvi, 1, 85, 160, 161n5, 164, 203
Johnson, David E., 175n1
Jonson, Jessica, xivn15

225

Index

Josephus, 127
Journals, xiii, 217
Judah (bar Ilai), Rabbi, 128
Jurisprudence, 67, 80, 84; Legal Theory, 61, 64, 76
Justice, 79–84, 80n35, 178, 182n14

K
Kalmin, Richard, 2n1
Kanarek, Jane, viii, ixn3, xxin33, xxii, 6n6, 57, 60n4, 70, 73, 75–76, 111n30, 116n33, 120n10, 125n28, 130n42, 164n22, 207, 207n4, 209n7, 213, 216, 217n12
Karet (Excommunication), 99
Katz, Steven, 2n1
Keene, Ellin Oliver, xvi, xvin22, xviin27, xviiin29–30, xxiv, 125, 127n35, 130n42, 132n46, 134n52
Kehati, Pinhas, 87, 87n3
Kelly, Ursula Anne Margaret, 193n31
Kent, Orit, xiin12, xixn32, 123n17, 124, 124n22–23, 124n25, 134, 134n49
Kindergarten, xvii
King Josiah, 97n16
Kraemer, David Charles, 61n6, 114, 114n31, 177n6
Krauss, Samuel, 135n56
Kress, Jeffrey, ixn3
Kulp, Joshua, 2n1, 118n6
Kutsch, Ernst, 97n16

L
Lasker, Daniel J., 118n4
Law, 34, 41–42, 45, 62–66, 69–70, 75–77, 80–81, 84, 87, 89, 105n23, 106–107, 118, 122, 130n43, 134, 145, 148, 204
Learning Experiences, xii, 36n1, 138, 155, 179
Learning How to Learn, 138–143, 155
Learning to Read, ix, xiii–xiv, xvii, xx–xxiv, xxvii, 5, 24–27, 57, 62, 66–68, 74, 84, 88–89, 92, 101, 103, 115, 119, 121–122, 128, 133–135, 139–140, 142, 156, 203–208, 212–213, 215–218
Lehman, Marjorie, viii, ixn3, xxiii, 60n4, 85, 120n10, 130n42, 164n22, 185n21, 203, 206, 212, 217n12, 218
Lerea, Douglas (Dov), 208n6
Lev, Sarra, xxvi, 175, 203, 206, 212
Levine, Dori, 202

Levisohn, Jon A., viiin2, ixn3, xn5, 6n6, 111n30, 118n5, 119n7–8, 123n17, 159n1, 203, 207n4
Lewis, Jennifer, xix
Lex Talionis, 65–66
Liberal arts, xx, xxv, 118, 121, 137–138, 157
Liberal Arts, xx, xxv, 118, 121, 137–138, 157
Lieberman, Saul, 161, 161n5–6, 162, 162n11
Literary unit, 37n2, 39
Literature, xv–xvi, xxii, xxiv, xxvi, 7, 40–41, 56, 59n3, 61–62, 64–66, 69–76, 80–81, 92n9, 107, 117–122, 127, 130–136, 144, 146–147, 156, 159, 161–162, 169–170, 177, 206, 207n4, 208, 212–214, 216; Law and Literature, 64–66, 76, 81
Logical coherence, 37–38, 46, 216–217; Coherent reading, xxii, 39
Lytle, Susan L., ixn4

M
Magid, Shaul, 204n1
Magness, Jodi, 132, 132n47
Manslaughter, manslaying, 41–44
Material Culture, 120, 133–135, 135n56
McCauley, Daniel S., 160n3, 169n26, 169n28, 170, 170n33, 170n36, 171
McCauley, Joyce K., 160n3, 169n26, 169n28, 170, 170n33, 170n36, 171
Meaning, xviii, xx, xxiii, xxvii, 5, 7–8, 10, 12, 14, 17–18, 21, 24–25, 35, 37–38, 46, 57–59, 72, 78, 84, 88–89, 99, 119, 124, 126, 139, 146, 152, 156, 164, 170, 172, 179, 184, 186–187, 198, 209n7, 210, 212–213, 215, 217
Mechon Hadar, 2n1, 35–36, 56n6, 118n6, 203
Meir, Rabbi, 21, 30–33, 50–53, 127
Meisel, Steven I., 192n29
Melamed, Ezra Zion, 5n4
Memory, 50, 93n12, 102–104, 149, 162, 163n20
Metacognition, 213–215, 216n10
Michaelsen, Scott, 175n1
Midrash, 123, 133, 139, 145–146, 149, 151–154, 205–206, 209
Mikveh (ritual bath), 95–96; Purification, 96
Milgram, Jonathan S., xiii, xxvi, 159, 203, 207, 211

Millar, Fergus, 130n43
Minors, 100
Mishnah: Mishnah Avot, 89–90, 92, 113; Mishnah Bikkurim, 108–113; Mishnah Eduyot, 89; Mishnah Hagigah, 89, 102; Mishnah Middot, 132–133; Mishnah Pe'ah, 123n18; Mishnah Pesachim, 97–108, 110n29, 113–114; Mishnah Shevu'ot, 149; Mishnah Yoma, 92–97, 105, 176n3, 185n21, 186, 194–196, 198, 200
Misreading, intentional, 210
Misreading, unintentional, 210
Morrell, Amish, 178n11
Morris, Christopher W., 61n6
Moscovitz, Leib, 134n53

N
Narratives (see Aggadah)
Nathan, Rabbi, 163
Neusner, Jacob, 88n4, 106–107, 107n26, 118n5, 122n16, 123n19–20, 162n10
Niddah (Menstruant), 105n23
Noddings, Nel, 192n29
Novick, Tzvi, 7n7
Nussbaum, Martha Craven, 178n10

O
O'Connor, Mary Ann, 178n11
O'Reilley, Mary Rose, 176n2
O'Sullivan, Edmund, 178n11
Ong, Walter, 168, 168n25
Oral Recitation, xxvi, 159–165, 168–172, 208, 211
Oral Repetition, xiii, 163, 169
Orality, 161–162, 168
Orphan, 99
Osterloh, Kevin, 90n6
Other, 177, 184, 196
Outline/Outlining, 3, 5, 18–20, 24, 29–30, 59–60, 80n34, 88, 97, 102, 113, 116, 122, 174, 174n50; Topical Division, 60

P
Paradigm, Paradigms, 7, 67–68, 76, 143, 154–155, 170, 205–207; Paradigmatic Text, 43, 206–207
Passover Seder, 97, 100–103, 113; Haroset, 102; Matzah, 102–103; Reclining, 100; Wine, 100, 100n20
Pedagogy, ix, xiii, xv, 8, 36, 39, 54, 159, 180, 208n6, 211, 217–218; Outlines, 3,
24, 97, 106n24, 113, 116, 174, 174n50; Study Guides, xxi, 4–9, 11, 13–14, 22–24, 26, 207, 209
Peleg, Yehoshua, 133, 133n48
Perek (chapter), 112; Perek ha-hovel, 59, 61
Peshat, 21, 119, 209
Peters, Jean Koh, 192n30
Piaget, Jean, 184, 184n19
Plagiarism, 23
Pomson, Alex, ixn3
PowerPoint, 14, 25
Practitioner Research, ix
Priests (Kohanim), 85–86, 89–92, 94–95, 97, 105–108, 113–116, 185, 188–189, 195, 199–200, 206; High priest, 92, 97, 101
Primary Sources, 110, 110n29, 120, 122, 128–130, 133, 136, 150, 217n12
Problem, problems, xi–xix, xxii, xxvii, 11, 22–25, 98, 130, 132, 138, 211, 214; Problem-seeking, 49; Looking for problems, 35–56
Process, xi, xv–xviii, xviiin29, xix, xixn32, xxi–xxii, xxv–xxvii, 6, 16–17, 24, 26, 35, 36n1, 37–39, 41, 47, 49, 53–54, 57, 62, 78, 80n35, 82, 92, 96, 110, 138–143, 147, 150–151–156, 161, 169, 173, 178, 180–182, 190–192, 195–197, 199, 201–204, 210–214, 218
Proficient Readers, xvi–xviii, xxiv, 125, 127, 214
Purification, 105

Q
Questions, ix, xn5, xii, xviin27, xx, xxii–xxvi, 3–4, 8, 14, 20–22, 24–26, 30–31, 36n1, 37–38, 40, 42, 57–59, 66, 68–69, 71–72, 79–81, 83–84, 86, 86n2, 88, 91–94, 96–110, 113, 116, 123, 125, 127, 139–141, 147–150, 157–158, 168, 180, 183, 189, 192–196, 198–199, 202, 204–205, 210–211

R
Rabbah, 165
Rabban Gamaliel, 103
Rabbinic Judaism, xxiii, 85, 95
Rabbinical Students, 1, 175; Seminary, xvi
Rabbis, viii, xn5, xx–xxi, xxiv–xxvi, 3–5, 27n18, 65–67, 67n12, 70, 79, 82–83, 85–87, 89–91, 91n8, 93–98, 100–116,

| 227

106n25, 110n29, 118, 126–127, 131, 134–135, 151, 154–155, 161n6, 169, 176, 185, 189, 200–201, 206, 209–210
Rashi (Rabbi Shlomo Yitzhaki 1040-1105), xvii, xviin25, 2, 4, 21n14, 26, 31–34, 51, 59, 75n20–21, 168, 168n24
Rav Kahana, 45–47, 50–54
Rava, 144–146, 165, 167
Reading Practices, xv, 24, 138, 146, 213; Reading Slowly, xviiin29, xxv, 93, 116, 146–150, 209
Rebbe, Mittler, 191, 195, 202
Rebekah, 70
Recitation, xxvi, 159–172, 163n20, 208, 211
Reconstructionist Rabbinical College, viiin2
Regev, Eyal, 131n45
Repetition, xxvi, 148–149, 159–165, 167–172, 168n24
Reportatio, 173
Reverence, xxii, 36n1, 41, 54–56
Richardson, Yael, 61n6, 66–67, 69–72, 72n16
Right Answer, 13, 152–155
Rishonim, 21, 40–41, 54–55, 160n4, 172–174; Rashba (Rabbi Solomon Ibn Adret, 1235-1310), 21, 21n14; Ritba (Rabbi Yom Tov ben Avraham Ishbili d. 1330), 21, 21n14, 49–54
Rogoff, Jason, 2n1, 118n6
Rosenblum, Jordan D., 117n1
Rosen-Zvi, Ishay, 110n29
Rubenstein, Jeffrey L., 27, 61n6, 72n17, 76n25, 123n21, 124, 127n34, 128n38

S

Santoro, Doris, 183n18
Satlow, Michael L., 119n7, 131n44
Schafer, Peter, 90n6, 125n27
Schlaff, Lisa, 160n3
Schneuri, Dov Ber, 191
Scholarship of Teaching and Learning (SoTL), xii
Scholes, Robert, xviiin26, 99n19
Schreiber, Peter A., 170
Schwab, Joseph, xin9
Schwartz, Joshua J., 133, 133n48, 135n56
Schwartz, Seth, 107n26, 131n44
Secondary Readings, xxii, 57–59, 76, 80, 83–84, 87
Second-language Acquisition, 218
Segal, Eliezer Lorne, 37n2
Self-esteem, 41

Self-Reflection, 178, 181, 183, 192–193, 198, 201–202, 206
Seminaries, viii, xv–xvi, 121, 203, 209; Teaching at Seminaries, 119n7
Sense-making, xvii–xviii, xxi–xxii, xxvi, 4–6, 12n11, 14, 17–18, 26, 27n18, 60, 208–209, 211, 214
Shame, 59, 61, 66–67, 69–72, 78n31, 83, 140, 199
Shulman, Lee S., xn6, xiiin13, xvn6
Siegal, Michal Bar-Asher, 7n7
Silverman, Rabbi Susan, 192n28
Skolnik, Fred, 97n16, 129n39
Slaves, 68, 73–75, 78–79, 81–82, 99–100
Smalley, Beryl, 173
Smith, Jonathan Z., xxiiin34, 6n5, 94n13, 108, 108n28, 110–113, 117, 117n2, 118, 135, 135n58, 200n36
Smith, Karen, xivn15
Socken, Paul, xxviin36, 118n5
Soloveitchik, Haym, 173, 173n44–45
Son, 101, 185, 187, 196
Spitzer, Rabbi Toba, 181n13
Steadman, Mimi Harris, ixn4, xi, xin7
Steinberg, Jonah C., xn5, 123n17
Steinsaltz, Adin, 39
Stern, David, 118n4
Stewig, John W., 169n28
Stuckey, Heather L., 182n14
Sugya, Sugyot, viiin1, xviiin25, xxi–xxiii, xxvi–xxviii, 7–8, 7n7, 10, 19–22, 25, 30–31, 35–42, 44–49, 52–60, 62–66, 68–69, 71–84, 73n18, 122–123, 144–145, 160, 163–165, 167–169, 171–172, 174, 174n50, 207, 213, 215–217
Sukkah, Sukkot, 3, 6–7, 7n7, 17, 21–22, 25, 28, 32, 160, 163–167, 172
Summons, xxvi, 177–178, 180, 182–184, 190–196, 198, 200–202, 206
Surface meaning, 35, 37–39, 41
Sussmann, Yaakov, 161n6

T

Talmud, viii–xiv, xivn18, xv–xxviii, 1–5, 7, 15, 15n13, 19, 21–28, 35–36, 37n2, 38–41, 47–50, 54–59, 67, 70, 76, 85, 91, 118–129, 133, 135–144, 146, 150–151, 153–159, 161–164, 168–181, 183–185, 189–191, 194, 196–197, 199–213, 215–218
Tanna, Tannaim, 20, 26, 55, 59, 88, 145, 159–163, 161n6, 168, 174n50, 189

Taylor, Edward W., 182n14
Technical Terminology, xxvii, 2-4, 9-10, 28, 33, 59-60, 165, 207
Technical Terms, 7-11, 15-16, 18-19, 24, 59, 207
Temple Judaism, xxiii, 85, 95, 115
Temple: destruction of, xxiii, 85, 94, 102, 107; Passover Sacrifice/Offering, 93-94, 96-105, 107-108, 112, 114, 123, 178, 187; Pigul, 104; Notar, 104
Temporini, H., 125n27
Text study guide/study guide, xxxi, 2-3, 20-24
Textual Details, xxv, 141, 143, 146-151, 156
Thalgott, Mary R., 169n27
Torah, xxiii, 7, 34, 41-43, 89-90, 113, 127, 135, 151-154, 167, 185, 212
Tosafot, 21, 21n14, 59, 77, 79, 79n32, 173
Transformative Learning, 178-179, 182n14
Translation, Translations, xiii, xx, xxv, xxvii, 8-9, 11, 14-20, 22, 26, 28-29, 33, 39, 44, 57-60, 77, 79, 88-89, 119-120, 122-128, 130, 135, 137, 144, 165, 167, 179, 182, 186, 188, 196, 207, 208n5, 210, 213-214; Problems with Translations, 14-18, 78, 129
Transliteration, Transliterations, 120, 186; Problems with Transliterations, 128-129, 132
Tucker, Ethan, xxi-xxii, 35, 56n6, 118n6, 203, 214, 216-217
Tzadok, Rabbi, 102, 188-189, 200

U
Uncertainty, 158, 182-184, 188, 196
Undergraduate, Undergraduates, viii, xiii, xvi, xviii, xxiii, xxv-xxvi, 1, 23, 85, 121, 137, 160, 163-164, 206n3

Universities, viii, xiii-xvi, xviii-xix, xxiii, xxv, xxvii, 118, 123, 137, 156-157; Teaching at Universities, 119-121, 133-135, 157n5, 174, 203, 206n3, 217
University of British Columbia, 203, 206n3
University of Virginia, xiii, xxv, 137, 156, 157n5, 203, 206n3

V
van der Meer, Jacques, 174, 174n48

W
Wayne State University, xix
Wenzel, Michael, 80n35
Westbury, Ian, xin9
Wilkof, Neil J., xin9
Wimpfheimer, Barry S., 76n25, 177n6
Wineburg, Samuel S., xivn17, 70, 86n1, 89n5, 90n7, 92n10, 94n13, 98n17, 115n32, 182n16, 188, 188n24
Women, 36, 100, 105n23
Workshop, xv-xx, 138

Y
Yeush shelo midaat, 144-145, 205-206
Yom Kippur, 92-94, 97; fasting, 92-93
Yohanan bar Nappaha, 128

Z
Zakkai, Yohanan ben, 125, 128
Zavim/Zavot, 100, 131
Zeira, Rabbi
Zeira, Rabbi, 20-21, 30-32, 165, 166
Zimmermann, Susan, xvi, xvin22, xviin27, xviiin29-30, xxiv, 125, 126n31, 127n35, 130n42, 132n46, 134n52
Zlotnick, Dov, 159

www.ingramcontent.com/pod-product-compliance
Lightning Source LLC
Chambersburg PA
CBHW051114230426
43667CB00014B/2576